DIVORCE:
IT'S ALL ABOUT CONTROL

How to Win
the
Emotional, Psychological and Legal Wars

Stacy D. Phillips
Certified Family Law Specialist

Illustrations by Jim Doody

WHAT HER COLLEAGUES ARE SAYING ABOUT THE BOOK:

"Stacy Phillips has done a masterful job in helping people steer clear of the typical wars that perpetuate the struggle for control. There's no question: Anyone going through a breakup should read this book."

Jennifer Openshaw
CEO, Openshaw's Family Financial Network (www.winningadvice. com)
Columnist—MarketWatch.com

"In many divorces, control is a major issue between the parties. *Divorce: It's All About Control—How to Win the Emotional, Psychological and Legal Wars* is a *must-read* for every person going through, or having been through a divorce. In explaining how the divorce process can overtake a person and completely consume them, Stacy Phillips is straightforward and very much on point. Her lessons are hard-hitting and insightful."

Dennis Wasser
Celebrity Divorce Lawyer
Wasser, Cooperman & Carter
Los Angeles, California

"From the perspective of an accomplished Family Law Litigator, this author's practical analysis of the divorce process exposes the clash between human emotion, psychology and the legal system. Ms. Phillips demonstrates why the devastation of acrimonious litigation should and can be avoided. *Divorce: It's All About Control—How to Win the Emotional, Psychological and Legal Wars* is not only essential for the many victims of divorce, but for attorney's practicing in the field."

Neil E. Kozek
Divorce Lawyer and Collaborative Law Practitioner/Trainer
Kramer Kozek, LLP
New York, New York

"Stacy Phillips captures the crisis of divorce. With brilliant perceptiveness, she shines the light on the monster under the bed - Control!"

Janet P. Brumley
Divorce Lawyer and Collaborative Law Practitioner/Trainer
Author: *Divorce Without Disaster*
Verner & Brumley, P.C.
Dallas, Texas

"*Divorce: It's All About Control* is a book that talks about winning in a losing situation! What I find most valuable about the book is that it provides a very personal experience for the reader by encouraging each of them to define their current status in the divorce wars and plan strategies to prevail in them. I also appreciate the way Phillips uses her sense of humor to enlighten the mood."

Robert C. Kaufman
Greenberg Traurig, LLP
Los Angeles, California

"Stacy Phillips is a pro. She takes an emotionally charged event, and with a no-nonsense, common sense approach, provides the road map to control. Her case studies highlight the dilemmas faced in divorce, then, in a way all her own, she provides strategies and practical solutions. This is a must-read for anyone facing divorce."

Jacqueline M. Valdespino
Attorney at Law
Valdespino & Associates, P.A.
Miami, Florida

"Divorce is a dreaded struggle for most of our patients who suffer the pain of loss, betrayal and abandonment in their relationships. As psychotherapists, we need to provide not only psychological and emotional support, but also guidance and understanding in helping them navigate the procedures of the legal system. Stacy Phillips' book, so easily readable, is an outstanding source for both therapist and patient in a comprehensive coverage of this often complex subject. It is simply a must for anyone working with couples."

LaWanda Katzman-Staenberg Ph.D.
Beverly Hills, California

"Stacy parses control from all angles. Her range of experience and down-to-earth style provide an accessible, user-friendly guide for anyone who is navigating the roller coaster of human relationships. She truly cares about people, especially children who are apt to be hurt the most by the folly of their elders. Her commitment to helping their parents find a better way shines through."

Tobi Inlander
Executive Director, Dispute Resolution Services
Los Angeles County Bar Association

"The desire to feel in control of our lives is rarely more acute than when we are challenged with the loss of our relationship. This book is absolutely essential reading for anyone who wants to engage in a mature and thoughtful split. "

Katrina Dewey
CEO of Lawdragon, Inc.
Los Angeles, California

"Fortunately, I have never gone through a divorce, but I do know many who have done so. After reading Stacy's book, I began recommending it to many I know—not only those going through divorce, but also those colleagues and acquaintances dealing with control issues in business-related partnerships. The book helps the reader make sense of the chaos and bewilderment that often accompanies a break up or relationship power struggle. I highly recommend it."

David Houston
Editor - *Los Angeles Daily Journal*

"If you're married, separated, unhappy in your relationship, considering divorce, in the process, even if you're already divorced, you've got to read Stacy Phillips' *Divorce: It's All About Control.* There is sound, practical, and not so obvious advice on almost every page. No matter where you are in your relationship, get this book!"

Paul Fedorko
Literary Agent
New York, New York

"I have seen a lot of television shows and read just as many books that deal with the complexities of relationship breakups but nothing can touch *Divorce: It's All About Control.* It digs deep and gives the reader a true perspective of what caused the breakup in the first place. If you are getting out of a relationship this book will guide you in powerful ways."

Denise Contis
Vice President, Production and Development
T.L.C.

"Finally, there's a practical and insightful resource to help people do more than survive divorce! Stacy Phillips' *Divorce: It's All About Control* not only clarifies the mysteries of the divorce process but also enlightens, nurtures and empowers readers, giving them the tools they need to be in control and to thrive. This book is for those who want to minimize their distress and maximize their success—a 'must read'."

Dr. Jana N. Martin,
Licensed Clinical Psychologist
Los Angeles, California

For My Mother and Father — Fran and Gerry Phillips
Throughout their marriage they
have always known how to share control,
keep the peace, and love one another

NOTE OF REFLECTION

I chose the complex area of family law because it provided me the opportunity to do the work I loved, yet handle caseloads that have a distinct heartbeat. I believe it's all about people…serving them. My wish as a family law attorney was that I would make a positive difference in helping my clients get through an incredibly difficult time and also help them reshape their lives.

When I set out to write this book it was my goal to offer an objective view of how destructive the divorce wars truly are and to offer the reader viable suggestions on how to deal with them. After all, I witness these wars every day.

Little did I realize that in the process of formulating, researching and writing this book, I would undergo such a profound change personally. I felt especially sad for many of the children of divorce and my work on this book gave me greater insight into how powerless and frustrated and out of control (and justifiably so) many people become when going through the divorce experience. I gained more patience and greater compassion for my fellow man.

Obviously, some of the characters and scenarios depicted in the following pages are real, while others are fictional, hypothetical or a combination of sorts. But, the stories and situations of many of the subjects of this book are real, and each of them made me keenly aware that much needs to be done to mitigate the pain and suffering one undergoes while in the throes of divorce, as well as the pain that often follows a divorce or significant relationship breakup.

While I am not a psychologist, and I do not pretend to be, I found myself dealing with delicate psyches—especially among the children. It is just the nature of the work I do. I realized that how we treat others, how we conduct ourselves, and how we communicate during difficult times, can alter the course of one's life. This is especially true in terms of children. This furthered my resolve to share my many years of legal expertise by funneling it into whatever means might serve others to find strength and peace and, more importantly, a roadmap to a more harmonious existence. I learned a great deal more about what I thought I already knew regarding what causes relationships to disintegrate, and moreover, what keeps people stuck in the need to keep battling.

When I finished the final chapter of this book, what struck me the most in reflecting on how this book had changed me was a nagging awareness of how much children suffer from their parents' inability to stop fighting over them.

The residual impact of my work on this book has spun me in yet another direction—it has prompted me to begin a sequel. My next book is specifically aimed at addressing how divorce and custody battles impact children and what can and should be done about them from a family law attorney's point of view.

I look forward to sharing it with you soon.

DIVORCE:
IT'S ALL ABOUT CONTROL
How to Win
the
Emotional, Psychological and Legal Wars

TABLE OF CONTENTS

DIVORCE:
IT'S ALL ABOUT CONTROL
How to Win
the
Emotional, Psychological and Legal Wars

INTRODUCTION

"Why did he *do* this? Why did he purposely bring the kids back late knowing we had a plane to catch?" asked one of my celebrity clients about her ex-husband.

I started to answer, but she cut me off with another exasperated comment.

"We missed the flight! He knew we would miss the flight! This is making me *craaazy*," she said. "He keeps *doing* things like this! *Constantly!*"

Once again I attempted to speak, but it was too late. She was already off and running again, spewing out a litany of other similar complaints.

"Two weekends ago, he was an hour late picking Greg up from daycare." She was snarling now through clenched teeth. "The time before that he got Greg's hair cut ridiculously short...or should I say a buzz cut . . . knowing full well we were having his picture taken the next day. And *then* . . ." She finally interrupted herself, stopping in mid-sentence to take a breath and ask again, "Why does he do these things? *Why?*"

"Control," I said softly. "It's all about control."

Most often someone is vying for it, I tried to explain to her. It happens especially when you are in the throes of divorce or experiencing its aftermath. "For you, it's your ex-husband. For others, it might be somebody else."

"Like who?" She seemed even more puzzled.

"For some, it's the former in-laws, the ex's new girlfriend or boyfriend. Could be a business partner, the children, a shrink, his or her attorney, and in some cases, the courts!"

She sat silently, but her expression said it all: A look that snowballed from anger to bewilderment, and then finally landed at defeat.

"But I don't get it . . . I mean I *get* it. I just don't know what to *do* about it," she finally managed. Helpless, she dissolved into tears.

Not that I wanted to further exacerbate an already overwhelming situation for this woman, but I then dropped the proverbial bombshell. "Sometimes it's even worse. Very often what's controlling us is our paranoia, our emotions, our need to win."

As I passed the tissues, a light bulb went on in my head: A real 250-watter. Certainly there are many excellent books on divorce, but no one has written the one that is long overdue (and much needed): A book that fully explains the single most important aspect of understanding what lies beneath the surface of the marriage wars—be they legal, psychological or emotional—the "X," or should I say "Ex" factor: Control!

"I know this is difficult to hear," I continued. "But the point is this: It's *you* who needs to be in control, *always*. And, if you can't be in control because he is, then you need to know how to deal with it to protect yourself." I tried to comfort her, knowing this was hard to swallow, but I drove my point home, making her take it in like bad-tasting cough medicine. "If you can learn to manage control of your business affairs, your feelings and your overall psychological well-being, you will not have days like today. You can minimize feeling as though you're always at the mercy of whatever is controlling you."

The objective, I stated as I wound down my argument, was to identify *who* was in control (if she wasn't), and utilize practical ways to regain and retain it.

"Okay, fine," she finally said, arms crossed defiantly across her chest in a pout. "So how in the world am I supposed to do that?"

"First by understanding the 'Control Factor'—what the nature of it is—its many complexities," I said flatly.

She seemed willing to continue to listen.

As I spent another forty-five minutes with her, I ran down my other thoughts on the subject of control. Without naming names, I told her some of the cases I had handled—and some I was still in the midst of—that illustrated my points about both the givens and mysteries of the control factor in personal relationships. Most specifically, as they related to marriage, but, of course, one could also apply these same principles to other relationships.

She was not the only person who had had a rough week, I told her as I walked her to the lobby of my offices. I had many clients who were in the middle of battles—their control issues.

For example, just that morning, I had been in a deposition in which my client (he) was trying to keep (her) from taking the children out of the country without his permission. Later, I was in a four-way conference with a client and her ex and his attorney. They were warring over their pet Labrador. Yes, the fight for control was over a dog! Likewise, shortly before the frustrated client had walked in, I confided, I had been trying to reason with an irate male who reported that his ex was throwing a birthday party for herself and had invited all *his* close friends and his parents. He insisted that I get a court restraining order to stop such behavior.

Not all my clients were as passive as she, I told her, and perhaps it had been a good thing that she had broken down in my office. Her "breakdown" and our resulting discussion helped her to begin to understand a problem she had been grappling with for three years—her ex-husband's ability to control her. It also affirmed something for me, something I had been wrestling with for years: Making a more concerted effort to write on the subject of divorce and the "ex" factor. Yes, on this head-banging Tuesday afternoon, I finally realized a book on the subject was clearly overdue!

What furthered my resolve to put these chapters together was the realization that not many individuals are as open and forthright as the client with whom I had just met. No, some can't even discuss it—instead they become extremely destructive. Very often they become hell-bent on "winning" at any costs. They can't seem to let go of the need to control. They may not rant openly or break down in tears in front of their attorney as my client had, or in front of their therapist—but they continue to go through each day completely out of touch with what or who is in control. In the end, many sabotage themselves. Such a damning thing! So I thought that if this book were available maybe I could reach others who I could not personally meet—people who would need the same tutorial. That, coupled with my client's outburst that afternoon, had cinched it. I decided then to make the writing of this book a front-burner priority.

My parting, and I hope consoling comments to this woman as we stood chatting in the lobby, was that her situation was not unusual, that there were many who shared a similar plight. They too were dealing with the bewildering frustrations only a broken marriage could present. I told her it was not uncommon for divorce to bring out the very worst in people. I said that I had clients—and knew of colleagues with similar ones—who even strongly resembled the main characters in the film, "War of the Roses." She had not seen it. I told her to rent it!

Now if you have seen this movie, you know exactly what I am talking about. Mr. and Mrs. Rose, portrayed by Michael Douglas and Kathleen Turner, had escalated their disagreements to such a furious "control" pitch that they lost all sense of reason and dignity and behaved in less than desirable ways, and that's an understatement! Granted, the warring couple may have portrayed an exaggerated version of what most couples are like when dealing with divorce issues, but the film provides an excellent example of what can happen when people get out of control with control issues. The Roses certainly lived out their issues boldly in graphic terms.

It is almost a given that every case I handle will have its share of "issues," many of which are not always practical. I am not referring to the task of writing up paperwork to evenly divide community marital property. Rather, I am talking about those issues that center around some urgent situation or chronic problem which is driven directly by the "ex" factor. (For example, the wife who refuses to give her husband contact information when she and the children are on a week's vacation, or the husband who purposely keeps bringing the children home late just to aggravate his ex.) No, at the heart of most contentious matters are those not unlike Mr. and Mrs. Rose's—they are disputes that involve the need or desire for one party to control the other. It becomes an obsession for one party—the need to always dominate the other.

What is especially difficult about most divorce and custody cases is that this tug 'o war over control does not begin or end in my office or the courtroom. It will go on for years, long after the divorce decree is official! As I stated earlier, the fight for control may not just be between the former husband and wife. It can also include various personal and business individuals associated with the couple.

I truly believe a better understanding of how to mitigate, bypass, overcome, handle or otherwise just downright outsmart or cope with control issues would be of great benefit to anyone about to go through divorce, those who are in the midst of one, and those who cannot seem to rid themselves of what I term "divorce residue."

With that in mind, and after the impact that particular client had on me that Tuesday afternoon, I set about gathering notes on the complexities of control and marital relationships. As part of my research for the book, I began talking to colleagues, therapists, judges, religious advisors and many who had gone through or who were still engaged in the frustrations often affiliated with marital breakups. I discussed with all these sources the "how come's" and "why for's" of control. Most importantly, I asked my colleagues for solutions they had found, and I also queried them on viable ways that would help people handle the angst, frustration, despair and a host of other emotions associated with control issues.

I asked couples engaged in the control "wars" what they felt they had gained or lost as a result.

The input I received was invaluable, the remedies sound and reasonable, and the advice precious. Obviously, all of it provided great reflections for this book, and to each of those I consulted, I am grateful.

As you begin to read this book, my first request is that you take a good look at yourself. Assess your root of frustration if you are one of those who is going through or has gone through divorce and is constantly or frequently feeling as though you are at the mercy of some person or situation.

As you travel through these pages, my goal for you is to first understand what constitutes control in the divorce process, past, present and future. Next, I will ask you to ask yourself: What about your current root of frustration? Is it due to factors or individuals? For example, what did your initial assessment reveal? Is it your attorney, your ex's new spouse, a therapist, your stepchildren? Is it you? (An often overlooked potential). Or, is it not a person at all? Could it be extenuating circumstances such as not enough money to live on, as defined by your own definition and experience or your volatile emotions?

Taking a first look at who or what is in control is geared to get you thinking before you move through the pages of this book. What if you cannot clearly identify who or what is in control? I will help you because I begin by delineating the differences between the legal, psychological and emotional wars, how those three overlap, how the lines can blur in battles that may encompass two or all three of them, and how control factors in.

I will also spend time with the "items" or "inventory" associated with control without the "ex" factor, such as children, money, friends, in-laws, and business associates. In other words, how to tally up those factors to determine whether one or several of them are heading up the control parade.

In this book, I also discuss what to do when you feel you are out of control, as well as how to clearly and objectively identify the real nemesis.

Moving forward, I make recommendations on how to fight the control wars productively and how to win them without diminishing anyone in the process. There is even a chapter on "threats," both real and perceived. I offer positive methods for dealing with both types.

Knowing that you, like so many others, will have to deal with those in the "enemy camp," I have even included a chapter on strategies to manage your former in-laws, mutual business associates, stepchildren (and, God forbid, even your own children), and others you just may not be able to avoid.

By book's end I am fairly confident you will have a real handle on assuming and taking control of yourself and managing the control conflicts that surround you. And if for some reason you cannot get control, you will understand how to better protect yourself.

More specifically, the book lays out like this: I offer case studies—real as well as hypothetical stories to illustrate my introductory point. I then move on to give workable strategies and practical solutions to such dilemmas. Through such stories I will expose you to a variety of dynamics. As such, you will come to a better understanding of what motivates and drives the control factor in different personalities. By means of a select choice of remedies, you will get to explore appropriate options—personal to you—for handling control problems, issues and disputes.

Also in each chapter, I offer a list of do's and don'ts. This checklist will come in handy, I am sure. I round out each chapter with a self-examination pop quiz and some helpful and practical homework tips. Throughout the book I also include ways to put good humor to use (an important element in helping you stay balanced).

When you have finished with this book, I am hopeful you will be armed with insight, information, and ways to handle those difficult and trying situations—those circumstances where control is at the heart of the matter or the dispute.

Before you turn the page to Chapter One, I would like to ask that you grab a pencil and paper—and maybe a highlighter to mark your favorite passages. Then you can be fully prepared to make this book not only what I hope is interesting reading, but a workbook of sorts, one that will provide a terrific source of reference and a practical roadmap to maneuver you skillfully down the many roads marked, "Caution: Control Ahead."

Your move.

Chapter One

THE ANATOMY OF CONTROL:
How It Manifests Itself
In Personal Relationships

"All I wanted was a six-foot, redwood fence! We live on a cliff."

I knew where she lived. It was high in the Hollywood Hills, where houses stack nicely on terraced bluffs, each one indented and angled slightly behind the ones below as they wind their way up to a pinnacle. Layered, they resemble a lopsided soft-serve cone from Dairy Queen, each one sitting precariously on top of the other.

I was not sure I had heard her right so I repeated her remark—in a patient tone—allowing myself to wrap my head around what seemed to be a rather harmless request.

"You wanted a six-foot, redwood fence."

"Yep," she said firmly. "To protect my toddler. My two-year-old plays in our rear yard and last week he was chasing his soccer ball. It got away from him," she said, cupping her hands close together to show it was a small ball. "I raced to stop him. Had I not been closer," her eyes were huge now, "he would have tumbled right off the cliff!"

I shifted uncomfortably in my chair. It gave me chills just to step inside the visual she had painted. I have two children. Though they are older now, I understood her fear.

Then she said: "My husband said 'No, you can't have the fence. It will ruin the view.'"

The sun was going down as she shared the disillusionment of her seven-year relationship with the man who had kept her fenceless. She

11

soon explained that it was the final straw that prompted her to sneak away to meet me without his knowledge. She had finally gotten up the courage to act on her thoughts of leaving him.

She told me about their whirlwind courtship, how he seemed so dedicated to making her happy. That he took care of everything for her. That no one had ever done that for her before. She also told me how, after three years of marriage, she had given up her career as an advertising account executive to stay home and, well, "home-make." Her husband told her she could because he would continue to develop property and build multi-million-dollar homes—that he would take complete and total care of her.

"When we got married, he told me I would never have to worry about money again and even took over care of all the finances," she said, making it sound like his doing so was some kind of a favor. "He just gave me money each week for groceries and incidentals."

"Hmmm," I replied, knowing what was coming next.

"It wasn't like that, at first."

"It wasn't?" I feigned surprise. Of course it wasn't. It usually isn't in cases like hers, at first. Well, actually it is, but she would not realize that until later.

"No. I had my own checking account. I had credit cards in my name only; even a small savings account, you know, $30,000."

"What happened?" I was just being polite. I knew what had happened.

"Well, when we got married, see, we had this agreement...."

"Written one???"

"No, just sort of an oral one, or oh well, not even an oral one. It just sort of happened. See, since he said he would just handle everything, it sounded okay to me. So I closed my checking account and cut up my credit cards and used my savings for odds and ends, Christmas gifts, you know, and gifts for him… It all seemed okay and now my savings are all gone." She struggled for a few moments to get out the next set of words, "but it isn't okay any more. I want…I want…I want a fence…dammit!"

Of course you do, I wanted to shoot back, and a heck of a lot more, but I didn't say it out loud! I only nodded understandingly.

What this woman really wanted was control. Not control of her soon-to-be ex-husband, but control over her life and herself, and the ability to make her own decisions, have her own autonomy, and in the end, to buy a redwood or any other kind of gosh-darn fence of her choosing.

Her story is not unlike the story of many a client. I represent people who often subjugate control in order to keep the status quo, at least for a time. But not all my clients (and those of any other divorce lawyer) are like the fence lady. To the other extreme, I have many clients just like her husband. Quite often, I am representing the side that is the controlling type, the one who wants to dominate the other party, have the last word—the one who wants to "win."

What I have learned as a family law attorney is that male or female, there is no established standard in terms of gender as to who may have control on any given issue. Also, control shifts, or the perception of it does, by both men and women throughout the different stages of the dissolution process. During pre-dissolution, she may feel he is in control. While during the dissolution process itself, she may think she is. Then, of course, during post-dissolution the balance of power, or view of it, can change once again. He may think he is now in control.

THE BODY OF CONTROL: FROM HEAD TO TOE

Control can be good, bad, or more often in between. There is no standard by which it can be measured. Sometimes control is a detriment when a person uses it to coerce, be it aggressively or passively. Sometimes it's good when used appropriately. Other times it can be a toss-up. The reality is, control is prevalent in any relationship. And when couples are jockeying for control, it *always* becomes a contest. Why? By nature, people are typically competitive.

Control is a fickle power. It can slip away from you, or it can be something you always have to have. It can change hands at the flick of a need or want, or it can change for other reasons. For instance, there are external forces, like job loss or health problems, or internal circumstances, such as falling out of love, or falling in love with someone else! What is important is that control is amplified in most personal relationships that fail. Generally, one person has the majority of control over the other, and when the other objects, day-to-day life can be one agonizing, protracted, and unrelenting taffy pull.

Without exception, when relationships are strained, someone is invariably in control, the other out of control, or the two are vying for control. More often than not when the relationship begins to unravel, both are out of control. Example: The Fence-Lady—the woman without the fence—she was clearly out of control until she finally considered taking control to do something about assuming control. She wants control over her life and the safety of her two-year-old child!

What is at the heart of this book is the notion that when marriages suffer it is because control has become an issue. And what manifests itself during the marriage is always exacerbated during and after divorce.

I have yet to see a divorce where control was not an issue or *the* issue!

AT THE HEART OF CONTROL: THE BIG SIX

Dealing with control issues, as I do every single day with my clients, I have come to realize there are six basic areas where control is, or can be, an issue. Understanding these six areas is key to your survival and well being. Often there are fights *over* these basic "areas," or the tensions in these "areas"—stressors that can cause control to *become* an issue.

Either people want control or they feel they have lost control. Or, for some couples, the break up is *over* control itself, or *because* of a chronic control battle that cannot be rectified. These control issues typically fall into a half dozen fundamental categories.

Before I list them for you, let me just say that in my experience, for every single case, one of the following has either prompted a struggle for control, or people are at war in that particular area over control. Some people feel they are out of control, while others feel they are being controlled. Then again, some are desperately in need of *more* control. Here are the six categories I have found:

1. Money/Property/Wealth
2. Children
3. Health (Physical and Mental)
4. Loss of Love/Intimacy
5. Growth (Personal and Professional)
6. Fear (Physical/Emotional/Psychological)

Although I will elaborate on each of these categories in subsequent chapters, for now I just want you to understand that in personal relationships—marital or others, where control is a problem—the control tensions fit "uncomfortably" into at least one of the Big Six, if not more. Sometimes all!

CONTROL EXPERTS

Webster defines control as "the power or ability to govern, regulate or direct." In some sense the one being controlled becomes somewhat a slave to the other's choices. British philosopher and sociologist, Herbert Spencer, a major figure during the Victorian era, best known for his theory that evolution applied to all subjects, said, "that which fundamentally distinguishes the slave is that he labours under coercion to satisfy another's desires." Face it, most people do not like to be a slave to another—to be under someone else's thumb.

Percy Bysshe Shelley, a 19th century English writer and political activist known as a strong proponent of individual freedom, including free love, said, "Man who man would be must rule the empire of himself." *He* certainly did not believe in any one person controlling another!

Spanish born playwright and philosopher born in 4 BC, Lucius Annaceus Seneca, best remembered for his plays *Medea* and *Oedipus*, said, "Most powerful is he who has himself in his power." As you can see, centuries ago, it was considered empowering and in vogue to be in charge of oneself, as well as one's life and destiny. I say it has not changed much!

Today, other philosophers and those that ponder the dynamics of intimate, personal relationships still pontificate on the same subject: Control. Arbie M. Dale, best-selling author of *Change Your Job, Change Your Life,* says, "To decide, to be at the level of choice, is to take responsibility for your life and to be in control of your life."

To be able to make choices for oneself rather than having them imposed upon us is a liberating thought and one that became magnified in a revolutionary Broadway musical of the late 1960s, "Hair." That play forever changed the way many individuals thought about their respective roles in personal relationships and helped to shape attitudes and influence future generations!

And though every expert and nearly every philosopher has touched on what constitutes control and how it manifests itself in relationships, to understand it thoroughly is still an ongoing psychological dig. No matter what the experts tell us—no matter how much study, research and attention it has been given—people still have power struggles. Some struggle to relinquish power to the party they wish to please—others covet the compulsive need to control their mate.

The dilemma is that when one person yields to the other, over time he or she may come to resent it. The truth is, if that type of arrangement is dissatisfying to the one being controlled, the relationship usually crumbles. With another type of personality—the domineering type—it is hard to let go of the desire or need to control his or her mate. So if that person cannot hold on to control, the relationship will also soon be over.

What else is very interesting is that assuming control for the immediate moment may not be the control one wishes to have or maintain ultimately. It is often all about timing and choice. Example: I'm reminded of one case, an affluent couple who was having tremendous problems over "him" treating "her" harshly, both physically and mentally. One day, she decided to take control of the situation and leave this man. It wasn't long, however, before she decided it was better to relinquish control and tolerate the marginal abuse and stay with him rather than miss perks—such as the mansion they lived in, limitless charge accounts and a lifestyle she was not about to forfeit. Ironically, in the end, she actually held on to a more meaningful form of control to her—or her perception of it—than the one for which she was about to trade. In this respect, the lifestyle became the controlling factor and choosing to stay with this man (in her mind) was her opportunity to exercise some semblance of control.

Whatever the situation, control can be as changeable as the people and the circumstances surrounding them. Whatever the dynamic, be it where one is submissive while the other domineering—or where both are vying for equal control—this controversy and mystery over control and how it manifests itself in personal relationships, and what it is that makes people choose what they choose—all this remains at the heart of a fascinating "autopsy," an in depth exploration that seems never-ending.

THE "REMOTE CONTROL" SYNDROME

In terms of personal relationships—the romantic ones—there is often an "agreement" going into the relationship, much like the one between the fence-lady and her builder-husband. Frequently, agreements like theirs are not verbalized, they just happen. They are born out of the dynamic that is set up early when two people meet and begin to date.

To define this more clearly, let's take a hypothetical. Let us say she always gets the last word on what movie the couple will see, and he always chooses the restaurant. The two fall into a pattern, a habit. It is what I term the "remote control" syndrome. Whoever is the boss of the remote control gets to change the channels. She has her hand on the device come movie time, and he takes the symbolic gadget away from her when it's out-to-dinner time.

But caution ahead: These agreements—those that tend to emerge non-verbally—can shift gradually as the relationship evolves. As the two begin to live together or get married, she may expand within her control "territory" by unilaterally deciding what color towels will be used in the bathroom. He, on the other hand, may get to make the selection of the gardener. Therefore control is continuously tossed back and forth. This is fine, as long as the two people are willing to hand it off.

There are those though who seemed willing to share the remote control at first but who have since changed their mind. They begin to like the feel of it and are suddenly reluctant to take turns with it—to pass it back. Then there are those who glom onto it from the get-go—they insist on holding on to the gadget from the start in an effort to make sure they get to choose *all* the channels!

These folks tend to want to control everything. Such was the case with the fence-lady's husband. In fact, the warning signs were there in their dating relationship. *The warning signs are generally there.* What she loved in the beginning—his taking complete and total care of her—became her silent prison.

A good example is the woman who appreciates her date ordering for her at the upscale restaurant. She thought it seemed romantic, and even chivalrous on his part initially, but over time she may come to resent being unable to order for herself.

Then to compound the situation, some people are afraid to snatch back that remote control openly, so they devise ways to get it back. For instance, the woman in the restaurant one evening tells her husband she is not hungry, rather than openly telling him she does not want him ordering for her any more. In an indirect way, by not eating at all, she's saying, "I'll sneak that remote control behind my back and you won't even know it!"

NOW WHO'S AT THE CONTROLS?

The relationship "agreement" is one that can change abruptly. A good example is when situations or circumstances force a change in the status quo of the marriage. Let's say a couple has a baby. Suddenly, she is telling him that he must take care of the middle-of-the-night feeding. If he refuses, then she feels she has lost power, or control, and he feels he is being controlled in a matter in which he wants free choice. He will feed the baby if and when he feels like it! For him to assert control, stating that he is not getting up in the middle of the night, or passively becoming "impossible" to wake, gives him control. If she cannot go with that flow, then she is left to feel powerless and subsequently out of control. So when couples are at an impasse—when they are struggling for control, whether it's over when they will engage in sex or who will take out the trash, generally control becomes the overriding factor in the relationship. Think of control as a centerpiece on the dining room table, everything begins to focus and revolve around it! Quite often fighting for control is what brings the marriage down.

WHO'S CALLING THE SHOTS

When you begin to understand what constitutes control and how it manifests itself in a personal relationship, you can either work out your differences, or you can let them split you apart. Sadly, in the course of my daily work-life, I see the latter repeatedly.

Fine, you say, you understand that, but how does one know when he/she is either in control or being controlled? For starters, ask yourself this: Who's calling the shots? Who has the last word? Whose decision reigns supreme! To be more specific: Who gets to select the movie, pick out the towels, change the channel, hire the gardener? Who feeds the baby according to his/her preferences. Who determines day and time of lovemaking? At an even deeper level: Who controls the money? Who controls the friends each person or the couple has (or does not have)? Who is the decision-maker on where, when and how the couple goes on vacation, when and where the children go to school, or who chooses the neighborhood where they live? Whoever it is, I consider this person the "Shot-Caller"!

How does one become a Shot-Caller? Well, that's a very complex question and always a gray area with no formulaic table to consult. And the balance of power can shift. Long ago, and still today, philosophers have pondered that query in a search for answers, for yesterday's Shot-Caller (Controller) can be tomorrow's Controllee. And how and why that happens is of great interest!

Each couple's circumstances and relationship typically evolves and changes—often dramatically over time. This is especially true where the "Big Six" are involved. So naturally then, the balance of power in the relationship can also evolve or change. It's truly mystifying. And, what is even more baffling is that two people can have control at the same time, but over different issues. That, too, can change. True it can provide a status quo as it transforms, but it can suddenly shift and shuffle and cause total chaos.

There is a defining factor in each control struggle: He who calls the last "shot" prevails or reigns as the Shot-Caller in that (whatever it is) issue. Indeed, the last "shot" is always the controlling shot. Yet if people willingly trade off calling the shots, the "who is controlling whom" dynamic can work nicely. Yes, the control baton *can* be passed back and forth, but when a marriage is in trouble, or even during the divorce process or the aftermath of a divorce, it is usually because someone inevitably yearns to be the General Shot-Caller. Often times, both parties do. In the latter instance, sparks begin to fly, igniting an emotional pyrotechnic display as each of them hold steadfastly to the baton, neither willing to let it go! For some it becomes a game—a competition, a contest—for others, a thrill!

THE GOLDEN RULE

I have my own theory and one that I have also proved empirically. It comes as a result of handling countless divorce and custody battles over the years.

When I refer to the Golden Rule, I'm not talking about The Golden Rule of "Do Unto Others." (Oh, how I wish!) Instead I'm talking about Golden Rule, defined as, "He who has the most gold rules." It is often true that whoever makes or has the most "gold"—the majority of the material things or perceived control over items such as money, property, investments and so forth—is usually the person who asserts or maintains control in the relationship. In our marital society, good or bad, the primary breadwinner is often the person who has the lion's share of the power or who calls the shots (The Shot-Caller). Such was the case with the lady who wanted the fence. Her husband was clearly Chief Shot-Caller! He had a pot of gold and he had literally and figuratively taken away her pot of gold.

Now, "gold" can hold value in other ways too, such as whoever has the most power, clout, influence, status, or celebrity. This "gold" standard could be a priceless commodity, like prestige. A good example: While the husband may be the major income-earner, the wife just may be the mayor of their town. Suddenly, her powerful position can knock him out of the power-box. Whatever is more highly valued in the relationship and whoever is in charge of "it" is the person who typically prevails in the Control Department.

In my experience, the Shot-Caller is often the person who pulls the strings. Having said that, there are also situations where a husband could be a mighty breadwinner, but the wife has the final say on how that income will be spent. Somewhere in their dynamic, she took over and assumed control. It could have been that he wanted her affection, but she was unwilling to provide it unless she was allowed to handle the checkbook. More often than not, though—and in your own situation if you examine it closely—whoever has the *most*...whether it's money, or an intangible commodity, like celebrity...is often the person who ends up with control over many aspects and things in the marriage.

Sometimes it goes like this: One person has control in one area, the other in another, i.e., she gets to manage the checkbook and he gets affection whenever he requests it. In some circles this is called "give and take," or *quid pro quo.* So, if control isn't bothersome, a relationship can stay together, unscathed; but once control becomes an irritant or a big deal, the relationship falters.

That final straw can be over something minor, too! I'm reminded of the story about the guy who stormed out the door and also his marriage. His final words: "Thirty years of burnt toast? I'm out of here!" Well, it wasn't the toast—the scorched bread. It is what the burnt toast signified. He had finally had it! This happens when someone reaches a limit—when someone is spurred to take control!

Such was the case with the Fence-Lady.

It was not the fence that threatened to dismantle the marriage between my client and her husband. The fence simply set off some deep-seated resentment that prompted her—motivated her to think about sticking up for herself and taking control. At first, she found it difficult to stand up to him, but we rehearsed how she would do it in my office.

The point is this: The fence incident signified her refusal to remain voiceless and powerless in her marriage and its "standard," one she had fallen into and had honored for seven years.

A CLOSER EXAMINATION

Let's delve into this anatomical probe of how control affects relationships even further. When personal relationships are not working, it is usually for two primary reasons. Either value systems are mismatched, or there is a power struggle over things, big and small. I once had a client who fought with his wife over what time the fish in the aquarium should be fed! When all was said and done, it had nothing to do with the fish, or values really, it had to do with the struggle for control. Control can be asserted in everything from what day to pay the monthly bills to what kind of stuffing should go into the Thanksgiving turkey.

Getting back to value systems for a moment, if they do not line up between two parties, a contest can ensue—both parties standing his and her ground on what they feel is right. A husband may not think it is important to sit down to dinner with his spouse regularly, while the wife believes dinner is a sacred time for "togetherness." To her it is a time to nurture their relationship, and therefore, a priority. In the end, if their beliefs about dinnertime are too disparate and they begin to manifest themselves in other value-oriented issues in the relationship, the couple will probably split—the negatives overtaking the positives in numerous ways. Whether it's values or power in the relationship, the result boils down to the same problem: He thinks it should be one way, she, another. So then, it becomes all about control!

THE BALANCE OF CONTROL

Naturally, there are always issues where couples will disagree or become polarized, but there can be negotiation and compromise rather than fierce competition for his or her way.

A difference of opinion as to how the children should be disciplined, who should take on what tasks if both parties work, and so forth, are often viewed as obstacles. Yet many couples find ways to work through those issues. But those who are unable or unwilling to find ways usually wind up in a tug 'o war. Sometimes this battle can be outwardly expressed. But what I find substantially more common is that these struggles are not always a 50/50 push/pull dynamic. Some are acted out more passively, more covertly. He may agree to be home to sit down to the dinner table, a nod that eating the evening meal together is important after all; but if he continually walks in the door an hour after he knows full well dinner will be on the table, that is a far more subtle way of maintaining control without declaring it, thus getting his way. In my experience, people opt for the latter control approach because it is a way to take control without declaring it.

Control, of course, is an issue in other relationships, too: With children, parents, in-laws, business partners, friends, and yes, even divorce attorneys. And each of these relationships can certainly affect your marriage or divorce. All this I will discuss and explore in a later chapter. For now, however, we are looking at what constitutes control in relationships between couples. Presently, I am addressing control as it relates to that dating relationship of yours, that marriage, or that divorce you are either going through or have been through—the one that still mysteriously and annoyingly lingers on.

BOTH AT THE CONTROLS

When things are going well with both at the controls, the relationship benefits. So, let me just take a moment to talk about when control *does* work. In most personal relationships that do work, one of three dynamics has to be in place: Either one party is designated as the "Controllor" and the other the "Controllee" —the dominate and the submissive—and they enjoy their respective "roles," or both have an understanding as to who will control *what* (like he handles the money, and she has the last word on rearing the children). Or in the idyllic relationship—my value judgment—both are equal partners, sharing in decisions and authority somewhat evenly. This is rather rare though; for where there are couples, there are differences.

I noted that control does not have to be a problem so long as the dynamic between couples is working. But I also said that I believe if couples can come to terms—if they can implement more equality in their relationship—control tends to take a back seat. Such couples stand a very good chance of keeping control issues under control!

Sadly, however, people coming together, negotiating, and divvying up control is not as common as I wish it were. Some couples function in a give and take mode for a while, or at times, but when people grow or circumstances shift so does the balance of power. So let's say that the wife agrees to be a stay-at-home mom, but when the children are grown or relatively independent, she decides she wants to return to the workplace or school. If her husband does not want her to do so, a control struggle ensues. This major change threatens the balance of power. Indeed, when change occurs, control can become a factor; and when it does, the relationship can quickly or gradually introduce a new dynamic, one that can readily dismantle a status quo partnership. Lots of Danielle Steele novels reflect this storyline. She takes a back seat, he runs the show, she steps up to the control plate, he challenges her, she leaves him, she goes out on her own—and in Danielle Steele's mode—she does so always very successfully. She generally then meets a new mate whom she can truly partner with—they share control—and he finds another woman whom, once again, he tries to control, with no success.

When control permeates the relationship's atmosphere, strife, discord and frustration usually follow. The process of vying for control is not only detrimental to most couples, it can also be extremely exhausting, especially if someone like the Fence-Lady or the Return-to-Workplace Mom has to expend a great deal of energy asserting herself. Some people just give in. Case in point: I had one male client who stumbled into my office, drained. He practically fell into the chair across from my desk. He had popped off two crowns just from gnashing his teeth at night and had gotten an ulcer. He looked as wane and worn out as if he had just run a 26-mile marathon. He looked at me lifelessly, and finally, through lips that hardly parted, ordered, "Give her whatever she wants. I'm just too tired to fight for what's fair."

You can only imagine the discussion we had in response to his exasperated words!

Unlike that client, some people do not give in. They fight for control another way: Through deception. Many people do not want a confrontation over an issue, and rather than face the partner with an announcement that could threaten the nature of the relationship, they may decide to become behind-the-scenes

Shot-Callers. This can be both dangerous and destructive. For instance, the husband who tells his wife she must stop running up the MasterCard account may think he has the situation under control, only to learn later that she has opened a second and third account to make purchases without his knowledge! Deception such as this can easily erode the trust in a relationship. If she deceives him with money, will she also deceive him in other ways? This dynamic can spawn an even greater need for him to feel he needs to control *her*! I do not have to tell you what the probable outcome will be. I am certain you know!

ADAM OR EVE: WHO'S IN CONTROL?

In the many years I have been a family law attorney—and I have always represented both men and women in approximately equal numbers—I can safely state that there is no one gender who wears the crown of Control. Again, the crown is passed back and forth as ceremoniously as the remote control, or control remains in one person's hands on certain issues. It just depends on the situation and the couple. It does not always hold true that all women control how the children will be raised, any more than it holds true that the men will always choose which football game to watch on Sunday! And, as I have pointed out, it can shift according to circumstances and personalities…and day-to-day!

What I do know is that people who feel as though they are being controlled maintain that the other gender is the one who always has control. The Fence-Lady was sure that all men were like her husband, while the Teeth-Gnasher had presumed that all women were likely to scramble for control and stake a claim to the driver's seat.

Naturally, thinkers have pondered this issue over the years, just as they have pondered the nature of control itself. The late Reverend Dr. Gene Scott, an internationally respected religious leader and scholar, asserts that in Genesis the serpent went to Eve, not Adam, because women are always in control when they want to be. But then you have diametrically opposing views on that claim. You have famous songwriter/singers like James Brown, who has emphatically stated: "This is a Man's World."

This might be a very good time to pause and ask yourself: Do you think men automatically own the control throne, or is it women? This careful examination is going to be helpful as you move through the lessons in this book. It is my goal that you keep an open mind, to not start out with biases or preconceptions of how you think the divorce and its aftermath is going to go just because you believe the other gender is the controlling type. This will have a bearing when you pick a therapist and when you choose an attorney.

Now would also be a very good time for you to ask yourself who is in control in your marriage or divorce. Also, ask yet another question: Who was in control in the beginning of your relationship? Did you have a pre-conceived notion about control, or did you acquire a point of view about it later on? Do you believe one gender or the other typically has the power seat? Of course, you can also look at the dynamic between your parents. That, too, will help you identify your frame of reference of how you view who is, should be, or can be, in control.

Answers to these interesting questions will help you as you move through these pages, for I think sometimes people are planted firmly in a belief that one gender or another will always have the "control advantage" no matter what. That is simply not true. Control is gender-less. Without getting too philosophical: Control just is! And so is a competitive nature among humankind, in general!

Having said that, I will admit that in many of the cases I have handled, it seems that the Golden Rule does apply; and generally, but not always, it is the *guy* who has the most "gold"! It's just the reality of the society in which we live. But I must admit that I have represented numerous women who controlled the gold and they still perceived that their ex, or soon-to-be ex, was in control!

Once again, I do not want to see you get stuck in a warped perception about control and what gender seems to dominate it! Instead, I want you to take a close and fresh look at what it really is, how it is at work in the dynamic of your relationship, and what it is that made you pick up this book.

OVERLOOKING OR LOOKING OVER CONTROL

As I have already mentioned, control is certainly something many couples do not notice (or are unwilling to acknowledge) early on in a relationship. They perceive what really turns out to be controlling behavior as something else entirely. For instance, what you now may point to as obsessive behavior or over-nurturing or bossiness, may well have been traits in your significant other you simply overlooked, or even adored, when the relationship was new and exciting. The bossy girlfriend may make her guy feel like he is being taken care of initially—looked after—when eventually he will come to resent her domineering. The caregiver who over-dotes is initially regarded as someone who really wants to cater to the other. Yet over time, it will probably mushroom into a series of suffocating scenarios. The person who thought he was being fawned over is finally going to go nuts from too much attention—and in the end will feel overtaken, smothered. Perhaps you loved being treated like a princess early on or you relished the fact that it seemed all your needs and wants were being met—like someone always willing and eager to cook your meals. But what did you have to relinquish in return? What did it cost you in "self" control? How do you currently feel about some of the things that seemed so wonderful and "right" at first?

When the initial "contract" suddenly changes—when one or the other party is suddenly behaving differently from the relationship blueprint that was once in place, or the other party does not want to change, something different will need to occur or the relationship will soon falter.

When he or she begins to assess similar situations to those just mentioned, that is when control issues begin to loom large and dismantle what once seemed to be a blissful and indestructible partnership.

As I said, behavior that is initially controlling is often overlooked or blocked out by the rose-colored glasses when two people come together. In other words, couples are blinded by the excitement a love relationship provides. But what was once exciting can become irritating and overbearing over time.

I had one client whose soon-to-be husband said, "I just want to devote the rest of my life to you and making you happy." Had I been her I would have run like hell! But she thought he was simply being loving and romantic. You can bet that eventually she would not have been able to make a move without his scrutiny and without him imposing his choices and beliefs on her. It would work only if she had remained complacent with that arrangement—if the soon-to-be wife were able to go along with the program. Otherwise, no way. You can be sure control is going to rear its ugly head the minute she says, "I can rely on myself to make me happy. I just want to share an equal relationship with you." You can safely bet a power-struggle will no doubt take place. If the two begin tugging for control—if he wants to impose his will on her and she wants some free choice—then, again, the relationship becomes all about control! Soon the good things will diminish and the focus will be on individual needs, like preserving "self, ideals and peace of mind."

When a relationship gets to this point, couples can get competitive and one-upsmanship takes over.

If you are beginning to think about divorce, in the preparation stages of divorce, in the midst of one, or still experiencing the after effects of one (even after many years), you know what I am talking about!

When couples suddenly begin to fight for control over things they were not hassling over before, the relationship is probably on its way out. When people begin to disregard the other's values and ideals, it may be time to part. When people just feel they cannot take any more struggle, up pops the burnt toast and divorce is probably their next phase of life.

Here is something else: The person who suddenly has control taken from him or her feels a sense of rejection, and that creates a need for one-upsmanship in many. It is a natural response, a way of regaining some control. So like the characters in "War of the Roses," the stakes get higher, and just as in their case, people behave in ways they never imagined or could have imagined. Oddly enough, for them, just like so many divorcing couples I know, they are suddenly turning over control to the process and no one wins! Typically, everyone loses.

A desperate need for control can bring out the very worst in people. I see it every day.

THE ART OF CONTROL

As we round out our probe, looking closely at control and how it manifests in personal relationships, we can study some of the great couples in time that struggled with it in their relationships. There were Antony and Cleopatra, Marie Antoinette and Louie XIV, Liz Taylor and Richard Burton, Sonny and Cher, and Charles and Diana, to name but a few. In nearly every case there was one-upsmanship! For some, having the bulk of control in the relationship became an art! Some people work hard at it, as ridiculous as that may sound. It has been a recurring theme for ages! In the case of Henry VIII, he had the "juice," so he asserted his control every chance he got with all his wives. An obvious fanatic about power over the women in his life, "ex" in this man's life meant execution, and so went the heads of Anne Boleyn and Katharine Howard.

While you are pondering couples whose relationships seemed contentious, also take a good look at those relationships where it is obvious the twosomes worked (or still work) at their control issues. Some good examples may include Maria Shriver and Arnold Schwarzenegger, Joanne Woodward and Paul Newman, Elizabeth and Bob Dole, and Mary Maitlin and James Carville. Who else can you think of?

The study of some pairs in comedy is another great way to get my point! Just look at a handful of the wonderful classic comic films and shows whose plots revolved around control issues. Laurel and Hardy were always at odds as to who was right and who would get his way. I will never forget the film where the two acted out their neuroses with control in a disagreement over how the piano would get up the stairs! In their particular dynamic, Hardy was more overt and outspoken about his intention to have control, while Laurel laid back, always robbing Hardy of it in more covert, passive ways.

When you watch "I Love Lucy," you can see the same dynamic at play; someone was always trying to run the show, or Lucy was trying to get some equal standing with Ricky. Even

Fred and Ethel got caught in the control trap when episodes focused on the couple's incessant need to outdo the other. The one-upmanship game was frequently part of the script, a recurring theme.

Looking at more modern day couples as typified in the favorite sitcom "All in the Family," Edith and Archie Bunker are certainly a great study in overt versus covert control. Archie was very outspoken about what he was in charge of, while Edith would feign ignorance, all the while getting the best of her thickheaded husband.

By comparison, look at "George and Gracie," a wonderful married theatrical couple who acted out their relationship before an audience. You will notice, to the outside world, Gracie Allen never butted up against George Burns; she simply went with the flow. Her character was oblivious to control altogether. So, the only tension in that relationship in front of their audience was Burns trying to get through to Gracie's perception of reality. You will also see that, he too, went with the flow. Perhaps this is why their characters were depicted as ones who had a harmonious relationship. They never struggled. Burns put up with Gracie's ditziness; Allen never let anything get to her. There is a great deal to be learned from this relationship—about how to keep one's cool and keep one's own sense of control without disparaging the other person in the relating process.

Look further: Abbott and Costello were always contrary. Dean Martin's and Jerry Lewis' characters battled for dominance, and "The Honeymooners" central theme *always* revolved around Ralph's need to control Alice. Today, that show would be viewed as sexist and politically incorrect, but it still tells us a lot about human behavior, control and how it manifests itself in personal relationships.

I strongly suggest you take time out to view some of these old-time favorites, many of which must have tremendous entertainment value as they are still on the air today! Even if you have seen them before, I am certain you will learn something new from watching them again. This assignment may seem trite at first glance, but it is not. It brings home many of the dynamics played out by couples everywhere.

Reading about some of the classic couples in history and viewing some of the great comedy classics listed above (or those of your choosing) are a couple of ways for you to get in touch with understanding control and how it manifests itself in your personal relationships. You can also begin to observe those around you—friends, family, and co-workers. By studying others, we learn a lot about the anatomy of control, what constitutes it, and how it manifests itself in personal relationships. In sum, my goal for you is first to understand the nature of control. Soon we will begin to look at how it affects your life and your relationships.

CONTROL YOURSELF

What I do not want is to see you getting caught up in the control traps that are so inherent in faulty relationships and especially prevalent when a divorce occurs. Keep in mind, these divorce-control issues can trail for years! Instead I want to see you assume and maintain control, and to do so in a positive way.

I am hopeful that the pages that lie ahead, and the lessons and the hands-on assignments in them, will serve to motivate you to take complete control, not of others, but of your "self." In so doing you will find that no matter how contentious your pending separation, the aftermath of your divorce, or how complicated the residual aspects of it are, such as fighting those emotional, psychological and legal wars—you will prevail.

It is time now to get down to work, to take a good look—a careful assessment of your current state of affairs. Focus in particular on the "Big Six" as we move from chapter to chapter.

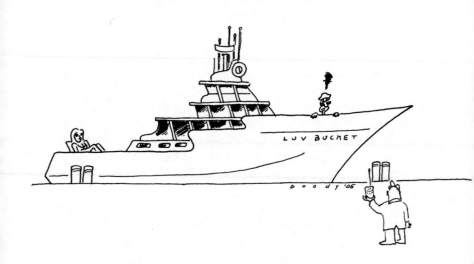

*It's your ex-wife's attorney. He says it's
time to "give up the ship!"*

Chapter Two

YOU AND CONTROL:
Assessing Your Current State of Affairs

"I think, I, uh, I…I don't know what I think," a well-dressed man in a pin-striped gray gabardine suit finally admitted.

"Well, Keith, you came to see me so that must mean you have concerns," I said, affirmatively, sans any condescension.

"Well, yeah."He stopped there, though I was hoping for more.

"Okay," I knew the ball was strictly in my court. "So, you say— Lucy—is that right? Did you say your estranged wife's name is…" before I could finish…

"Yes, Lucy."

"And, how long have you been separated?"

"Well, actually…" His voice trailed off again. "Well, I moved out a while ago, but I still go over there, to our house," he pointed, index finger skyward in a northeasterly direction, like I would know where his house was.

For lack of anything better, and caught somewhat off guard, I replied, "Ah, I see…"

"Well, I go back there like when she needs something."

"When she needs something." I said it without a question mark since I wanted to make it sound like our dialogue was actually going somewhere other than this conversational cul-de-sac.

"Yeah, like if she wants me to relieve the sitter, ya know, like if her tennis game runs over, or if she has to work late, or if she wants to go out with her friends."

I hated to ask this next question for fear the answer would be what I thought it was going to be, but I asked it anyway. "How long…" I found it necessary to clear my throat, "how long have the two of you been separated, Keith?"

"About 14, 15 months."

"Uh-huh. Anybody…uh, …Lucy…you…file for a legal separation or dissolu…" He butted in.

"No, Lucy thinks we should wait."

"And you?"

"Well, that's why I'm here. I do not know what to do and I'm kind of feeling like I have no control over the situation."

If I had had a bullhorn I would have jumped up on my desk like a crazed cheerleader and blurted, "And you don't! You absolutely don't! D-O-N-'T Don't!" but my professionalism stopped me. Instead, I listened intently (a prerequisite to being really good at this practice of law) while he told me how he hoped if he went "along with the program" she might change her mind; that they just might reconcile.

I felt genuinely sorry for the guy. By all outward appearances he looked like he had everything going for him. He was an Internist, and not just any Internist, but one of the top doctors in Southern California, one whose patients would travel to see him from as far away as India and China. This high-profile doctor was making $1,000,000 a year, had a medical degree from Harvard and had done his residency at New York's prestigious Mount Sinai Hospital. He had won countless awards for his charitable works and had built a thriving medical practice in Beverly Hills. This dignified mid-40's father of three was not only intelligent and very nice looking, but he dressed well, looked fit, and had a very pleasing personality. No wonder he had such a fine reputation, his manner radiated patience and understanding.

After talking to him for about 90 minutes I realized that these very qualities were what had gotten him into trouble with Lucy. He considered her feelings first and foremost—foregoing his own wants and needs. He was clearly out of (his own) control. There was no balance in their relationship.

As we talked further, I learned that the two still had a joint checking account and that Keith had not changed much in the way of their *routine when they were living together. He still handed over a hefty amount every month—his entire pay check—to replenish that joint checking account from which she paid the mortgage, the household expenses and the sitter—not to mention whatever else she wanted. When I asked if he had receipts from these expenditures he said, "No." When I asked why it was they had such an arrangement, he lowered his head and without looking up said, "Well, Lucy lets me see the kids pretty much whenever I want to."*

When he told me how often that was—usually every other weekend (Friday night to Sunday night), one night (really dinner) during the week, sometimes two dinners—I explained that that is what the court would generally order—at the bare minimum.

The Doctor-Husband-Father did admit that he hoped they would reconcile at first, but after six months he had come to the realization that Lucy showed no signs—no interest, in fact—of even discussing it. Though he tried several times to coax her into joint counseling, she refused. As hard as it was for him, he confided that he knew it was time to do something more "formal" about the situation.

NOW HEAR THIS

Hearing him say that, I was ready to give him as much assistance as I believed, or he believed, he needed. Indeed, it was time to have that lawyer-to-client chat letting him know what his options were. But first things first: We needed to have a talk about control and the ex-factor (Lucy). I provided him some insight on the subject and soon he began to see how it had impacted his relationships with Lucy and their children. I attempted to help him identify which of the Big Six over which he had some semblance of control and which areas he did not.

What was listed in the "In Control" column? Nearly zilch! He did, however, feel that he had some control over his blossoming career—that he had definitely grown as a physician and businessman and done so on his own. He managed his practice well, we both concluded. I asked him to "hold that thought." I told him that if he could be in charge of one area of his life, he could certainly do the same in other areas as well. We set about discussing each of the remaining Big Six and attempted to identify where he stood.

We also discussed a legal separation, filing for dissolution and his legal rights with regard to his children. I suggested he discuss these options with his therapist. I also asked him to take a closer look at each of the areas in his life where he did not feel he had much or any control, and make a list of just how he thought he could gain control in ways that would not be harmful to anyone, including himself.

Because my work is never a "one-size-fits-all" approach, I wanted to be certain that The Doctor chose the best solution for his individual circumstances—for what resonated with him. Only then, I explained, would he be the Captain of his own Ship of Control.

I wanted to help him sort out his legal affairs, but felt it was also my duty as a family law (aka divorce aka matrimonial) attorney to provide additional guidance. I certainly was not trying to play "shrink" with him, quite the opposite. I was merely trying to get him to understand the anatomy of control and how it plays itself out in personal relationships. I also wanted to prepare him for what lay ahead in regard to what would soon become his legal affairs.

With him, just as with so many other clients, I had come to realize that when a client can identify the control factors in the relationship or relationships with which he or she is grappling, only then can he or she make judicious legal decisions—choices that are bound to have a substantial impact on the future.

The Doctor's children were four, five and seven years of age, so he had a long road ahead in terms of dealing with Lucy, both regularly and productively. I wanted to make sure he did not become a control "victim"—setting himself up for constant control *battles*, many of which, of course, wind up on my desk and often go the distance all the way to the courtroom. I explained that if he took a stand to gain control over his life and his affairs, he was bound to get some resistance from Lucy. I also told him he had to be ready to face those challenges—those tug 'o wars—head on; but I stressed he do this in a positive and "high road" way.

We talked a long while about the various aspects of his situation—from money, to in-laws, to children. When he tried to vote himself another control "yes" in the Big Six department, he finally understood I was not just talking about physical well-being, I was also talking about mental well-being as well.

He finally admitted he was not sleeping well, and he was beginning to experience severe anxiety attacks at times, even though he continued to do a masterful job at the office. "Work," I told him, "focus on work," and all the many ways he enjoyed piloting that portion of his life. It would come in handy, scrutinizing how he did that, I explained, for he could begin to adapt some of the same strategies into other important areas of his life. There was no reason he would have to continue to have little "self" control in any department—in any of the Big Six—where he had the *right* to lots of control and certainly more say. My goal was for him to become his own Shot-Caller while creating a winning dynamic all the way around, or at least, doing his part to facilitate that happening.

TAKING STOCK

In addition to weighing all his options and discussing them thoroughly, I also asked him to do something else: I asked him to make a careful assessment of his current state of affairs in each of his "deficient" Big Six areas and to determine where he felt he had even a modicum of control. I also asked him to be very candid with regard to the areas in which he noticeably lacked control.

I asked him to decide where he thought and felt he *wanted* or *needed* control. I explained that by doing this "homework" assignment he would gain a better perspective on what he needed in order to "regain" his "Self," yet all the while keeping a reasonable status quo with his estranged wife and an excellent relationship with his children.

I told him how important it would be to have a workable relationship with his ex. Having a positive relationship with his ex would continue to be a requisite since he would be inextricably tied to her because of the children they shared. I told him this was a harsh reality and one that is difficult for people to come to terms with.

I told him there would be additional and more complex "control" issues with which to deal in view of the fact that both he and Lucy would undoubtedly enter into future intimate relationships with new significant others, and it was probable both of them would eventually remarry.

He flinched when I said that.

The truth is—I told him—you are always linked to the former significant other when children are the result of a personal relationship, so it is important that you keep control of your affairs. Not of others and their affairs, I stressed, control over your situation—your circumstances. Not just now, in the present, I repeated several times, but always.

WHEREVER YOU ARE, WHOEVER YOU ARE...

You can do the same as The Doctor. You, too, can take stock of your situation whether you are pondering divorce, about to go through a divorce, are in the midst of one, or have already gone through one a year or ten years ago.

In our last chapter, I attempted to help you understand the nature of control and how it manifests itself in personal relationships. I also introduced you to the Big Six—the areas where control can become, or is, a factor—and now it is time to see how all that information lines up with what is going on in your life.

It is time now to get to work on your first assignment, a quiz that will help you identify where you rank in the Big Six on the "Control" scale.

I have broken this "quiz" into four sections in order to address the important questions that one should ask of oneself—issues that will help you determine what needs changing, what currently works in your favor, what's tripping you up, what's causing you angst and sleepless nights, and ultimately, where control seems to be important to you. I have presented these with a keen focus on doing nothing more than getting you in touch with an awareness of what you are in control of, what you have a semblance of control over, and where you are clearly out of control.

It could very well be that you have been avoiding a candid assessment, hoping that "things" would simply change all by themselves. In all my years of practice, I have come to know that each client of mine has had to be in charge of his or her affairs in order to move forward with a productive and harmonious life. It could also be that by answering each of these questions thoughtfully you may find you have had far more positive control over your circumstances than you first thought. I also think the answers to these questions will help you as you meet with your family law attorney, saving both of you time, and as a result, hopefully money.

By the time you are finished, this self-examination should aid you in making a candid (and sometimes brutal) assessment of what you need to work on! In some areas you may have complete control, in others you may have none. You will find that some areas are difficult to delineate; control is not always a black and white thing.

So depending on whether you are still married (like The Fence-Lady), in marriage limbo (like The Doctor), going through the chaos of a divorce like so many (you are not alone!), or still feeling the effects of one, (you may be one of those divorced for twelve years asking: "will this ever be over?"), you will be able to identify where control is an issue or at issue. The results of this "test" will be very important as I later discuss which ones can benefit from legal remedies and which ones you can manage on your own without the help of an attorney. The following is what you should accomplish with your answers:

1. Identify where you are in terms of control in the geography of the Big Six;
2. Pinpoint *who* or *what* is in control;
3. Evaluate whether or not you want or need control in each of the categories of concern;
4. Pave the way to introduce opportunities that will aid you in reclaiming, asserting and maintaining control in positive ways.

Be mindful as you go about engaging in this "pop" quiz, and others in the book, that there are no right or wrong answers. No one is going to judge you.

My wish is that you not be reluctant to answer any of these questions truthfully. Rather, I want you to use this chapter of the book as a welcome place to finally look your situation squarely in the eye and report back what you see! The questions are simple and basic. I have a table at the end of the chapter that allows you to tally your scores. I will also offer comments on your scores in each category. Depending upon your circumstances, you should consider whether completing these questionnaires should be in anticipation of conveying them to a lawyer, whether you currently have one or not. The goal here is to protect these statements from discovery, if the worst case scenario proves to be the reality. Therefore, if you have a lawyer, address the answers to your lawyer. If you do not have a lawyer, perhaps you should label these answers "privileged for my lawyer." Please understand that I am not giving you legal advice. Consult with a lawyer in your area before deciding what to do, write or not write. Regardless of your decision, answering these questions to yourself will be *very* helpful.

So then, here we go:

MONEY/ASSETS/LIABILITIES

The first part of the assessment has to do with monetary issues and assets. The first series of questions are for those of you who are thinking about or beginning the divorce process.

1. I have a bank account(s) in my own name:
   Yes ____
   No ____

2. I have a bank account(s) with my spouse:
   Yes ____
   No ____

3. I have no bank account(s) at all ____

4. I have real property, such as a home, land, time-share condo or other dwelling in:
   My own name ____
   Joint title with my spouse ____
   All property is in my spouse's name ____

5. Was this property acquired:
   Before marriage _____
   After marriage _____
   During marriage _____

6. The money for this property was acquired from:
   Joint funds _____
   Funds I/spouse had pre-marriage _____
   A gift to me _____
   A gift to my spouse _____
   A gift to both of us _____
   Inheritance by me _____
   Inheritance by my spouse _____
   Neither of us owns property _____

7. I have stocks and bonds and other investments in:
   My own name _____
   Joint title with my spouse _____
   All assets are in his/her name _____

8. These assets were acquired:
   Before marriage _____
   After marriage _____
   During marriage _____
   Neither of us have investments _____

9. These assets were acquired from:
   Joint funds _____
   Funds I had pre-marriage _____
   Funds my spouse had pre-marriage _____
   A gift to me _____
   A gift to my spouse _____
   A gift to both of us _____
   An inheritance by me _____
   An inheritance by my spouse _____

10. I have credit cards in:
    My name only _____
    Joint accounts with my spouse _____
    Credit cards are in his/her name only _____

11. I have a prenuptial or postnuptial agreement that includes stipulations for all my property and assets as separate property:
Yes _____
No _____

12. I have complete knowledge with regard to all joint liabilities and the liabilities of my soon to be ex:
Yes _____
No _____
Not sure _____

13. If your answer is yes, please list them.

_____

_____

_____

14. Do you have any lines of credit, ATM cards, or open accounts where cash can be made available?
Yes _____
No _____
Not sure _____

The following is for those of you who are completing the divorce process or who have been divorced for one or more years.

1. I am financially dependent upon my ex for:
Child Support _____
Spousal Support _____

2. I have property and assets (includes cars, boats, etc) in:
My name only _____
Still jointly with my ex _____
Everything is in his/her name _____
I have no property or assets _____

3. I have credit cards in:
My name only _____
Jointly with my ex _____
Credit Cards are in his/her name only _____

4. I have credit cards (lines of credit, ATM cards) of my own:
   Yes ____
   No ____

5. With regard to the Golden Rule, who has the greater financial net worth?
   Me ____
   My ex ____

6. With regard to the Golden Rule, who has the greater income?
   Me ____
   My spouse ____

If the answers to the above questions reflect autonomy from your ex, that is, you have bank accounts, property, assets and credit cards in your name only, then flip the pages to the end of the chapter, and under "Money, property, wealth," give yourself one point for each question that indicates your independence under "In Control." If you have accounts, property, assets and liabilities jointly with your ex, give yourself one point in the "Somewhat in Control" space. If the property and assets you share (shared) with your ex are in his/her name only, put a "1" in the section for "Out of Control." If some of the assets that rightfully belong to you are in his/her name only, that is another reason for a point in the space allotted to "Out of Control."

If you are divorced and financially dependent upon your spouse to pay your monthly living expenses, add one to "Out of Control." If, on the other hand, you have a job with income you can rely on to pay some, or a good portion, of your living expenses, give a number one to "Somewhat in Control." If you stash your ex's spousal or child support payments in an interest bearing account and use it at will, mark a number one down under "In Control."

CHILDREN

The next set of questions has to do with the children that are a result of your relationship. If you have no children, or your new significant other or new spouse has no children, or grown children, then skip this section. Otherwise, answer each of these questions because they apply to you whether you are still married or living with your significant other, living with a new spouse or even if you have been divorced recently or for some time.

1. With regard to the major decisions in the children's lives, such as choice of medical practitioners, where they attend school, the governing of their day-to-day routine, what church/synagogue/religious facility they attend, or disciplinary action, who would you say is the Shot-Caller?
   Me _____
   My ex (soon-to-be ex) _____
   Both of us _____

2. If you are divorced, do you have:
   Sole legal custody? _____
   Joint legal custody? _____
   Sole physical custody? _____
   Joint physical custody? _____
   Visitation only to you? _____
   Visitation only to your spouse? _____
   Court ordered supervised visitation to you? _____
   Court ordered supervised visitation to your
      ex (soon-to-be ex)? _____

3. If you are currently separated, what percentage of the time are the children with:
   Me _____%
   My Ex _____%

4. If you are not yet separated, what percentage of the time are the children with:
   You _____%
   Your soon-to-be ex _____%

5. Are the children influenced by:
   Your ex (or soon-to-be ex) who openly displays his or her opposition to you _____
   Your ex's new significant other, spouse or other family members on his/her side _____
   Your new significant other _____
   Your new spouse _____

6. Are the children influenced in positive ways by:
   You _____
   Your ex (or soon-to-be ex) _____
   Your ex's new significant other, spouse or other family members on his/her side _____
   Your new significant other _____
   Your new spouse _____

7. Are the children influenced in negative ways by:
   You _____
   Your ex (or soon-to-be ex) _____
   Your ex's new significant other, spouse or other family members on his/her side _____
   Your new significant other _____
   Your new spouse _____

8. What residence do the children consider their primary residence?
   My home _____
   My ex's home _____
   Both homes _____
   There is no primary residence _____

9. To whom do the children go to for money?
   Me _____
   My ex _____
   Both of us _____

10. Who is involved in the children's day-to-day activities?
    Mostly me ____
    Mostly my ex ____
    Both of us equally ____

11. How many days a week, or month, do you spend with the children?
    Weekly ____ days a week
    Monthly ____ days a month

12. If you fit within the stepparent category, how much say do you have in the decisions of your significant other's/ new spouse's children's lives?
    Equal in decision making ____
    I take no part in decision making ____
    I give them money or take care of
       other needs such as living expenses ____

If you are the Shot-Caller in the major decisions in your children's lives, have sole legal or physical custody or primary physical custody, spend the majority of the time with the children, tend to their day-to-day activities, and it is you they come to for monetary needs, chances are you are in the control seat. Place a big "1" under the Children's category beneath "In Control."

If you or your ex, or your soon-to-be ex, tend to share major decisions (joint legal custody), and the children spend time with both of you as a pattern during your marriage (if you are not separated/divorced), or under some mutually agreed upon custody arrangement, and they tend to ask both of you for money, or rely on both of you to meet their day-to-day living expenses, then scratch down a "1" in the "Somewhat in Control" column. If, on the other hand, you do not spend much time with your children, or post-separation you visit your children, have little or no say in major decisions affecting them, are not involved as a rule in their day-to-day activities, but on special occasions only, you and only you provide them some monetary boost other than child support (and your ex doles out the money to them), then give yourself a "1" in the "Out of Control" space under the Big Six "Children's" section.

Also, if your ex's significant other, spouse or other family member on his/her side, or your new significant other or spouse influences your children, this is one more reason to add a point to either the "Somewhat in Control" or the "Out of Control" column. In your scoring, it is up to you to decide whether the influences from significant others, spouses and extended family are positive or negative and how much impact such influence(s) have on your children.

An important note about the Big Six "Children's" section: This area of control is one that can shift radically and constantly. Because you are dealing with "the little people," and in actuality these little youngsters belong to both of you, the control over them can shift from time to time. As you make your assessment relative to the above, know that these answers can change when circumstances change (i.e. your son suddenly goes to live with your ex). So when they do, the control dynamic can shift right along with them.

HEALTH (Physical and Emotional)

Physical Health:

This next set of questions takes a look at your health. A change in health circumstances is one of the leading factors that can cause divorce, for the change in the relationship dynamic is dramatic. Typically, the one who is ill always feels completely out of control. His or her partner may feel like he or she has been given too much control, or the one who is not ill can be made to feel uncomfortable (and out of control) merely because they suddenly find themselves with too much control! Hopefully, you are not one of those who have suffered due to a difficult illness. But if you are, cut yourself some slack; soon you may be back on your feet. For those of you who have been fortunate enough to be in relatively good health, this new set of circumstances just might be taking a toll on you! Take good care of yourself. You also need to address some hard questions about your emotional well-being—that is also part of good health—and we will get to these in the second part of this query section.

Let's start this round of questioning though by first assessing *your* physical condition:

1. I have been sick and unable to work ____days in the past year.

2. I have had a debilitating illness in the last several years:
   Yes ____
   No ____

3. I have developed health problems as a result of the problems in my marital or cohabitation situation:
   Yes ____
   No ____

4. I was in better health until this marital discord started in my life:
   Yes ____
   No ____

5. I would rate my physical well-being as:
   Excellent ____
   Good   ____
   Fair   ____
   Poor   ____

6. I would rate the way I take care of myself with regard to nutrition and exercise as:
   Excellent ____
   Good   ____
   Fair   ____
   Poor   ____

7. My ex, or soon-to-be ex, physically abuses me:
   Yes ____
   No ____

8. I abuse myself through drugs and alcohol or other excesses:
   Yes ____
   No ____

Now, answer similar questions with regard to the physical well-being of your spouse or your ex.

1. My spouse has been sick and unable to work____days in the past year.

2. He/she has had a debilitating illness in the last several years:
    Yes ____
    No ____

3. My spouse or ex has developed health problems as a result of the problems in our marital or cohabitation situation:
    Yes ____
    No ____

4. I would rate my ex's physical well-being as:
    Excellent ____
    Good ____
    Fair ____
    Poor ____

5. I would rate the way in which my ex takes care of him/herself with regard to nutrition and exercise as follows:
    Excellent ____
    Good ____
    Fair ____
    Poor ____

6. I physically abuse my ex:
    Yes ____
    No ____

7. My ex abuses him/herself through drugs and alcohol:
    Yes ____
    No ____

If you are *not* in good health, give yourself an automatic "1" in the "Out of Control" section. Do the same if your ex is abusing you physically, if you are taking poor care of yourself (drinking too much, etc.), or lacking in sound diet and exercise.

If you take some care of yourself—your physical well-being—yet you have been plagued with physical ailments, perhaps you are not eating right, not working out regularly, but you are able to go to work and function normally: Chalk up one point under "Somewhat in Control."

If your ex is in poor physical shape, abuses drugs and/or alcohol, and you are dependent upon him or her financially for spousal or child support, or if he or she has been ill in the past year or so or developed physical problems as a result of your breakup (or just not taking good care of his/her physical well-being), write the number "1" under "Somewhat in Control." Even if he or she is over the scale in this department, it does not mean you will crash if he or she does. It just means you better have a back-up plan to meet financial needs if he or she can no longer honor commitments in this way. Also, if you have had thoughts of abusing your ex physically, or have done so, scratch a down a point in the "Out of Control" category, and get some help, pronto!

If you are fit as a fiddle, are weathering this marital strife with no physical toll whatsoever, (strife can affect people physically), sustaining a good appetite and taking good care of yourself despite your circumstances, enjoy a big sigh of relief and chalk up one point under the "In Control" section.

Let's move on now to do a cursory check of your emotional health.

Emotional Health:

Here are the questions that will help you determine where you rank with respect to your emotional well-being and control:

1. Do you sleep through the night, soundly?
    Yes _____
    No _____

2. Are you sad, depressed, and angry and/or frustrated a good part of every day?
    Yes _____
    No _____

3. Have you gone into therapy as a result of your marital upheaval or continue in therapy to get a handle on keeping your emotions in check?
Yes _____
No _____

4. Are you taking prescribed medications to manage your emotional woes?
Yes _____
No _____

5. Are you taking medications in excess of their prescribed dosages?
Yes _____
No _____

6. Are you taking illegal drugs to manage your emotional stress?
Yes _____
No _____

7. Are you drinking to excess to manage your emotional woes?
Yes _____
No _____

8. Do you overreact to things your ex or others say?
Yes _____
No _____

9. Do you obsess or think constantly about your ex?
Yes _____
No _____

10. If you go to therapy, do you feel it has helped you maintain a more centered and balanced emotional state?
Yes _____
No _____

11. Are you able to function productively even on difficult days?
Yes _____
No _____

12. Do you have thoughts of suicide, murder, or any other type of violence?
    Yes _____
    No _____

13. Do you have feelings of self-doubt, failure, guilt, regret or remorse?
    Yes _____
    No _____

14. Do you take your anger or frustration out on others?
    Yes _____
    No _____

15. Do you inflict psychological abuse on your ex?
    Yes _____
    No _____

16. Are you behaving in ways you never imagined (i.e. rifling through your ex's personal belongings, concocting ways to "get back at him," scheming to "out-do" "him/her," etc.)?
    Yes _____
    No _____

17. Are you inflicting emotional abuse on your ex or soon-to-be ex?
    Yes _____
    No _____

Let's now take a quick look at how you perceive the well-being of that of your ex in the same category.

1. Is he or she noticeably depressed, angry, and/or frustrated when you come in contact with him/her or through communications, both written and verbal?
   Yes _____
   No _____

2. Is your ex in therapy?
   Yes _____
   No _____
   I do not know _____

3. To the extent you are aware, is your ex taking prescribed medications to manage his/her emotional stress?
Yes _____
No _____
I do not know _____

4. To the extent you are aware, is your ex taking prescribed medications in excess of the prescription dosages?
Yes _____
No _____
I do not know _____

5. To the extent you are aware, is your ex taking illegal drugs to manage his/her emotional stress?
Yes _____
No _____
I do not know _____

6. To the extent you are aware, is your ex drinking to excess?
Yes _____
No _____
I don't know _____

7. Does your ex overreact to things you or others say?
Yes _____
No _____

8. Does your ex appear to be obsessed with you?
Yes _____
No _____

9. If your ex is in therapy, do you feel it has helped his or her emotional state?
Yes _____
No _____

10. In your estimation, is your ex functioning productively?
Yes _____
No _____

11. Is your ex abusing you in any emotional way?
Yes _____
No _____

12. Is your ex abusing you in any psychological way?
    Yes _____
    No _____

13. Is your ex behaving in ways you never imagined
    he/she would?
    Yes _____
    No _____

I am sure you may already know that one's emotional well-being is *the* area in the Big Six that takes the biggest hit, for it is impossible to go through serious struggles in a marriage or experience a marital breakup without encountering some emotional problems. Remember what I have stated all along, these types of issues only become more amplified *after* the divorce—sometimes for years after. So do not be hard on yourself if you scored high in the "yes" department. It is very common to do so. It is also common for your spouse to be experiencing similar symptoms and if his or her emotional state is affecting yours in any way, give yourself another point under "Somewhat in Control," or (in severe cases) under "Out of Control." For instance, if he/she is inflicting emotional pain on you, the children, or others close to you, or talked of committing violent acts, threatened suicide, seems obsessed with you, or is constantly instigating fights, then you are eligible for a point in the "Somewhat Out of Control" slot. Remember that emotions play a huge part in personal relationships, and when feelings are out of control they can manifest in many ways and completely throw people off kilter. So ease up, there are ways to deal with your emotions (and those created by or from your spouse) as they impact your relationship breakup. Take heart, we will get to those in Part II, Chapter Five.

If you are sailing through your situation, then by all means, chalk up one "In Control" point in your favor. If you are managing to get through the day productively, going to counseling to help deal with your problems, keeping circumstances in perspective, and not abusing others or yourself out of disappointment, hurt, or anger, then go ahead and give yourself a "Somewhat in Control" point, or even an "In Control" point. If you are giving your spouse low grades in this section, rack up another "Out of Control" or "Somewhat in Control" point, depending on how strongly you are affected by his/her negative emotional behavior.

If you are lashing out at others, unable to sleep at night, taking prescribed drugs in excess of their prescribed dosages, taking illegal drugs, drinking to excess, feeling as though you have no hope, or having thoughts of any type of violence - self-directed or otherwise - give yourself an "Out of Control" point and make a beeline to your nearest therapist! And, if your spouse is in similar shape, ask your therapist for positive ways to deal with those issues. You may also have to decide whether his or her emotional state rates a "Somewhat, or Out of Control," point or two.

LOSS OF LOVE/INTIMACY

This is another area that is difficult to deal with, but one that warrants careful scrutiny. When a marriage begins to fall apart, it could be because one party has fallen out of love with the other. Quite often, when the marriage begins to fall apart, or when the couple separates, a loss of intimacy—and I do not mean just sexual intimacy—is the main culprit. Control then becomes an overriding factor in all aspects of the relationship. Though this is another tough round of questions to answer, they are very important to your perception and sense of control. All of these questions apply to you no matter what category you fall in to—be it the person who is on the verge of divorce, the one still trying to get past the bewilderment of what happened to cause the relationship to fail, or the person who has been dealing with the angst of divorce for years.

1. Are you in love with your ex or soon-to-be ex?
   Yes _____
   No _____

2. Was sex, or lack of it, a factor in driving a wedge in your relationship?
   Yes _____
   No _____

3. Do you still discuss intimate details about your wants and needs with your ex or soon-to-be ex?
   Yes ____
   No ____

4. Are you still in a committed relationship but having an affair with someone else?
   Yes ____
   No ____

5. If you were the one turned off to your spouse, did you experience a better sense of control, or lack of it, after you were no longer intimate?
   Better sense of control ____
   Lack of control____

6. If your spouse let you know he or she was turned off to you, how did you feel?
   Out of control ____
   Very much in control ____
   Not sure ____

7. Who called off the marriage (or relationship)?
   Me ____
   My Ex ____
   Both ____

If lack of sexual intimacy is (was) a factor in your breakup and you were the party who refused to be intimate, you are in the "In Control" column. Also if you were turned off by your ex—if you were the one who pulled the plug—you probably are/ were more the Controllor. The caveat to that is if you felt you were forced to withdraw from sex, or moved to break off the relationship because your significant other was having an affair. In that case, you can put down a few points in the "Somewhat in Control" category.

If you are still in love with your spouse and you are either thinking about divorce or starting the process of one, but intent on going ahead with the separation (if you feel it is for the best), you can also add a point to the Loss of Love/Intimacy category. If you have been separated and divorced for a couple of years and still in love with your spouse, I am afraid you would have to tally up one big garish point under the "Out of Control" column.

Remember what I said in Chapter One: Some of the categories in the Big Six are areas in which you feel in or out of control, partially in control, or control was a factor in your relationship in the first place and is now affecting your after-marriage relationship. When one party gets rejected, that person can feel completely out of control, and not always after the marriage ends, but when you're in the beginning stages of the relationship's demise. The "area" regarding Loss of Love/Intimacy is one of those! Do not judge yourself harshly in this category; most people who experience a breakup have had a number of "ghosts" in their Loss of Love/Intimacy closets. What is important is that you do not let the rejection, or the need to reject, become an issue that is controlling you in any way.

GROWTH (Personal and Professional)

Personal Growth:

Most people grow in one way or another during the course of a personal relationship. Sometimes the couple grows internally— in personal ways—and they do so together. A good example would be a couple that decides to practice a particular religion, and they join a church or synagogue together. Through their joint experience they evolve spiritually, and again, if they do this together they will continue to relate with like minds.

Sometimes a couple will grow, but separately. She may take up the study of Buddhism, while he decides that Golf is his "church." If there are no conflicts, there may be no control issues, but just as soon as one of them thinks his or her way of communing with a Higher Power is the "right" way and there is no give, the couple can grow apart. Sometimes, when divorce is looming, it is probably because their personal growth was highly individual and their new interests, points of view, perceptions and such have caused them to grow apart.

This first set of questions is geared to get you to define to what degree you have evolved personally, and whether some of that journey has been made in tandem with your significant other, or if you have set up a dynamic where the two of you have (or are) growing apart. Bear in mind, personal growth can readily impact the relationship—cause a shift that begins to stimulate control issues. Let's see where you stand:

1. Are you the same person in thought and belief you were when you began your relationship with your ex?
   Yes _____
   No _____

2. Have any dramatic changes taken place that have caused you to change the philosophy by which you live; or have experiences put you mentally, spiritually and emotionally in a different place?
   Yes _____
   No _____

3. How has your personal growth impacted your marital relationship?
   Positively _____
   Negatively _____

4. Is your personal growth a contributing factor to the breakup of your relationship?
   Yes _____
   No _____

5. Did you "outgrow" your spouse?
   Yes _____
   No _____

6. Did your spouse "outgrow" you?
   Yes _____
   No _____

7. Did either of you opt for control or relinquish control due to the impact personal growth had on your relationship?
   Yes _____
   No _____

8. Did you abandon the relationship because of your personal growth?
   Yes_____
   No_____

9. Did your ex want out of the marriage due to his/her personal growth?
   Yes_____
   No_____

If you have grown personally, but feel your significant other has not, and you have chosen to leave the marital partnership, you can settle up under "In Control." Add one point.

If your significant other walked out because of his or her personal growth and you were traumatized by the breakup, you are probably standing knee-deep in the "Out of Control" section. Add one point.

If you grew apart and both of you knew it, and the growth created a chasm in your bond, and you both agreed it was better to go your separate ways, then tally up a point under "Somewhat in Control." Just because we grow and feel we need to "move on," and doing so does not include taking your significant other with you, it doesn't mean you are fully in control. I sometimes think the clients who suffer the most are the ones that realize they just cannot stay together because they have become two very different people. I think the answers to the remaining questions in this portion of the test will make it pretty obvious where you are and are not in control.

Professional Growth:

Let's now look at professional growth, often a major factor in causing a rift in a personal relationship, and one that creates all kinds of havoc in the control department. Like the woman who wanted to return to work despite her husband's protests, many individuals enter into control battles when one or the other starts to climb the proverbial workplace ladder. Change is hard for anyone, and there are times and there are people who just can't seem to advance with what is needed in a relationship to keep it together. Nothing can suddenly start the Control Wars faster than an upward move in career goals. I am reminded of the client I had who had been pounding on doors to sell his first screenplay. He and his wife seemed quietly content when he was still struggling to get a show biz break; however, the minute he sold his first script, everything changed in their relationship. The two finally split up.

Let's see if professional growth has impacted control in your relationship:

1. Have you or your significant other, or both of you, experienced professional growth since the two of you got together?
   Yes ____
   No ____

2. If the answer is "yes," did the professional growth belong to
   You ____
   Your ex ____
   Both of you ____

3. If you were the partner who experienced success and professional growth, did your success spawn control issues with your ex?
   Yes ____
   No ____
   Not sure ____

4. Was it your partner who has had a steady growth pattern professionally, and if so, did it stir up power struggles between the two of you?
   Yes ____
   No ____
   Not sure ____

5. Did a professional growth spurt cause the relationship to fall apart?
   Yes ____
   No ____
   Not sure ____

6. How was the impact from professional growth felt?
Suddenly ____
In intervals ____
Gradually ____

7. Are you the same person professionally you were when you began your relationship with your ex?
Yes ____
No ____

8. How has your professional growth impacted your marital relationship?
Positively ____
Negatively ____

9. Did you abandon the relationship because of your professional growth?
Yes ____
No ____

10. Did your spouse leave you because of his/her professional growth?
Yes ____
No ____

If professional growth was not a factor in your marital breakup, you need not weigh in on the scorecard on this one! I am willing to bet, however, that professional growth may have played a vital role in creating an atmosphere where one or both of you may have been jockeying for control. For instance, like the woman who wanted to return to work: If she suddenly expects her husband to pick up some of the slack in running the household, it is very possible that she and her husband would get into control issues over who is responsible for what. Or even if she does not expect him to pitch in, the dynamics have changed and the result is a change in perceived control.

If your job, or that of your significant other, changed the landscape of your relationship (or is in the process of doing so presently), and you wind up (or have wound up) in fights over what was "fair," or over one seeming to have more "gold" (wanting a higher lifestyle, a new home, more clothes while you are together or wanting more of it for child or spousal support, for instance, and you are not getting what you want), you can also put yourself down for one point in the "Out of Control" ledger.

If you were the party who benefited substantially from professional growth and it has not created any push/pull dynamics with your ex, go ahead and chalk one up for "In Control." I would be surprised if you or your ex experienced professional growth and you had no control battles, but then anything is possible. If you are a reader who has been caused tremendous grief in your personal romantic relationship by your career advancement, or that of your ex, put your point in the "Out of Control" box. For instance, if you suddenly became president of your company while your ex remains in a middle management position, and this has caused an underlying sense of friction; or if you finally got that doctorate degree and everyone now refers to you as "Dr. So-and-So," and your spouse cannot make the adjustment, these may be professional growth spurts that you felt you could not fully enjoy. Perhaps one or both of you had to stifle your enthusiasm about them. One of the biggest causes of discord over professional growth is when the "lesser-earner" suddenly becomes the "higher-earner."

If control issues have been resolved in spite of growth by either of you (let's say you're divorced and both doing well financially and there are no "gold" issues), then go ahead and weigh in under the "In Control" slot.

Growth, whether it is personal or professional, is hugely responsible for marital and relationship breakups. I am guessing, no matter what your situation, some "growth" circumstance has caused control issues to be a problem. It is inherent in most partnership breakups of a personal nature.

FEAR (Physical, Emotional and Psychological)

Though we talked a good deal about the Golden Rule being a huge factor in the face of control, fear is nearly just as great. When we are fearful, whether we think someone is going to hurt us either physically or emotionally or psychologically, we are truly playing out the role of the Controllee. Not that it is not inherent in most divorces—I see people every day who are either physically frightened of their ex, or terrified of additional emotional barrages or psychological ploys coming their way.

Fear breeds insecurity, and when people are insecure they naturally opt for control because they are so afraid of losing equilibrium, or they are afraid of being vulnerable in any way.

Prior to the divorce there is also tremendous fear regarding the marriage falling apart completely. So when this happens, people are similarly frightened and often fall victim to the other partner (the one who lives in fear) as they begin to verbally, mentally or physically attack.

The objective, however, is to stave off any additional injury—physical, emotional or psychological—and not let the *fear* of it control you. This section is also designed to help you identify if, in fact, you are caught in a need-to-control trap due to fear, or to identify if you are the one being controlled, be it physically, emotionally or psychologically.

As we get into the next chapter where I discuss the three types of wars one can wage in the divorce process, I will delve heavily into fear and emotions. For now though, let's continue on and take a look at physical fears by answering a handful of questions to see where you stand as the Controllor or the Controllee:

Physical Fear:

More people are threatened with bodily harm than most typically think. Statistics tell us that battered person syndrome is growing in alarming numbers. If you are a victim of domestic violence, or afraid you may be, look at this Big Six "area" candidly. Some people simply choose to ignore viable threats, or take physical abuse rather than take precautionary or necessary measures (and I am not just referring to restraining orders). True, some people are all squawk and no "walk," but the point to this next query is not to determine whether or not you are in danger (we will cover that later in another chapter), rather this part of the assessment is to reveal whether or not you are fearful, and how that does or does not have bearing on the control you have in your life. See where you rate with regard to the following:

1. Are you, or have you ever been, a victim of domestic violence?
   Yes _____
   No _____

2. Have you been a perpetrator of domestic violence or thought about inflicting it?
   Yes _____
   No _____

3. Has your ex made physical threats against you?
   Yes _____
   No _____

4. Do you worry about these threats being acted upon?
   Yes _____
   No _____

5. Have you ever threatened your ex?
   Yes _____
   No _____

6. Do you worry constantly about being harmed by your ex?
   Yes _____
   No _____

7. Do you constantly think about taking revenge—in physical terms—against your ex?
   Yes _____
   No _____

8. Has your ex ever threatened your children?
   Yes _____
   No _____

9. Have you ever threatened the children or had thoughts about doing so?
   Yes _____
   No _____

10. Have you ever harmed the children physically?
    Yes _____
    No _____

11. Has your ex ever harmed the children physically?
    Yes ____
    No ____

If you answered "yes" to *any* of the above, you are clearly "Out of Control" in the Physical-Fear realm. If you occasionally think about physical harm against someone, or worry about it being done to you, you can rank yourself "Somewhat in Control." If on the other hand, no one has made any threats against you, you have no reason to believe your ex would harm you, and he or she has never displayed any violent behavior in the past, then you are probably safe to put yourself "In Control" on this one. Know how powerful threats of physical violence can be in terms of feeling controlled. You may be one of the readers who is quite used to living in fear. That is no way to live! More on this in Part III, Chapter Nine.

Fear of Emotional and Psychological Harm:

As you can imagine, there are many who live in constant fear of having emotional or psychological distress inflicted upon them, for they are clearly the most common weapons people use against one another while in the throes (and before and after) of divorce.

As I pointed out in the Introduction, the main characters in "War of the Roses" exaggerate the problems often associated with the emotional-fear or psychological-fear syndrome. Each character was teetering on the brink of sheer panic, waiting for the next emotional or psychological "shoe" to drop. If you have seen the movie, you know that their emotional/psychological "damage" built to such a frantic pitch it finally gave way to physical harm. After they had exhausted all other means, the two tried to kill one another, and they succeeded. They both fell to their deaths from the chandelier!

Living in a state of fear of what someone may do to you to impart emotional or psychological harm, or having him/her do it to you, is an untenable way to live! If you are the Controller in this Big Six category, know that it is a serious problem simply because your need to inflict emotional or psychological distress on your partner means you are clearly "Out of Control." That said, I have seen few divorces where it was not just par for the course for each partner to inflict some type of emotional or psychological harm on one another. Unfortunately, in the divorce process it just becomes the norm—it's human nature. When people are hurt at such deep, personal levels, they behave in ways they never could have imagined. This does not mean you have to tolerate such abuse, or that you cannot get a grip on your need to inflict it. I merely point this out because I know it ranks up there as a headliner in the Big Six line-up; and at one time or another, I am willing to bet if you are going or have gone through a marital breakup, you have definitely been "Out of Control" in this category at some point. Some people get stuck in that groove and can never get out! Again, more on that later!

Keep that pencil sharpened as you check off the answers to this next set of questions:

1. Do you feel emotionally or psychologically vulnerable to your ex?
   All of the time _____
   Some of the time_____
   Occasionally _____
   Never _____

2. Do you still have positive "feelings" for your ex?
   Yes _____
   No _____
   Some of the time _____
   Occasionally _____
   Never _____

3. Do you still have romantic "feelings" for your ex?
   Yes _____
   No _____
   Some of the time _____
   Occasionally _____
   Never _____

4. Does your ex play "games" with you?
   Yes ____
   No ____
   Some of the time ____
   Occasionally ____
   Never ____

5. Do you believe your ex goes out of his/her way to hurt your feelings, embarrass you, or make you feel uncomfortable?
   Yes ____
   No ____
   Some of the time ____
   Occasionally ____
   Never ____

6. Is your ex able to "push your buttons"?
   Yes ____
   No ____
   Some of the time ____
   Occasionally ____
   Never ____

7. Do you feel anxious or panicky at the thought of seeing your ex with another mate?
   Yes ____
   No ____
   Some of the time ____
   Occasionally ____
   Never ____

8. Do you live in fear that your ex will "turn the kids against you"?
   Yes ____
   No ____
   Some of the time ____
   Occasionally ____
   Never ____

9. Are you afraid you will never have a fulfilling and satisfying, intimate relationship again?
   Yes _____
   No _____
   Some of the time _____
   Occasionally _____
   Never _____

10. Do you find the need to hurt your ex's feelings, push his/her buttons, or cause him/her duress?
    Yes _____
    No _____
    Some of the time _____
    Occasionally _____
    Never _____

Once again, if you have checkmarks in the "yes" column on most of these questions, then clearly you are sitting in the Controllee seat—you have fallen into the "Out of Control" column. If you find yourself constantly worrying about your ex hurting you in some emotional or psychological way, then that is one more reason for you to chalk up a big one in the "Out of Control" slot. Similarly, if you feel the need, or cannot resist the temptation to inflict emotional or psychological damage onto your ex, then you are also "Out of Control."

If you answered "yes" to just two or three of these questions, it could be you're experiencing perceived fear, and that may abate. If this is the case for you, put yourself in the "Somewhat in Control" slot. Many people may feel vulnerable early on— when they are starting the divorce process or going through the storm of it—but eventually those feelings subside and the fear or need to punish diminishes. If you have fear in this area, or a tremendous need to "get back" at your ex in emotionally hurtful or psychologically twisted ways, then this is one area you will want to spend some time getting in check.

If you marked "some of the time" or "occasionally," you can rack one up for the "Somewhat in Control" column. But keep in mind, you still have work to do!

If you answered "never" or "no," you are in a poised and enviable position! Yes, if you are strong, centered, unfettered and otherwise untouched by your ex's emotional abuse, or never feel the need to inflict it, then give yourself a high five and a point for "In Control."

SUMMING UP

As you go about tallying up your scores in the table below, bear in mind that keeping tabs is not a way of judging yourself for better or worse. Instead, this "blueprint" is meant to serve as a guide and useful tool in doing the other assignments in this book, all of which are designed to help you pay heed to what needs work on your part in order to keep you and your life "controlled" or better managed.

Congratulate yourself for making a positive identification of what it is you need to handle. This first assignment took time, soul-searching, and the courage to face things that may have seemed uncomfortable at first.

Now for your score: In category one, **Money, Property, Wealth** there was a potential for 17 points. If you scored 13 or more in the "In Control" slot, I feel relatively secure that you are secure! However, if your "Somewhat in Control" has the bulk of your points (8 or more), then you have work to do to gain some financial autonomy. If you have more than 4 in the "Out of Control" column then it is time to get to work in establishing some financial independence.

In category two, **Children**, here's where you stand: Of the 12 possible points, if you scored less than 8 in the "In Control" section, adjustments, clarity or a "take charge" attitude is your number one task. If you scored more than 4 in "Somewhat in Control," it is back to the drawing board on taking your power to be an "In Control" parent. If you scored more than 3 in "Out of Control," major work on your part to take back the reins is your next order of business.

Next, I asked you to grade yourself on **Health** issues, both Physical and Emotional. In terms of Physical, there were 15 questions. If any of these are in the "Somewhat" or "Out of Control" category, then shape up in every way. This is true unless you have a debilitating illness. In that case, get help. You need and deserve it. If you suffer no substantial handicap, realize you need to muster as much stamina as possible to handle the many stresses of divorce. If you could tally up the 15 points in the "In Control" box, you should be very pleased. Being well gives you an edge in keeping control. In terms of emotional well-being, there were a possible 30 points. If you scored more than 19 in the "In Control" column, you are doing okay, but can improve (and probably will) as you process your divorce. If you have less than 16 in the "Somewhat in Control" section, you need to go to work on yourself to get your mental well-being in better condition. If you have any points in the "Out of Control" slot, get to the nearest mental health practitioner and work on getting those points transferred to the "In Control" box.

Next is **Loss of Love**. There are 7 points to be tallied. Anything in the "Out of Control" section requires that you get a good therapist or trusted mentor to work through these issues. If you are "Somewhat in Control," having scored more than 5 in this category, I am relatively certain you will gain ground as you move through the chaos of divorce. If you have more than 5 points in the "In Control" section, I would say you are in pretty good shape; however, try to gain the other two points as you move forward with your life.

The next category had to do with **Growth**, both Personally and Professionally. There are 9 possible points for Personal Growth scores. If you have all 9 in "In Control," then you are home free on this one! If you have less than 6 in "Somewhat in Control," keep your eye on this area, for it needs work. If you have any point at all in "Out of Control," do not despair. Chances are you will be moving those points to the left two columns as you do your assignments laid out in subsequent chapters. In terms of Professional Growth: No sliding on this one either. I would like to see all 10 points summed up in "In Control." If, however, you have at least 6 in "Somewhat in Control," there is hope! If you have more than 2 points in "Out of Control," then worry! You want to see that column in this category empty, so get to work!

Lastly, we have **Fear**—fear for your physical well-being and that of your emotional and psychological status. All 11 points should fit in the Physical slot under the "In Control" section. If not, then get busy. You need to focus on safety. If you have points in either "Somewhat in Control" or "Out of Control," know there is no margin for error in this section. Lack of Emotional and Psychological fear is also important, and of the 10 points possible, I would like to see you jot them down in the "In Control" section. If you did put 3 or less in "Somewhat in Control," it is quite possible that this fear is simply transitional, and it too shall pass! If there is even one point in "Out of Control," see a good shrink. He or she can help you stave off any emotional or psychological zings, whether such fears are real, perceived or imagined.

As you may have guessed, ultimately by book's end, my goal for you is to be "In Control" in all of the Big Six areas. For now though, cut yourself some slack. No one who has ever taken this test has scored a perfect "In Control" total!

Now, as you line up your status in the three columns below, I want you to do one more assignment. Decide in each of the Big Six if you want:

1. Complete control
2. Some control
3. Equal control
4. No control

Answering these questions candidly is important as you move forward in the book. Know that where there is freedom, there is also a great deal of responsibility that goes along with assuming and taking full control (being the Controller and Shot-Caller). There is also a great deal to give up if you are *not* willing to assume any control (remaining in the Controllee post). There is also a lot of "bend" if you want some control or to *share* control. And, there is no triumph at all in having no control. Naturally, I am hopeful you will not make that an option! As you answer these four questions, you may find that your point balance may shift regarding how you graded yourself in the Big Six. Maybe handing over control makes you feel more in control; that could be the case in some instances. Giving thought to all this, and coming to terms with where you stand with "control" and how much of it you want or need, is a great start.

So give thought to each of the components in the Big Six to see what best fits your "control" needs. Coming to terms with where you want to be will help chart the course in your "Control Program."

Whatever you decide means that you've taken control and that is a great first step; that is what really counts!

	In control	Out of control	Somewhat in control
• Money • Property • Wealth			
• The Children			
• Health: Physical/ Mental			
• Loss of Love/ Intimacy			
• Growth: Personal/ Professional			
• Fear: Physical/ Emotional			

In Chapter Four, we will delve further into control, the different people within your "circle," and how to handle control issues with each of them (not just your ex). For now, though, give yourself another pat on the back. This initial task was an important one!

Petitioner, Respondent, Counsel ...
Let's get ready to R-R-R-RUM-M-M-M-BL-L-L-E!!

Chapter Three

THE CONTROL WARS:
The Typical Three

"*And you can tell her attorney that I will be picking my son up at the house, not at daycare!*" *screamed an irate, joint-custody dad, forcing me to hold the receiver as far away from my ear as my arm could reach.*

"*I hear that, but...*"

"*...and that's not all. You can also tell her attorney to tell her that the last time we had a conversation, I did not overlook the fact that she asked me three times to repeat the name of our son's baseball coach.*"

"*What are you saying, Herb?*" *I inquired, though I already knew where he was going with this comment.*

"*What am I saying?*" *he repeated.* "*What I'm saying is that Lindsay is losing it. I told you that. I tried nicely,*" *he continued, with the calm flatness as that of a blasé airline pilot informing the passengers of an updated arrival time,* "*to ask her to get help. You know her mother had an early onset of Alzheimer's, and she's always worried about that. And, well,*" *he went on, unable to hide the condescension in his voice,* "*I, too, have wondered if maybe it would be best for our son if she underwent a thorough mental exam.*"

"Herb..."

"Ms. Phillips..."

"Yes..."

"Please help Carter, please." Carter was their eight-year-old.

"Help Carter?"

"Yes. You can tell her attorney to tell her that Carter has expressed fear about his mother's forgetfulness."

I believed Herb was talking about the "cupcake incident." A few weeks earlier Lindsay had totally spaced when she forgot to drop off the desserts to Carter's second grade teacher for the Thanksgiving fest.

"You mean the cupcake thing?"

"I mean the cupcake thing."

"Well, don't forget, Herb, it was the day after you had Sarah drop Carter off for the first time..."

"Huh?"

"You remember: The day Sarah introduced herself as your fiancé."

"So?"

"So some people are traumatized to learn that their ex is dating so soon, let alone engaged."

I tried to make the next statement diplomatically. I said it rather quietly, "Herb..."

"Yeah?"

"You've only been separated for seven months. Let me tell you something. Sarah making that announcement and flashing that ring...well, that's quite a shock." I tried to say it with a little laugh, hoping he might respond with some compassion.

"Well, whatever," he said coldly. "Look, I don't care how much it costs...the reason I called was to tell you to tell her attorney that I won't do a four-way conference. I want to litigate. I want you to take my case to trial. I want custody of my son."

"It's probably going to get expensive, and your chance of prevailing is not all that great." I made one last attempt at a peace summit.

"I don't care. Money is no object. I have to go now," he said almost in the same breath, "Just about to close that deal on the hotel chain."

I said goodbye on top of a dial tone.

A DECLARATION OF WAR

Well, Herb had done it. He had declared war on every divorce front: Psychological, emotional and legal. And, in the end, it was going to cost a bundle, both in money and mental duress. And, as is typical, everyone would end up paying, especially Carter.

Herb had launched not one attack on Lindsay, but three. As frail as Lindsay may have appeared to be, somehow she had chosen a good attorney—a formidable opponent—who knew how to fight her battles. I tried to reason with Herb in a series of follow up phone calls and a lengthy letter, telling him a trial would be draining in many respects; but he told me to proceed and that he didn't care what the tab would be. And although I told him he really didn't have sufficient grounds to get the court to shift the physical child custody order to him, he emphatically instructed me to "try." I also told him "forgotten cupcakes" did not constitute a "psych eval" by the courts. Further, I cautioned him that when Lindsay found a new significant other, he might take it hard. After all, he had not wanted the divorce, Lindsay had. She filed only after repeated unsuccessful attempts to have Herb seek marriage counseling. She had become a successful stockbroker after working her way up the financial ladder at Merrill Lynch, and that had infuriated Herb. He wanted someone who was dependent upon him, and he resented the fact that she no longer was.

Herb's reasons for launching the bellicose assaults on Lindsay had little to do with reality. As in so many other cases that land on my desk, Herb's case, at the core, was all about control. He was out to "win"—to show the woman who left him that he would have the last say—and to punish her for jilting him.

Taking their eight-year-old son from her would even the score. Marrying someone else would add a few more points to the "Control Board," and waging a pre-emptive strike in the courtroom would certainly send Lindsay into a divorcee's tailspin.

Ridiculous? Yes, but not unusual.

This dynamic is played out daily in hundreds of divorces throughout the nation every day. People get emphatic, irrational, competitive, angry, mean, depressed, forgetful, and, indeed, litigious.

As I mentioned earlier, people tend to show their "shadow," their worst side, as they hunker down for any one of the three typical wars. Herb was no exception. He was ready to launch a full attack. What he did not anticipate, however, is that as vulnerable as he thought Lindsay might be, she was not afraid to go up against him. Through her attorney, she was fully prepared to defend her position. She dug in her heels on the custody issue, believing that Carter would be better off with her as the primary physical custodian.

HEAD TRIPS

Based on the phone conversation I just recounted, you can probably see where Herb was headed. He had clearly declared war on all of the three typical battlefronts with Lindsay. He had "locked and loaded" his intention to make her downright miserable. Like so many other people who go through divorce, he was not thinking rationally. He was thinking irrationally, to say the least. Interestingly, Herb, who so desperately wanted control, was out of control. I finally told him I could no longer represent him, unless he stopped his game playing. It is my custom to dismiss clients whose antics are distressing, harmful to the children, self-destructive, or unreasonable. True, I represent many difficult people. I am not suggesting I do not. But I draw a line between those who are waging war just for the hell of it—those who are doing so because they are out to get a spouse, for no productive purpose—and those who have a goal worth fighting for. Neither will I represent a client who feels the need to call all the shots. When you hire a qualified attorney, he or she is on deck for one reason only: To do his or her professional best to get positive results.

Initially, it was my understanding that good counsel is what Herb signed up for, and I was not about to get into a slug fest over unreasonable requests or be a party to his game playing.

READY, AIM…

Herb began his power struggle with a psychological attack by suggesting that Lindsay might have inherited early onset Alzheimer's. True, she had given birth at 42, and now at 50 could be considered a possible candidate for this cruel disease. Since a child was involved, this concern was not to be taken lightly; but I tried to convince Herb I did not think it was likely, even though she was sometimes forgetful. People get distracted and thoughts become muddled when a person is in shock or under grave mental distress, I told him. And believe me, there are few stresses in life more traumatic than going through the divorce process. He was not buying it; or if he was, he was not letting on.

I shared with Herb that I had one client who had put the Cheerios in the refrigerator, another who backed over her vacuum cleaner in the driveway, and yet another who mistakenly and accidentally put his frozen grocery store foods in the pantry cupboard. It does not necessarily mean, I told Herb, that someone has dementia or Alzheimer's when they forgot day-to-day things. It is simply that the mind can be so preoccupied with the stress of all the divorce variables that it functions in ways it otherwise would not.

Herb still was not buying it.

He insisted Lindsay's mental stability should be checked out. Herb's need to push this point—to put questions in many people's minds (including their own son's)—was clearly a direct hit on the psychological war front. If he had good reason to think his son was in a precarious position because of it, I would have been the first to step forward and defend his position. But after a careful probe on the issue, there just was not enough evidence for me to suspect Lindsay was suffering from anything other than "divorce."

Again, Herb also attempted to get me to buy in, but I am always skeptical when these wars begin. I have learned that when such allegations are put before me they are probably not accurate. Herb was not fooling me. My job was to resolve his matter as efficiently as possible without making him more hostile by thinking I was not his advocate. I certainly was up to that point. I am with all my clients. I feel I can do a greater service to them, though, if I can help them see reality and get through their divorce with as little collateral damage as possible. I do believe in going to trial, but only after all other options have been exhausted.

If you have ever seen the movie "Gaslight," where the main character (played by Charles Boyer) tries to make his love interest (played by Ingrid Bergman) think she is crazy, you will get a very clear picture of psychological warfare.

In brief, it is when one person (or both) tries to make the other question his or her sanity, or when one or the other attempts to persuade others that his or her opponent is not mentally fit. Psychological Warfare extends beyond these boundaries to include any attack that plays havoc with one's peace of mind and mental well being or focuses on the object of ruin. In the Psychological War, "mind games" are the order or the day!

Psychological warfare can be one of the cruelest forms of combat since it is sinister and deviant. Unlike many emotional wars, which I will discuss soon, psychological wars take plotting, planning and time. Those who choose this path often do so by carefully calculating how to effectively hurt their soon-to-be or ex spouse, in a deep and often vicious way, by disturbing their mental equilibrium. Indeed, most people who choose to use weapons of "mind destruction" play out a chess game of sorts in their heads beforehand, strategizing and even carefully plotting eventual counterattacks. They can play out a scenario anticipating a response, then offer another attack, aimed at further maiming one's mental well-being, or destroying it altogether.

That said, it does not mean that people who engage in this type of divorce war are necessarily bad people or evil, by any means (although, yes, some can be). It is simply another unfortunate phenomenon of what happens to the human psyche—what can happen with human nature as the divorce process begins to take its toll. Desperate people do desperate things. And, again, when one is in the throes of divorce, the sky is the limit for uncharacteristic behavior and desperation. Odd, I know, when you consider that the person waging this war was undoubtedly the same person who swore "to love, to honor, to cherish…!" Oh boy!

What you need to know is that psychological warfare, like any other warfare, is all about control. So whether you are the one perpetrating it, or whether you are the one forced to defend yourself in it, it is a tough situation. Often no one wins this type of war. It is insidious; psychological war breeds emotional contempt and reaction, and ultimately can lead to a full-blown legal war.

Psychological warfare is a powerful way to attempt to keep the upper hand, especially when the person who is being attacked has already shown signs of being in a weak mental state. These include individuals such as Lindsay, who absentmindedly forgot small details, that ordinarily she or others would, at any other time in their lives, have likely remembered. When Lindsay asked Herb for the name of the baseball coach three times (if, in fact, that was true), it could have meant she was rattled and upset. Perhaps he had dropped some kind of mental bomb on her that shook her up and made it impossible for her to concentrate.

In this case, it was Herb versus Lindsay in the psychological war; yet in many instances both parties play head-trips back and forth, and just as in the movie "War of the Roses," it can become ugly and irretrievably destructive. Here is something else to consider: It could very well be that unknown to Lindsay, she was engaged in inflicting psychological assaults onto Herb. Case in point: Retaining custody of their eight-year-old son, Carter, was driving Herb nuts! Having left Herb was another source of torment, and he was ostensibly acting this out with this "Lindsay is certifiably deranged" game.

I always try to steer my clients away from playing such detrimental head games or imparting such irreparable damage because, just as in many other wars, such efforts are nonproductive and futile in the end, and the mental carnage can leave permanent scars.

I caution all my clients to take the high road, to wear the proverbial "white hat," because I am sure they will come off looking better for it to everyone involved, from the children to the judge. I also know that they ultimately will feel better about themselves—if they will not allow themselves to get sucked in.

You may be asking why I am in this business if I tend to be "anti-war." Well, no one feels more strongly about going to court when absolutely necessary than I do; but I do not believe in psychological warfare as a means to settle disputes. It is wrong, and more importantly, it is a dangerous game to play. It becomes like a business dispute between two powerful corporations without the budget and with far more collateral damage, i.e. the children! I know couples who play psychological warfare "chicken" over long periods of time, and I have yet to see anyone ever win! I will have more on this in Chapter Six.

HEART ATTACK

When Sarah, the fiancée, showed up at Lindsay's to drop off Carter after a visitation weekend, she knowingly or unknowingly declared a war of the emotional type on Lindsay.

Whether Sarah realized it or not, Lindsay was deeply shocked when she suddenly learned that her husband, from whom she had been separated for only seven months, was engaged to be married to someone else. The couple's divorce had been filed only weeks before!

One way to assert control is for one or the other party to keep the other off guard and off balance emotionally. This is exactly what Herb tried to do to Lindsay. It was not just one attack, either. He confided in me that the ruby ring that belonged to his grandmother—the one that Lindsay wore on her right hand for all the years the two were married, and the ring she returned to him at his insistence—was given to Sarah who flaunted it proudly (on her right hand, along with her new engagement ring on her left hand). Chances are Sarah did not know this heirloom meant a great deal to Lindsay (or maybe she did), but in any case it was another successful attack—a powerful missile launched by the "Herb" camp—intended to inflict emotional damage onto Lindsay.

Often when people engage in the wars of the emotional type, they do not wage one targeted attack. They hit their opponent from many sides simultaneously. Wreaking emotional havoc, of course, is one more way to fight for and gain control. And, do not forget what I have stated all along: When it comes to most divorces, control is the central issue. If you can keep someone in a state of upset, then you have truly found a way to control them—to lord power over them. I tell my clients who get embroiled in these emotional wars—whether they are the instigator or the victim—that their time is better spent on other things. Lindsay knew Herb well. He was vindictive in business dealings apparently (or so I later heard), so it came (or should have come) as no surprise to her that he would seek vengeance on her. But even when one knows a person has a tendency to inflict emotional damage, one never knows when it will strike them. Such was the case with Lindsay opening her front door to see Carter and Sarah, and both the engagement and the heirloom rings! Catching someone off guard with an emotional zing, by the way, is a powerful way to beat down the psyche, leaving it vulnerable to a psychological attack.

I had one female client who, after so many emotional attacks, began to question everything about herself. Each emotional jab beat down her sense of mental well being and self-worth, until finally she began to experience severe panic attacks. She wound up spending three months in a mental institution and had years of therapy to "regain" her "self"!

As you can see, sometimes emotional wars can segue into the psychological ones. This is when the two wars very often meld together.

RETALIATION

What most people who inflict emotional damage do not bargain for is that the other party will return the emotional "fire" at some point and quite possibly in a bigger and grander way. When people feel they are losing a grip on control in emotional wars, they will up the ante. They will find ways to make the counterattack that much more dramatic and hurtful. For every one salvo in an emotional war, the perpetrator can expect one or more in return.

Emotional wars are those marital-type conflicts geared to hurt another's feelings. They are the divorce war "variety" designed to penetrate one's feelings at a very deep and painful level.

Playing upon one's insecurities, frailties and vulnerabilities is at the heart of an emotional attack. I have yet to handle a divorce where an emotional war was not involved, and I doubt I ever will. You may think that is because I handle celebrity clients, but not so. I also handle others who have no notoriety and who cannot seem to resist the need to start an emotional battle.

Emotional wars are often fought to gain an advantage in court (which usually backfires), and if there are children involved, they are fought to gain allegiance toward one parent over the other. This, too, is a very dangerous war because it has severe repercussions.

Emotional wars are awfully tempting.

Emotional wars are the most common of all divorce wars. Often one or the other party may wage one unintentionally. A good example is the type of damage Herb may have inflicted on Lindsay via Sarah. For instance, let's say Herb had suddenly showed up at Carter's Little League baseball game with Sarah. Let's also say he was callous to the thought that when Lindsay encountered Sarah there for the first time it might surprise her and hurt her feelings. Perhaps Herb did not premeditate this event, did not really think about it and the hurt it would cause, but still, his doing so could serve as a great kick-off for an emotional war!

Like a recklessly tossed hand grenade, one never knows where an unintentional emotional rocket will land. Some people don't give thought to launching this type of war; they just do it mindlessly. Yet, others launch the emotional war intentionally. And once they do—whether mindlessly or intentionally—the retaliation often begins.

Had Herb not considered how Lindsay might react when Sarah dropped off Carter that evening, that incident would still have been enough to launch a legitimate emotional strike. I will say, however, when it comes to divorce, most strikes in emotional wars are planned. I feel strongly that Herb knew exactly what Lindsay's reaction would be. He had always been the one to drop off Carter, and setting both women up for this emotional "moment" was something he must have known would be painful to his soon-to-be ex wife. It may have also made his soon-to-be wife extremely uncomfortable, unless of course, as I alluded to earlier, she was in on the evil maneuver. Whoever the instigator is (whoever was in "control" in this attack), I must point out, will bear the brunt in time, for as corny as it must sound, what goes around comes around! I have been doing divorce law for enough years to notice that without fail, he or she will "get theirs" at some point. It is Universal Law, I suppose. So then, one must always consider when strategizing and gearing up for a premeditated emotional attack what the consequences will be.

What is important to note, is that intentionally or unintentionally, when a party is attacked in an emotional war, he or she may retaliate with even greater force. It is simply human nature. It is painful to have been so intimate in a relationship then suddenly shrink back when someone hurts you in your "deep parts." And so, one emotional bullet can invite two in return. From there the battle escalates.

Something else: Whoever thinks they are prevailing day-to-day in an emotional war thinks they have an advantage in the control department. If a person is constantly attacked emotionally, he or she will undoubtedly feel the loss of control and therefore emphasize the need for "emotional equality." He or she will find it necessary to even the emotional score. When that happens, people begin behaving in uncharacteristic and shameful ways. "Tit-for-tat" is what I constantly see. Most people in the throes of divorce (and those who carry the baggage from it well after the divorce) have knee-jerk reactions to the emotional missiles fired at them, and they cannot seem to stop their Pavlovian reactions.

What I find disheartening is that these emotional wars can last a long time—or a lifetime—for both parties and their children as well. The children, of course, become prime "collateral damage." The bottom line is this: Once this type of war gets underway, it is very difficult for people to stop the destructive momentum.

Emotional wars are not always fought on the porches of couples' homes or Little League fields; they are also fought in mediation sessions, Conciliation Courts, and Four-Way Conferences (meetings where both attorneys and their clients attend), or Settlement Conferences, as well as during court trials. I have seen more free-for-all fights in settlement conferences than I care to recall! Often one person will hurl a caustic or hurtful remark at the other, and though we attorneys attempt to stop the bullets, or deflect them before they really begin to cause major damage, the fallout can be devastating.

I had a colleague who told me about a client who turned to her attorney during one such meeting, and in front of her estranged husband made a crack about her husband's impotence. The man turned crimson out of both embarrassment and rage. One month later he showed up at the follow up conference with a woman 25 years his junior—a starlet type who he carefully placed in the lobby for his ex to see. In order to level the playing field, my colleague supposed, was her client's reason for having an affair with her ex's business partner shortly after *that* meeting. Yikes!

You may ask: What is the difference between psychological and emotional war? Though, as I stated the lines are often blurred, a psychological war is one that is often planned, contemplated, and geared to mess with a person's *mind*. An emotional war is geared more toward messing with someone's *feelings*. An emotional war is often fought in the heat of passion, but can also be fought sans passion; it is just triggered by an emotional response. A psychological war, on the other hand, comes at the expense of the person or persons involved on the opposing side (such as the children or other family members). It is most often designed to win "in the end"—to call the last shot. Both these wars, however, can intertwine, and both can be waged simultaneously. The most important thing to consider about either of these wars is that they always have to do with control; the bottom-line purpose is to get or maintain control, or to keep from being controlled!

COLLATERAL AND OTHER DAMAGE

The third most common war in this trilogy is the legal war. Sometimes a legal war is legitimate; other times it's fought simply as a way to escalate the psychological and emotional wars and jockey for a stronger hold on control.

Whether or not the case ever goes the distance, a legal war is one that is fought when legal papers are drafted and/or filed for the purpose of resolving issues inside the courtroom. A legal war can be costly in both emotional and psychological terms, but then add to that dollars and cents, and this type of war is the most difficult and costly of all—albeit in dollars. The psychological and emotional wars can indeed be more costly, but not to the wallet. A legal war is one where neither side has much control because they relinquish it to the discretion of a judge or in some states, to a jury.

When a war over assets, real property, a prenuptial agreement, child custody, spousal or child support is necessary, a legal battle may be the only remedy, and that is where I certainly come in—and for good reason. But what I tell all my clients is this: Legal battles—the ones that wind up in the courtroom before a judge—can be extremely costly. And even if a case is settled before trial, what is involved and what it can cost can be mind-boggling. The mental and physical tab is draining enough in a legal war, but add to that the price tag of financial drain! The toll associated with this type of war cannot be measured or budgeted for in advance.

Most legal wars, nearly 90 percent of them I would say, are settled on the courtroom steps, or shortly before a trial is due to begin. But those that are waged on the courtroom floor can be brutal, because no matter how well someone is prepared, no matter how good one's attorney, no matter how solid they feel their case is, no matter how much money they spend funding it, the outcome is still in the hands of a judge, and one never knows how she or he will rule. The judge then becomes the "Controller!"

My advice, always: Work it out. Settle your case if you can.

If you launch a preemptive legal strike against your spouse you had better be ready for heavy artillery, because most courtroom battles are fought between attorneys representing those who have declared the war.

Attorneys—generally—know what they are doing!

War is their occupation.

So, if you stand up and scream, "We're going to court!" get ready for a big battle! Be prepared, I tell my clients, for a difficult time. Also be prepared for delays and frustrations, for they are the norm. A trial set for June may not be heard until the following year; or the trial may be heard a few days at a time over several years. Attempts to get financial records—the ones you thought would be a breeze to get your hands on—may take weeks and thousands of dollars to track down. And if you were certain the case would go your way, well, it may turn out exactly the opposite! I have seen judges switch physical custody arrangements. I have seen one party ordered to pay the other far more than they had anticipated in a modification of child support. I have also seen others made to relinquish assets and holdings they were certain would be awarded to them.

The legal war is often an ugly war. No one on either side walks off the battlefield unscathed.

Court appearances can cost big bucks—and there could be several of them in a legal war. The paperwork alone is expensive and overwhelming. There are written declarations (called affidavits in some states), document productions and subpoenas (forms of obtaining documents that back up your case), interrogatories, requests for admissions, depositions, as well as property and business appraisals, custody evaluations, psychological evaluations, trial briefs, schedules, charts—not to mention hiring experts, preparing witnesses for court, etc. In certain cases, it could also mean tracing financial assets, a marital lifestyle analysis, and in some instances, the equivalent of a fraud audit.

All this work takes an inordinate amount of time. When the attorneys are involved—and they almost always are in a legal war—time is money! The payment for a legal war can cause a large deficit in your mental, emotional and financial pocketbook!

Here is the kicker: Even when you are fully prepared for that court appearance, it does not mean your case will be heard and/or resolved as you finally get to court! Your case could be continued merely because of the court's busy calendar. When it is, the time between appearances may necessitate your attorney's need to update many of the documents, exhibits and records, for circumstances can change in the interim and these materials may need updating. Also, your attorney will no doubt need to bone up again for the hearing if too much time has elapsed. Think of it this way: It is akin to being prepared to take an exam, having the test postponed, then once it is rescheduled, cramming again to be totally prepared. You, too, may have to re-prepare your thoughts and testimony.

Once in court, your case may not be heard on consecutive days. There may be additional continuances in order for your attorney or opposing counsel to revisit certain issues brought before a judge. All this could take days, weeks and sometimes months or years. Also, the waiting time can be grueling in other ways. Each time an issue is brought before a judge the attorney-meter starts running all over again. Your attorney may have to gear up by updating those financial records, paperwork, briefs and summaries.

The legal war is what I, like many of my colleagues, do best. However, a legal war—court action—should be your last resort, as I hope this chapter has demonstrated.

If you elect to engage in a legal war, know what you are starting! If you are the one declaring it, your first order of business is to sit down with your attorney and do a complete evaluation of what such a war will cost, both in dollars and collateral damage (i.e., how it will affect the children, grandparents, business colleagues, etc.), before you launch that first attack. If you are on the end of having a war waged against you, a pre-emptive strike may be your best defense. Again, confer with legal counsel.

FIGHTING FOR A WORTHY CAUSE

One reason so many seek court assistance in divorce matters is because the emotional and psychological wars are out of control. And sometimes it is just because the parties are unable or unwilling to compromise. But a legal war to get more money may gain a person very little when attorneys' fees, court costs, and perhaps missed work is considered. Let me explain. Not too long ago, I turned down a client because I assessed the financial pros and cons and determined that it would not be advantageous for him to seek a reduction is his child support payments. That client then hired other counsel and spent $40,000 in legal fees to get a $150 per month reduction in his child support payments. Yes, he got the reduction, but he was also ordered to pay his ex-wife's attorney fees of $25,000, as well as his attorney $40,000! Well, you do the math! You can see that fighting over money can sometimes cost more than it is worth.

I know people who sought modification of their child or spousal support payments because they learned their former spouse's income had increased. Sounds sensible when you consider that the court makes rulings on support payments based, in part, on a person's ability to pay. But what if the person who is making more money hides it? This happens every day. Sometimes it is hard to prove. Yes, people lie. They can go to great lengths to hide documents, finagle money, or move it around. All in all, some people get very creative when the time comes to divulge those new earnings.

So then by the time you do your discovery (depositions, interrogatories, etc.), go to court and pay a forensic accountant to analyze all the financial records (which he or she may not be able to access to substantiate your claim), the fees can become astronomical. Naturally, the toll becomes even greater when you consider the amount of stress you go through to gear up for such a war. It is positively exhausting. I prepare for hearings and trials on a regular basis. It is my job, so although I am used to it and often thrive on it, it also can be physically draining for me. But the average person hasn't a clue as to how tiring it can be to participate in the process.

Talk about a drain! The lesson here: Do not head off to a legal war you cannot handle, may not win, or cannot afford! Also do a cost benefit analysis with your attorney to make sure what you are spending will likely garner a viable return for money spent and get you the results you are after. But then again, there are no guarantees.

Many times, a legal war is the only way to resolve issues. Sometimes it is a matter of simply getting an answer—a concrete resolution to an issue that has been argued over for months. A good example might be the parents who are at odds over what school the child should attend. In those cases the legal war may be the only viable solution. I have clients who would rather have a definitive answer, even if the outcome is not what they wanted, just so they can finally put the dispute to rest.

Sometimes a legal war is necessary because all other avenues have been exhausted without resolution. For instance, there are times when child custody issues require a court hearing. This happens in instances when the parents may have made genuine attempts to find a solution, but just cannot come to terms. Perhaps the dispute is over whether the child should be allowed to move across the country with one parent, or whether the child should be on a particular type of medication or be in therapy, or what daycare the child should go to, or whether to home school the youngster or send him to public or private school. I know people who were willing to spend thousands just to have the right to pick the pediatrician.

Another instance where a court hearing may be necessary is when dealing with the negligence of one parent—whether it has to do with physical or sexual abuse of the child or neglect in making regular child support payments.

What I do want you to realize, however, is that the legal war is not unlike the psychological and emotional war. Often at the root is a maniacal need for control! I know many people who go to court just to topple their ex by hitting him or her in the pocketbook—not necessarily an effective way of getting retribution. In many instances, the Golden Rule litigation prevails; in other instances, it backfires. The courts may see one person as greedy and rule in the other's favor. If you are the one with the most "gold," you might consider every plausible avenue of settlement rather than winding up in court. Don't forget: The courts are also there to enforce the law. Judges very much dislike it when those who come before them are just there to waste judicial time. Think twice!

Something else: When my clients insist on going to trial, I caution them to be ready for the unexpected in terms of rulings because there are so many variables. What often stops people from taking a case the distance—going to trial—is that they realize they have less control than if they were to try to work out issues between themselves with the assistance of their attorneys. Ironically, going to court to gain control over an issue could set up a situation where there is little if any control over the issue being contested, because as I mentioned, the outcome will be decided by a judge. Very often the law can be interpreted to the judge's preferences. The judge may not see the merit of one party's case or point of view over the other. What often happens, without both parties realizing it, is that they have virtually turned over control to a third party—the judge—someone they do not even know and who does not know them!

I have a dear friend who called me for help after the following occurred: She had gone to court to rectify the issue of her husband continually being late in picking up their son for visitation. During a court proceeding, my friend wanted the judge to sanction her ex-husband for causing such unnecessary disruptions and for costing her money in babysitting fees. Her ex argued through his attorney that he was working hard to make the child support payments she was given, and because of demanding work commitments could not help but be late in picking up their daughter. The judge sided with the husband, sympathizing that the burden was on him to pay a hefty chunk of change every month! The judge appealed to my friend to be more lenient. Rather than giving her babysitting fees and sanctioning her ex, he instead ordered that the husband be given a two and a half hour window for picking up their child. Naturally my dear friend was livid, but this case makes my point: While she certainly had a valid complaint and her requests seemed equitable, since courts often allow a window for visitation pick up (say 30 minutes), the judge ruled from a completely different point of view.

This is not to take away from real issues where both parties have legitimate positions that cannot be resolved by compromise, and it is ultimately up to the judge to make the call. For example, if one party wants to move across the country with the children. That is often a situation that the parties cannot resolve themselves.

When legal wars are waged, psychological and emotional wars often follow, for it is hard to avoid these other wars with the friction and competitiveness that takes place in a legal battle.

If you are a reader contemplating court action, I would urge you to make an evaluation as to whether or not such a war is to your children's benefit, helpful to your financial situation, or good for your personal welfare. I will discuss this point more thoroughly in Part Two, Chapter Seven when I have you make that determination through a series of very pointed questions.

If your ex is insisting on the court's involvement, do what you can to settle, because legal wars are draining even when you emerge victorious.

WAR IS NOT GOOD FOR CHILDREN AND OTHER LIVING THINGS

As I have already stated, I am not opposed to fighting in the courtroom if the battle to be fought is a legitimate one; yet I would far sooner see my clients settle all their disputes reasonably, especially when children are involved. No one is more vulnerable to becoming a casualty than the child who innocently gets pulled into the war.

Children are among the first and biggest casualties in a legal war, yet they are hardly ever willing combatants.

A poster in the 60s read, "War is not good for children and other living things." It became very popular and formed a consciousness about the horrific detriments of war with regard to the physical and mental well being of children. I believe this philosophy aptly applies to marital wars and the importance of protecting the child. One judge in Orange County, California, proclaimed that involving the children in a couple's "war" was blatant child abuse! He certainly made a thought-provoking point! For in many cases, the skirmishes, battles and all-out wars are extremely detrimental to the children.

Children tend to think they are at fault when parents fight. When they are aware of a psychological or emotional war, or dragged into a legal war as unwitting participants, the toll can be devastating. Many times, children are yanked emotionally and psychologically (as well as legally) back and forth by both parents, and in the process, and for years to come, scars are deeply etched.

What is even of more concern is that those parents who are so embroiled in their need for control use the children or recruit them to help fight their wars. I am not passing judgment on anyone when I say this, for most people going through divorce do behave bizarrely and unusually when under such duress. But I urge you to keep the children out of any and all wars.

Having made that statement, I realize that emotional wars often include the children. For instance, they may feel your hurt when your ex shows up at the Little League game with his or her new significant other. They may also be dragged into the war when they see you in tears or in a fit of rage over something that happened between you and your ex. I understand how difficult it truly is to keep things separate, but you must, especially if you want to maintain control of both yourself and the situation!

My request is this: That you try very hard not to involve the children in your wars, *ever*—be they psychological, emotional or legal. As the judge in Orange County so emphatically pointed out: As a parent, one's job is to protect and nurture children. Taking them onto the battlefield is irresponsible, indeed, abusive.

I knew of one warring couple who were engaged in a horrific tug 'o war over the children, a boy and a girl, 11 and 13, respectively. The mother had been awarded primary physical custody of the children, though her ex wanted that custody arrangement. Rather than participate in making the children miserable, she finally handed over physical custody of her children, opting to see them once a week and every other weekend. In the end, she knew that the wars would have been chronic—endless—had the children stayed in her physical custody. What is interesting is that her husband felt he finally had "control"—he finally "won." Ironically, she won. She was able to love her children in a very unselfish way. She was still able to see them regularly and involve herself in their daily lives, and even though it was a painful adjustment, she gained tremendous peace of mind. From her vantage point, the wars were just too costly to both her and her children. She could foresee that she would have stayed embroiled in all three of the "Typical Three Wars," with no end in sight. The direction in which her situation was going was like that of King Solomon, and she was not about to allow her children to be symbolically cut in half!

In making her choice this woman retained complete control of her well being and ultimately felt she had a more solid sense of control over the well being of her children, as well. Eventually, I might add, when the children were grown, when they were of college age, they distanced themselves from their father who they came to realize was (in their words) manipulative and controlling. My client may have given up a lot, but when all the dust had settled she prevailed in a very positive light. The children opted to spend holidays with her and she was the source they consulted when they needed sound and mature advice. If there was any winning to be done, I suppose in the end, she was the victor.

STOP THE WAR, I WANT TO GET OFF

What I most want you to come to terms with is that once a war gets started, it is very hard to stop. Just as in the film, "War of the Roses," (those parties just could not help themselves after a while), the sheer force of the wars themselves seemed to propel and sweep them into deeper crevices of destruction. So, choose your battles carefully and make a conscious decision that you will be able to handle whatever war in which you enlist! If you are on the receiving end, do what you can to stop the war from raging before it gets really out of hand.

If you are one of the readers who finds it impossible to stay out of the line of fire no matter how hard you try, do not give up; you will find tips in each of the separate "War" chapters in Part Two to help you avoid stepping on psychological, emotional and legal minefields. So, stay tuned.

IN SUM

The most important point I wish to make in this chapter is this: Everyone usually suffers in war. Ask yourself right now: Is a war necessary? Will it get you what you want? Is it productive? Can you handle losing? Will you think less of yourself if you walk away from one? And most importantly, must you really fight a war to maintain a healthy sense of control? The art of control comes in the ability to find equitable solutions and to make peace, both with your ex and yourself.

Let's move on to Part Two now of the book for a discussion on others who may have control in your divorce situation and advice on how to handle them. Keep in mind, these three types of wars are not always launched by your ex. They can also be waged by friends, in-laws, the children, business associates, and others caught up in your marital web.

You picked a bad day to forego mediation.

Chapter Four

WHO'S IN CONTROL—
YOU OR THEM?

"Look, I suggest you go along with my recommendation to file an ex parte, Maria," said a loud divorce attorney through a raspy, baritone voice over the telephone.

"But, I would rather you contact Jason's attorney again and see if we can try, just one more time, to get him to give me the address where Jason and the kids will be in Aspen," said a nervous, timid woman, her voice trailing off with the word "Aspen." "Just one more time, plea…"

"Please don't tell me how to do my job, Maria!" he belted.

"But a court hearing will just set him off again and he's already made me and my children's lives miserable. I'm concerned he'll take it out on…"

"Look, I can't be responsible for your ex-husband's behavior," he shot back through a snarl. "He has to comply with the law."

"But, I want to explain something…"

"I'm afraid I have a meeting and I'm running late, Maria." Losing patience, "Meet me in Department 48 tomorrow morning, eight forty-five sharp."

"But it will be too…"

"Have a nice day, Maria." He was gone.

Maria was left holding the receiver against her ear, frozen in despair and resignation, a feeling that was becoming all too familiar to her at the conclusion of her phone calls with her divorce attorney.

Maria, like so many others, found herself hopelessly stuck in a client/attorney relationship that made her feel anxious and uncomfortable. Ironically, Maria picked an attorney just like she picked a husband; she had a penchant for choosing men who were domineering and terribly uninterested in her concerns.

Maria is not alone. There are hundreds of divorcees just like her. I am not saying they all pick an attorney like their ex's. But, many of those dealing with divorce do experience similar control issues—both with their ex and with their attorney. It is not unusual for people to be thrust into relationships where the same control frustrations they tried to get away from are nearly identical to the ones they encounter with the very person they hired to do their bidding! It is crazy, yes, but oh so common!

Ostensibly, Maria hired Mr. Hubert P. Doddard to protect her interests as she journeyed through the travails of her divorce, and in good faith in that contractual arrangement, she figured that would include his taking into consideration her points of view and utmost concerns.

Though she had specific anxieties about her former husband's reactions to her attorney's actions, her attorney seemed to care less. He, like other attorneys of his character, was interested only in winning. He was not keen on hearing or discussing Maria's fears. And so it goes, often between clients and attorneys.

In this type of dynamic, the client is clearly not in control.

But, you might argue, didn't Maria hire Mr. Doddard to represent her interests, and wasn't he doing just that? Further, wasn't he the professional, and shouldn't he have been calling the shots on Maria's behalf?

Well, yes and no.

He was the professional with the legal expertise, but he was not exactly functioning as her advocate in the true sense of the word.

I have alluded to it in all of the previous chapters, but I will say it again: I firmly believe it is people like Maria who should have the control. Sure, Doddard, as the attorney, needed to assert a certain amount of control. It is his job to take the lead and see that things get done for her benefit—but based on what she wanted for herself and her family, not what he wanted for Maria and her family. Yet when Doddard failed to listen to Maria—to take her concerns into account—he left her feeling frustrated and vulnerable to yet another salvo by her ex. Had he offered options that would have made Maria feel more comfortable, he would have been of greater service to her.

Doddard did nothing to see the situation through Maria's eyes. A really good divorce attorney—at least by my definition—will do that.

I am not suggesting that Doddard was not a polished and knowledgeable attorney. To the contrary, he was probably well known for his ability to prevail in court proceedings. But I am suggesting that he was not in Maria's corner in other ways.

You might also argue that Maria could have asserted herself. She could have resisted by politely explaining that she disagreed with Doddard's approach. Yes, Maria could have taken control of her situation. Unfortunately though, for her and many others faced with similar delicate situations during divorce transitions, Maria had become intimated by her attorney—just as she was intimidated by her husband. And the same holds true for others—they are often reluctant to speak up.

Maria could have also taken control of her situation by finding another attorney, one with whom she was more in tune. Like others in her quandary, Maria was having to deal with the enormity of such a major life transition that she probably did not have the energy or the wherewithal to find someone else. So Maria did what others tend to do: Just stay put. Sadly, it is not unusual then for those who do so to feel constant aggravation and ultimately regret because they are rendered somewhat helpless.

Of course, helplessness is the neurotic twin to no-control.

People going through a divorce should select an attorney carefully to find the one who suits their needs. Clients should also decide how much control they want or need as they deal with issues presented to them and wade through the murky and often rocky waters of divorce.

Though there are a variety of divorce attorney types, Doddard is what I would categorize as the "Warrior." It seems that his answer to handling divorce issues was to slug it out in a Legal War. Many divorce attorneys are like that. That may be effective for some clients, but not for those like Maria. She may have needed to shop around for another lawyer whose approach and advocacy better suited her personality and mental well-being.

You should pick the *type* of divorce attorney who serves your needs, but also leaves you with a comfortable feeling. That includes a say-so, if you want it, in decisions you may feel strongly about.

For some, having an attorney take full control, oddly enough, may make them feel *they* are in control. Some people not only want that, but they need that. As such, a Doddard might be the man for the job. However, I have learned through colleagues and from my own personal client experiences, that most people dealing with divorce and its many complicated facets have the need to *feel* they have some control, some power throughout the course of the divorce process. And, most want a say in decisions.

So, the key then is finding the type of attorney that works for you! Or, if you already have an attorney on board, deciding whether he or she is the right choice. In some cases, your choice may depend upon not only your personal preferences, but also your objectives. For example, you may single out a specific lawyer based on his or her expertise in handling cases that involve child custody issues; or you may choose one who is known for getting large financial settlements. Indeed, some attorneys will not handle any child custody matters but only financial matters. How does one go about finding the right attorney? I speak on this topic often and always tell those I speak before to ask trusted business associates for a referral. These sources might include your CPA, your business attorney, or your therapist. When you get these names, make an introductory appointment with the attorneys that pique your interest. Ask questions. Inquire as to how they would handle your case. See if your goals line up with his or her approach. This initial meeting will provide you the perfect opportunity to gain a sense of whether your goals and his or her approaches to your case will line up. Also, be sure and ask about retainer agreements and costs. Interviewing a handful of potential attorney-candidates will be well worth the time and money spent.

Since everyone is different, I want you to ultimately decide what type is best for you and how much control you want or need, to be comfortable in your dealings. Also, if you already have an attorney in place, this is the perfect time to ask that very important question with regard to that attorney relationship: Who is in control?

To aid you in making an appropriate choice, I have provided a brief description of what I think constitutes the most common divorce attorney types.

Lawyers are as diverse in personality as any other group of business service professionals. I have studied my peers and the following depicts what I think make up the other general categories, i.e. types of lawyers, and of course, these types overlap.

See if you can identify your attorney (the one you have or the one you want) in one of these descriptions and most important of all, assess whether that type is best for you and where you stand on the control front.

The "Warrior": This is the type like Doddard. They plow full speed ahead, usually winding up in a courtroom on a regular and repeated basis in each case. This is their modus operandi: They prefer playing the divorce game in the courtroom. The Warrior likes competition and he likes to win. Warriors have no qualms about taking off for the battlefield at the least provocation. A Warrior is terrific when your last resort is a bonafide Legal War, but often times this species can create more havoc and chaos than good. The Warrior may not always choose his battles prudently, especially when he gets knee deep in the front-line trenches.

I believe every good divorce attorney should have a Warrior "within" (I certainly do); but to behave bellicose 24/7 is not necessarily the answer.

The "Parent": This type is the "father/mother figure." They are known to "caretake" throughout the divorce process; but just like Mom and Dad, they may have a tendency to tell you what is best for you and insist on your following their lead regardless of what you think or feel. Now, this approach may work just fine for you; but keep in mind, the hand-holder type is not terribly willing when it comes time to relinquish control.

The "Wimp": This person backs off from any confrontation, whether it is coming from you, opposing counsel, or the judge. He or she would rather just settle the case and collect fees. Beware of the Wimp, for he or she is not likely to take a stand when taking one is necessary. From my experience, and quite possibly from those around you who have gone through the divorce process, the Wimp is the type that wants no control. The Wimp would just as soon you keep control, preferring the path of least resistance.

The "Lazybone": The way in which this lawyer type differs from the Wimp is that the Lazybone just cannot seem to get the job done. He or she is notoriously late in returning telephone calls, tardy in filing the proper paperwork, forever losing important documents, cannot seem to remember details, and, to the extreme, can also be known to nod off in a deposition or lengthy court proceeding. There is really no control problem with the Lazybone—he or she is often more than happy for you to take charge.

The "Egomaniac": This is an interesting type, for he/she often wants control since it bolsters his/her ego. With this type, if he/she cannot run the show, they would rather have no show at all! They, like the Warrior, *need* to prevail. It is driven by a basic instinct in them! These types are incredibly conscious of what others think, and therefore may do an excellent job on a client's behalf, just to make one more overwhelming impression. The Egomaniac, however, is not apt to give away much control, preferring to use it as a means of saying, "See, how perfectly *my* strategy worked out!" The difficulty with the Egomaniac is that if they are "shown up" by opposing counsel or the judge, they can sometimes react negatively by wielding power randomly (in order to stay on top), and suddenly control becomes a real free-for-all!

The "Bait and Switch": This type often rests on his or her laurels—a fine reputation or that of a celebrated one—but shuffles you over to a firm associate or partner. The Bait and Switch usually charges big bucks and may even try to warrant those hefty fees, though you come to find out that one of his/her attorneys is actually working your case. When you hire an attorney be clear on what you want. Do you want Bait and Switch's reputation for façade purposes, or do you fully expect him/her to do the work? If your expectation is the latter, make sure that prerequisite is clear when you sign the retainer agreement. Maybe the attorney who is handed your case is with Bait and Switch's firm, but he/she is really a better match for you—often a less expensive match.

The "Partner": This type of attorney encourages the client to participate in his or her divorce process on all fronts. Teamwork is the bylaw of this attorney's approach, making sure the client plays an integral part in the making of all decisions. A strong partnership between client and attorney is established from the get-go, and this type of attorney is adroit at listening to the client and taking into consideration his and her needs, as well as making clients feel comfortable. Good Partners rarely employ "plays" from the same old playbook; instead they tailor their approach for what is wanted and needed in each particular case and instance. The Partner does the Control Dance well because he or she knows when to lead and when to follow. The Partner is always goal-oriented and results-driven. The Partner's strategy is to build trust first (with the client) and then to move forward to implement an agreed upon course of action—a course of action that may change by the "partnership" decisions over time. However, beware of the "Pseudo-Partner," the one who claims he or she wants you to have a say but swings the bulk of the decisions his or her way in the end. A sub-category of the Pseudo-Partner is one who only allows you to participate in some of the major decisions but makes others based on his or her preferences, not yours.

Now that you have had a glimpse of the attorney categories in a broad sense, see if you can identify into which category (or categories) your attorney falls. Know there is no right or wrong type in general, only a right or wrong type for you. My request is that you make a clear-headed decision on which of the above types will make you feel most at ease and secure.

After choosing your attorney type, please answer the following pop quiz questions, all of which are geared to help you determine who is (or will be) in control: You, your attorney, or both of you.

1. Does your attorney listen to and address your concerns?
   Yes _____
   No _____

2. Does your attorney impose his or her strategies upon you (tell you how your case will be handled)?
   Yes _____
   No _____

3. For the most part, does your attorney advise you, yet allow you to become part of the decision-making process?
   Yes _____
   No _____

4. Does your attorney return your phone calls within 24 hours?
   Yes _____
   No _____

5. Is your attorney on time for scheduled appointments?
   Yes _____
   No _____

6. If you have been involved in court proceedings, does your attorney spend adequate time with you well in advance of the hearing to go over all the details with you, or does he/she explain the "game plan" on the courtroom steps?
   Well in advance of the hearing _____
   On the courtroom steps _____

Just a few questions, yes, but this handful is very revealing!

Keep reading. I will get to the scorecard at the end of the chapter!

THE EX TYPE

Join me now in listening in on a conversation between a man and his ex. See if you can tell who is in control!

"Jeremy, please don't try to make me feel guilty," she said kindly, *feet firmly planted, standing erect and steady.*

As her twelve-year-old twin daughters darted through her ex's threshold and headed for her SUV, she instructed them to buckle up. Then as soon as they were out of earshot, she exclaimed, "I can be a working professional and a good mother, too."

"Oh, yeah? Well, you and I both know the kids would be better off with me, Tammy. I'm a stockbroker. My day ends at three just in time to pick up the girls from school." He thought he was finally playing the right card.

"It is perfectly fine for you to pick them up at three every day. In fact, spending every afternoon...perhaps helping them with homework until I can come for them at five is a great idea."

"No, if I'm going to pick them up every day, then I want custody, dammit!"

"You have custody," she stated, still no hint of animosity.

"Not that kind of custody. Not joint legal custody. I mean physical custody. The kind of custody you have." His pseudo confidence was wearing thin.

"Sorry, Jeremy." She held her ground. "We worked that out eighteen months ago. They are doing fine with this custody arrangement," smiling as she backed away, and still no edge in her voice. "It was an arrangement you preferred, remember? And I think we both agree, the last thing we want to do is disrupt the girls' lives any more than we already have."

Heading away from the doorway, she turned and threw him a sincere smile. "And thanks for helping the girls finish their science project. It's awesome."

Jeremy tossed back a lifeless smile and a limp wave. He shut the door.

Jeremy is not unlike other divorced parents who suddenly want to change the custody arrangement. For some, like him, it signifies a way in which to gain more control. Obviously, he felt lacking—he felt deficient in the Control Department! Shaming his ex-wife into turning over physical custody would have signified a huge "Control Victory." Also trying to get her to question her worth as a mother was another way for Jeremy to gain control. Try as he may, he had not been able to throw her off her consistent platform of handling their affairs so sensibly, and, I might add politely, each time he tried another guilt tactic. For if Jeremy could get Tammy to question her ability to be a better parent, he might rattle her; and if he could do that, then in his perception, he would have gone from being the Controllee to the Controller.

No such luck. Tammy was not having it. Guilt was a constant tool Jeremy pulled out of his covert tool belt to try to gain control. If he could launch a successful psychological attack—make Tammy think she was faltering in her motherly duties because she was a working business professional—then he might feel, well, mightier. And, once again, that would translate to more control.

My colleague told me Tammy was familiar with Jeremy's tactics—using the children to "get to her." However, Tammy had worked through that issue and was able to keep the guilt from penetrating her "control shield." She rolled right through his battlefield, her resolve as tough as a Sherman tank.

It took time and hard work. Tammy was intent on keeping control. She had no desire to control her ex, yet she refused to allow him to control her. It was what had caused the demise of their marriage.

I am sure you know my next suggestion: Examine your situation to determine who is in control, you or your ex. I might add it does not have to be either/or. Both parties can maintain a healthy sense of "self" control.

TYPE A...or B, or C...

As I get into the section that more fully describes each of the Typical Three Wars, you will have the opportunity to make an assessment as to which Wars you are about to begin, those in which you are involved, or may have already fought. To be at "Marital War" of course, you need an opponent or enemy. In keeping with that fundamental theory, I have taken the liberty of defining various opponent or enemy types, or even conspirators or allies (the players), you may encounter. Don't forget: The "attorney types" can be in such a "camp," too, since they are all part of the "Who's in Control?" faction. I believe your own attorney should be solidly on your side though, no matter what. But keep in mind even attorneys can end up as less than advocates if your selection is not a sound one.

Looking closely now at the potential enemy of those around you—those who generally assert, take or maintain control—let's start off with the "ex" types.

Though there are many different types of behaviors ex's may employ to wrestle for control, I have narrowed the field to an interesting few.

The "Intimidator": This is the ex who goes out of his or her way to make you think he or she is more powerful. They do things like make inferences that you are less than worthy, that they are better off than you—this could be financially and personally (i.e., a better paying job, a more prestigious occupation). This type often does not bully openly, but finds covert ways to assert himself or herself and always feels the need to play the "one-upmanship game." Jeremy is the ideal Intimidator, for he tried to get Tammy to think he was the more available parent. He tried to make her feel "less than."

The "Passive Aggressor": I know people who would rather have a serial killer as an ex than a Passive Aggressor, because they are the hardest type of all to handle. They are also the most devious of all the ex types. They volley for control by engaging in passive acts like showing up late with the children (like our "control perpetrator" in Chapter One) to try to disturb one's equilibrium. They "set you up" by playing the "who, me?" game with tactics like out-spending the other parent on the children for holiday or birthday gifts. Where the Intimidator might boldly enter a parent-teacher conference with a new mate on his or her arm, the Passive Aggressor will sit down to the conference and a few minutes later have his or her new mate show up. Or he/she may have her/him waiting outside, stationed precisely where the ex will cross his/her path. This type often uses quiet methods to snatch control, and you never know when they might launch an attack in any one war. They often stay off the front lines. Instead, they craftily strategize in the background using friends, family, business associates, and the truly innocent victims, the children, to carry out their attacks.

The "Terrorist": Now, this type is usually very vocal and obvious about intentions to assert or gain control. The Terrorist often makes open threats—physical, mental and emotional—and can act on them. Terrorists should be watched carefully and taken seriously, for they tend to be fiendish and compulsive about maintaining control. The Terrorist will stop at nothing to steal control. Sometimes this type will veer away from their ex after becoming exhausted, but usually only when they find a new target—like a new ex spouse or ex significant other! Keep a close eye on the Terrorist. They may threaten to turn you in to the IRS, tell the children your darkest secrets, or even suggest that they will kill you. Do not ever let this type think they can control you. Stay strong and calm, always, no matter what attack they launch. If you feel you are in physical danger, do not hesitate to seek assistance, and I mean immediately.

The "Manipulator": This ex type is clever, charming and often seductive. This group can lure an ex in, only to pounce or pummel him/her. The Manipulator, similar to the Passive Aggressor, plots and carefully plans control strategies. Manipulators want one thing: Control and more control. They can use the children (or unsuspecting others) in their quest to gain it. That includes those who interact with the children such as caregivers, teachers, coaches and others. If no children are involved, this ex will use the couple's friends and business associates to rally for control. One way is to hire away those who you thought were loyal employees, like the housekeeper (for more money). These types are adroit and they never seem to run out of ploys to get what they want. It is best to stay clear of their grenades when they are symbolically tossed for they can cause irreparable damage to one's psyche. This type can never seem to relinquish control. The more they get the more they want!

The "Victim": There are more control Victim types than most would think. This type sets up their ex to make them feel as though they are always being abused by their ex. Closely aligned with the Passive Aggressor, they control through the back door, so to speak. They may attempt to make you feel guilty. They may greet you at the door in tattered clothes when you drop off the children. They may purposely lose their job, have their car repossessed, or be seen sitting forlornly in familiar places like the country club, the family restaurant, at weddings, funerals of mutual friends, etc. They want one thing: Pity. If they can evoke such an emotion from you, they have emerged victorious in the control department. Anyone going through a divorce has an opportunity to make his or her life better; yet those who go the opposite direction are called Victim types.

The "Cooperator": This is the ideal ex, the one most people complain that they do not have—the ex type everyone longs for! The Cooperator is the person who is so "self-contained" he/she neither feels the need or desire to control the other person. Cooperators are flexible with plans and arrangements regarding the children, thoughtful and gracious in all dealings with extended family and friends, and sincere in a desire to work through the "aftermath" of divorce (whether it is dividing assets, paying off bills, or working out differences with a mediator, counselor or lawyer). The Cooperator is the ex type that wishes to move forward in his or her life productively, and even wishes the same for his or her ex.

See if you can identify which ex type you have! Keep in mind, your ex may overlap into other sub-types. For instance, your ex may display characteristics of the Victim, yet be masterful at the Manipulator game. The object is to identify the type as closely as you can, so I can instruct you on ways to best manage your type productively. Naturally, my goal for you is to stay in control without toppling your ex's right to his or her own sense of control. Though we covered a good many questions about you and your ex in Chapter Two, "You and Control: Assessing your Current State of Affairs," answers to the following two questions will be reminders of where you stand in the Control Department with your ex.

1. Does your ex say or do things that disturb your equilibrium?
   Yes ____
   No ____

2. If your ex uses the children to "get to you," do you allow it?
   Yes ____
   No ____

SHRINK RAP

In addition to examining your relationships with your attorney and your ex to ascertain whether either of them is robbing you of your rightful sense of "self" control, it is time now to do the same with your marital therapist or mental health professional assisting you in your dissolution process—the individual whose help you have sought on personal and emotional issues. Take a close look as this scene unfolds to determine who is in control.

"...so I really don't know what to do," a guy in his late 40s said, *tugging relentlessly on his Armani necktie and nervously licking his lips.*

"Well, if you give her the house and you take the business, where do you suppose that leaves you?" a bespectacled woman in her 60s probed.

"Where does that leave me?" He seemed distracted.

"Yes, where does that leave you?"

"Uh, well, I guess if the business continues to thrive, I'd make out okay. But, if it doesn't, well, I'm screwed. I will be left with nothing."

"What do you want?"

"Everything."

"That's not practical, Gil."

"Yeah, I know, but you did ask." Gil tried to laugh, oblivious to the fact he was now about to yank his tie off altogether.

"You have a lot of decisions to make, Gil, and..."

"Can't you make them for me, Dr. Thompson? I mean that's why I come here isn't it? To have you help me make these decisions…these are tough decisions."

"Yes, I know," her voice was authoritative but gentle. *"And they are your decisions. I can only assist you in weighing the pros and cons to making them. I can't make them for you. The final decisions rest with you."* She smiled sympathetically as she tapped the face of her watch. *"I'm afraid our time is up today, Gil."* She stood to usher him from her dimly lit office. Gil popped off the sofa and headed for the door. In parting she said, *"You got yourself thinking this session and that's good. That's progress."*

"Yeah, I guess so." He seemed exhausted, defeated.

"See you next Monday evening, same time."

Dr. Thompson did what most good therapists do: She was attentive to her patient, but put the onus on him to ponder his options and then make decisions that would work for him—decisions he felt he could live with, comfortably. Good therapists are like that. There are others, however, who clearly try to force the solutions, or impose their belief systems on their clients and patients. And during such precarious times—when one goes through a divorce—the vulnerable patient may put more stock in the leanings of a therapist than any other person.

Since we are looking at types, I have also listed a few therapist styles to better help you decide where yours fits in, and more importantly, to have you identify who is in control in your counseling: You or your therapist! Here goes.

The "God": These therapists tend to think they are omnipotent. You can pick that up from their demeanor and attitude. Often times, this category of shrink tries to instill his or her dogma into a patient's psyche. They can range from gurus to astrologers, cult leaders to talk show hosts. Beware. If anyone claiming to be a bonafide therapist is intent on getting you to handle your divorce his or her way—actually telling you what you must do—slide off their sofa immediately and gracefully excuse yourself.

The "Zealot": This type of therapist can be almost over-zealous about his or her belief systems. No matter your psychological makeup, they seem to rally round a one-size-fits-all approach: Theirs! These extremists often cause more harm than good. Check out their credentials and affiliations. If they speak publicly, try to take in a speech or two to learn more about his or her approach to divorce. Do not jump into therapy with both feet with a Zealot, until or unless you are sure this individual lets you hold the reins.

The "Manipulator": This type of therapist is crafty! Manipulations may not outwardly express opinions on how you should run your life, but they will hint at what they want you to do as you handle your divorce affairs. They may instigate more controversy in your already contentious situation with your ex or others in your extended circle (the kids, in-laws, business associates, etc.) by openly instructing you on how to confront those who are aggravating factors in your divorce. Be skeptical of any counselor-type that eggs you on in any of the typical Three Wars. Your therapist should be helping you find ways to create peace and balance, not more grief and discord! Types like the Manipulator stand out, as they are deceptive in their ability to get you to play out their fantasies.

The "Guide": This therapy model can be a positive force in helping you cope with divorce. The guide neither judges nor nudges, but rather assists you in productive ways to keep you on the right path. The Guide can be subtle and understated in pointing you in the right direction, or quietly and diplomatically persuasive in getting you to see the light. The Guide's main mission is to help enlighten you.

The "Facilitator": This variety is possibly the best, for he or she has a constructive way of moving you forward on your own terms. The Facilitator differs from the Guide because he or she is a bit more active in the ability to stimulate action on a patient/client's part. These types are determined to get their charges to think through choices, rather than make them based on feelings. The Facilitator always approaches a patient with long-term goals in mind. Facilitators often join with the others in the patient circle (the attorney, social worker, mediator, etc.) to aid them in setting a course that will bring peace and harmony, both in the short term and the long term.

Conferring with a marriage counselor, psychiatrist, psychologist or seasoned clergy person is an excellent way to handle complicated decisions. However, be wary of such professionals who do more than attempt to facilitate your ability to make your own decisions. As set forth above, some of these professionals often have their own agenda, and you become their pawn.

Your Professional Trusted Confidante can have more influence over you in this period of your life than other any person. Since divorce is such a pivotal milestone, such influence and the decisions made because of it can last a lifetime. My advice: Choose wisely. I mean that literally—choose someone who is well regarded for his or her *wisdom* in handling the divorce candidate. My yardstick for measuring the appropriate therapist or counselor is this: Find one who assists you in coming to conclusions and decisions that feel right, but who never attempts to impose his or her own will, beliefs or ideals on you. If you find yourself in the company of a therapist who doesn't do just that, switch camps. A good therapist does not impose his or her beliefs or opinions, but rather helps you get in touch with your own. You certainly do not want someone dictating his or her philosophies and putting you under some type of Svengali spell! One more comment: So that I am not misunderstood, I do want to say it is my opinion that when shopping for a marital therapist, or any therapist for that matter, exploring (in an initial visit) their values and points of view is very important. I feel strongly that entrusting a person's psyche to another human being is a major decision.

Like the attorney types, choosing the one that suits your personality is strictly your call. But just as with an attorney (and in the case of dealings with your ex), being at the Control Helm should be your foremost objective. Find a mental health professional with whom you resonate and one that allows you the control to which you are entitled.

Here are a few questions that will help you determine whether it is you or your mental health professional type that is in control:

1. Are your visits to your counselor all about you?
   Yes _____
   No _____

2. Are you comfortable in the presence and with the counsel of your chosen therapist?
   Yes _____
   No _____

3. Does your therapist talk in terms of "should have and could have"?
   Yes _____
   No _____

4. Does your therapist give you the impression he/she is your unconditional advocate?
   Yes _____
   No _____

5. Is it obvious to you that your counselor not only listens to you, but can also anticipate your needs?
   Yes _____
   No _____

6. Are the decisions you are making a result of your own choices?
   Yes _____
   No _____

I believe a good therapist not only helps you deal with feelings, but also champions ways to get you to deal positively and realistically with your feelings. I also believe an effective therapist can coordinate efforts with a good attorney in order to bring about continuity and resolve issues. A good therapist will leave you with the feeling that he or she is only a phone call away, if you find it necessary to contact them.

Summing up in this category, keep that pencil and paper handy. You will want to tally up your score at the end of the chapter, right along with the other "Who's in Control?" types.

It is time now to peer around the corner and sit in on a discussion between a parent and her child. If you have children, see if any of this conversation sounds familiar!

YOUTH ORIENTED

Megan half skipped, half ran, to greet her waiting mother at the door. Her father had just dropped her off from a weekend visit. The nine-year-old could not reach out to hug her mother because her arms were full.

"Hey, what's all this?" Her mother tried to hide her irritation. Megan had obviously been deluged with gifts. She followed her mother into the kitchen.

"Well, the movie is for scoring a point at soccer on Saturday." Megan was hyped and revved. "The bracelet is for helping Dad clean out the garage. The posters are for having perfect manners at the dinner table, and don't get mad Mom, but the jacket is..."

Before she could finish her sentence, "That jacket! Megan, I told you I would buy you that little suede number for your birthday next month, remember? You asked me specifically to buy that for you. Did you not?"

"Yeah, but..."

"But, what? What's going on?"

"Well, we were at the mall and I showed it to Dad and he said... well, he didn't say, actually. I told him I wanted that for my birthday."

"So you got him to buy it for you? You didn't tell him you had already asked me to?" Megan's mom was incredulous.

"Well, yes, it's an early birthday present. Dad and I, well, we decided. That's what I told him I wanted and...but Mom?"

"What did you say? We decided?" She was ready to blow.

"That's okay because that means you can buy me...you can get me that DVD player," Megan couldn't hide a wide grin.

"Possibly not, Megan." Her mother was spinning!

"Well, fine then." Megan turned on her heel to head upstairs with her things.

Her mother instinctively began to follow her.

"Then I'll just ask Dad for one. He'll buy it for me!"

Megan's mother stood at the foot of the stairs, fuming and speechless.

Well, well, how often do children attempt to run the show in divorce, playing one parent against the other? More often than most people think. Sometimes it can be subtle, other times it can be blatant, as in the case of Megan. Children can be the most provocative forces in the Control Department. Yes, they are often casualties of the Divorce Wars, but then again, they can actually manipulate or even *instigate* them! I have seen more second, third and fourth marriages break up because of conflicts with, or over, the children. Their power can be nuclear!

I have listed a few varieties of child types to see if you can identify where your offspring or your stepchildren rank, and also to get you in better touch with who it is that is in control, you or your child.

The "Opportunist": This type of youngster is like Megan. He or she will look for the right time/place to take advantage of one parent, grandparents or others in his or her immediate circle. Many children of divorced parents cannot resist seizing opportunities to get what they want. Getting what they want might include not only material things (the largest percentage of opportunists use their charms for just that purpose), but also extended curfews and other privilege-oriented perks they may not always get with one parent or the other. They may also want more affection.

The "Dualist": These youngsters go out of their way to placate both parents, not wanting to offend either of them or fall out of a parent's good graces. The Dualist wants peace at any cost, and he or she may try to play both ends against the middle in a quest to achieve it. Unlike the Opportunist, these children are not so much out for themselves as they are out for making a favorable impression on each of their parents. Dualist children are often in deep inner turmoil, for if their parents are at odds, they seem to be caught, innocently, in the middle. They often feel it is their fault.

The "Plotter": These "children" can be people of any age, minors or grown-ups, who spend hours strategizing how to control their parents. They may launch mini-wars just to gain control. For instance, a Plotter may drop an emotional bomb on mom about dad's new girlfriend, just to check out her reaction. When they find they can throw mom off center, they feel powerful. There is nothing more seductive than power, especially to children. Stay straight-faced and steady in the face of the Plotter, and he or she will soon learn you cannot be controlled by his or her games.

The "Trickster": I would consider these youngsters "Plotter-Lite." Though they try to fool mom or dad into falling for their tricks, they do not necessarily spend hours or days plotting strategies. Their actions are often more impulsive, glomming onto an immediate opportunity (yes, they are somewhat an Opportunist) in order to get what they want. They are quick thinkers and planners and extremely crafty. One example: The teen who does not want to go to mom's for weekend visitation, so he purposely takes off after school with friends when mom is due to pick him up. When he shows up at home, dad scolds him for blowing the weekend with his mother. He says he thought it was next weekend. Keep your eye on the Trickster! This type is the Passive Aggressor of the young set.

The "Navigator": These children, young or old, work hard at staying out of the crossfire caused by their parents, and they also make efforts to stay out of the Marital Wars altogether. Their goal is to wade through the everyday parental conflicts of warring parents with agility and grace. These children are often the ones who quietly leave the room when dad is yelling at mom on the phone. They are also quick to change the subject at the dinner table when mom starts complaining about dad. These children are considered the diplomats of divorced parents, for they are brilliant at finding safe detours around the landmines of parental controversy. The Navigator usually takes these skills into other areas of his and her life and benefits greatly from them. These children take little interest in controlling either parent, but rather spend time and energy on positively managing themselves.

The "Resilient": These are the children who bounce back no matter what injuries they suffer in a Divorce War! In fact, they seem to show strength and depth of character in spite of the marital carnage around them. They elect neither to control nor to be controlled. They seem to flourish and grow even in oppressive circumstances. These children are saints in my book, for most often they are sunny in disposition and always see the positive rather than the negative. They are known for not taking advantage of a parent's weakness by playing one against the other; they are also not apt to try to use tricks or plots or opportunities to gain control. They have a marvelous sense of inner control, and it shows!

While I realize that most children will easily dart back and forth between several of these category types, or overlap, most display predominant characteristics of one of the types. Also, when there is more than one child, there can be just as many types among them. Just because little sister is a Trickster, does not mean big brother will be. He could very well be a Navigator.

It truly does not matter what type your children are. Instead, what is meaningful is whether or not you feel *they* are in control. Here are a few questions to help you scrutinize your "control" barometer when it comes to the Children Department:

1. Do your children try to intimidate you regarding issues with your ex?
   Yes ____
   No ____

2. Do you make parental decisions just to please or impress your children?
   Yes ____
   No ____

3. Do you find yourself upset, frustrated, or anxious over things your children do or say regarding you and your ex?
   Yes ____
   No ____

4. Have your children played you against your ex?
   Yes ____
   No ____

5. Do you get caught up in the "one-upsmanship" game with your ex over issues with the children?
   Yes ____
   No ____

6. Do your children know your "soft spots" or how to push your buttons?
   Yes ____
   No ____

7. If you answered yes to #6, do you allow them to do so?
Yes ____
No ____

8. Do you find yourself reacting or overreacting to circumstances that involve your ex and your children?
Yes ____
No ____

9. Do you typically give in to your children's demands?
Yes ____
No ____

Just as before, keep those answers close by. You will be grading yourself at the end of the chapter as you discover how much, if at all, your children control you!

Let's move on now and look at another potential group of "Controllers." These I have lumped together in an extended category since it does not matter what group they are in. Each of them has the potential for running your show if you let them!

CIRCLE OF INFLUENCES

Step inside this phone conversation:

"Theresa, now don't you hang up. I have one more suggestion," a brittle, tense voice shot through the phone. *"Call Josh Thorgood and tell him I recommended you. Next, I want you to stop greeting David when he brings those children home. You have other people in that house who can answer the door, like, oh, what's her name…"*

"Her name is Bonita, Mother."

"Yes, well, that's your housekeeper's job…to answer that door."

"Yes, Mother."

"Theresa?"

"Yes,"

"Now don't forget what I told you about that money. You take your savings and whatever else you can get your hands on and you put it in my account. When all this is over I'll give it right back to you." There was a *"hummph"* at the end of that matriarch's last order.

"I can't hide assets, Mom. David will find out and it's really not legal."

"Legal-smegal, Theresa. We're talking about your financial future, here. Now...you take my advice...who knows you better than I do, huh?"

Theresa had listened to her mother on many occasions and followed her guidance; but she decided this would not be one of those times. Instead, she chose to humor her.

"Mom?"

"Yes, dear."

"I'll think about it."

"Well," she said, in a supercilious tone, "let me just suggest one more thing..."

Theresa changed the telephone receiver to her other ear. She knew it would be awhile before she would be able to hang up.

Theresa is not unlike other women who get well-intended counsel from outside influences. There are dozens of people who truly want to help those they love and care about during tumultuous marital breakups; but like Theresa's mother, in the end, they are quite likely to cause more damage than good!

Those going through divorce should learn to lean on trusted confidantes—and yes, among them there might be a mother or father. My suggestion is to listen to those you respect, but never let them control you! Arguably, this is what Theresa's mother was trying to do, even though I am sure she believed that her intentions were in the best interests of her daughter.

Your circle of influences could include more than your parents and your siblings. Often they might also be your ex's family, your extended family, your friends and even business associates. I know of one client who kept getting unsolicited advice from her hairdresser!

While these folks may mean well, they can also create more strife and discord in an already tenuous situation. Some people going through divorce will not make a move without consulting their mother or business partner or friend or others in extended circles of influences. That is all well and good, but, to repeat: It works only as long as *you* are leading the parade, not them!

See if any of the following fit into your circle of influences.

The **"Meddlers"**: These individuals may mean well, but they often cause more grief than good. It could be the mother-in-law who wants to meet for lunch to discuss what she thinks will be best for the children, or the business partner who tries to persuade you to meet with him or her to talk over giving up your interest in your spouse's business. Perhaps it is even an uncle who has been through divorce and thinks he knows the ropes. He would like to sit you down for a good old-fashioned, "here's what you should do" chat. Listen to these people, but the trick is to not allow them to control you or make your decisions for you. Always smile appreciatively, but keep the steering wheel for control in your hands.

The **"Troublemakers"**: These people seem to pounce on you when you least expect it, trying to wreak more havoc than already exists. This could be your mother, who decides she will go after your ex herself, let him know the children do not like him very much, and finally put him in his place! It could also include your secretary, the one you thought you could trust, who is suddenly into a "he said, she said" dynamic to act as the go-between for you and your ex when you are too busy or angry to speak to one another. Try to anticipate or block the Troublemaker from entering your divorce sphere, because the clean up could take years and be extremely costly! Troublemakers love control. In fact, they thrive on it; but remember, this divorce is your drama, not theirs!

The **"Pot-Stirrers"**: These folks can take Troublemaking to a whole new level. Not only do they start out creating a problem, they keep stirring it up! The Pot-Stirrer might be a brother or sister who makes harassing phone calls to your ex, or it could be your ex's sister who lunges at any opportunity to verbally tear you down in front of your children. These people seem to thrive on upping the ante in a good Divorce War, apparently, very stimulated by the power they wield. The Pot-Stirrer can be more dangerous than the Troublemaker because while the latter is often in the game for a one-hit Control Attack, the former typically likes to keep the strife going. Steer clear of the Pot-Stirrer, or humor them. Never fall into a Pot-Stirrer's Control Trap. The climb out will feel like a trek up Mt. Everest! Children, by the way, make great Pot-Stirrers.

The "Neutrals": Also known as the "Hands Off-ers," they can be more helpful than you may think. They include the parents who let you know they are in your corner but refuse to get involved in any of your squabbles. The friends who let you know they do not wish to take sides are also part of this collection and may be demonstrating more loyalty than you think. The business associates who direct you to handle your own affairs yet let you know they are behind you all the way are also considered Neutrals. There is a fine line between those who take a position and those who do not. Often those who do (like Theresa's mom) cannot help but want to sneak in a little control as they do. But again, the last thing you want is anyone else imposing his will on to you!

The "Supporters": This group makes up your staunchest allies, but ones who never meddle. You know who they are, for they never judge you, only gently point you in the appropriate direction. They listen intently, they comfort you when you have an "I cannot cope day," and they keep their personal opinions to themselves. If they do provide advice, it is sage advice. They never bad-mouth the other side, instead they keep you positively focused or redirect you down the right path. Take comfort in knowing that everyone usually has at least one Supporter in his or her circle and quite possibly more. Be cautious, since sometimes Meddlers, Pot-Stirrers and Troublemakers will attempt to pass themselves off as Supporters. While the line may be fine, there is a very definitive demarcation between these types.

Here are a few questions to make you think! See whether or not any of those in your extended circle have taken any control in your affairs:

1. Do you find yourself making decisions regarding your marital situation based on input from your "Circle of Influences?"

   Yes ____

   No ____

2. Which of the above "types" seem to be embroiled in your divorce situation?
   The Meddler ____
   The Troublemaker ____
   The Pot-Stirrer ____
   The Neutral ____
   The Supporter ____

3. If you have relied on the advice of any of the above, do you have any regrets?
   Yes ____
   No ____

4. Do you rely on anyone of the above more than your therapist or attorney?
   Yes ____
   No ____

Now for a look at our last group of the extended collection—the Court. These are the types that can have more control than any of the others listed on this menu. In some observers' view that is a good thing; in others', it is not. Scan the list below and get acquainted with the control types that exist, or perhaps the types you have already encountered.

All rise as we listen to this courtroom repartee:

"Mrs. Adelman, please ask your client to restrain himself," said a tight-lipped, red-haired, middle-aged woman as she fiddled with the pearls that touched the white collar of her black robe. "This is my courtroom and I will not tolerate another outburst. Is that clear?"

An obedient servant of the court replied, "Yes, Your Honor. I am sorry. My client is under tremendous duress over this divorce."

"Well, so are the hundreds of other husbands and wives who walk through these doors! What, Jamison vs. Jamison is something new? What am I missing here?"

A small outburst of laughter from the gallery.

"If it pleases the court, Your Honor, no, not exactly something new. But I would like to ask the Court to grant a continuance until after the holidays."

"What? Are you kidding?" the Judge shot back, shifting her weight to the other side of her chair and peering down from her platform. "This place will be packed after the holidays."

"But, if I may, Your Honor..." Adelman tried.

"No buts, Counselor. You have until after lunch to prepare your case. This case is going forward. It will be heard today."

"I ... would ... but ..."

"Court is adjourned until 1:30 p.m.!" The Judge landed a gavel on top of Adelman's last "But..."

THE BALL IS IN WHOSE COURT?

The "Heard-It-Alls": The Judge referenced above is known among her peers, and those who stand before her in the courtroom, as a Heard-It-All type. This category of judge has little patience for the daily routine that goes on in the courtroom, between counsel, or for that matter, the parties, and refuses to grant continuances for "frivolous" reasons. Heard-It-Alls become easily fed up with standard excuses and can see past every histrionic ploy. They often roll their eyes in an "I've heard that before" response to the ridiculous. Don't try to pull anything over on a Heard-It-All because they already have heard it all! This moniker suggests a negative connotation. However, the label can equally apply to a very experienced, no-nonsense, truly fine judicial officer who, indeed, does know it all.

The "Peacemakers": Contrary to the Heard-It-Alls, the Peacemaker is the type of courtroom boss who attempts to get the parties to come to terms and may even suggest the case be continued until additional settlement discussions can take place. The Peacemakers are known for being big on child rights. They also tend to be more sensitive to the perils only divorce can bring. As such, they try to minimize the trauma of the courtroom experience on the parties who come before them.

The "Technocrats": This group tends to care less about the "people" side of the hearing and rules by the book. They typically have no "heart" and could care less about the parties personally. The way the Technocrat sees it, they have one duty and one alone: To uphold the state codes under which the marital laws fall. Do not try the emotional plea or pray to the Technocrat for mercy. A Technocrat will rule right over you!

The "Equalizers": This group always wants to do what is fair to both parties. They usually come from a "one for her, one for him" point of view. They take a seat on the bench each morning with a "split down the center" mentality. As such, they are calmly focused on dividing everything equally—that includes responsibility for the children, assets and liabilities! Their focus is on equality, whether it means ordering each party to pay his and her fair share of attorneys' fees or picking up responsibility with regard to the children. Though equitable, this judge does not have any patience for antics, so save any outbursts for the hallways.

The "Solomons": They are partial to the Solomon theory and implement it regularly. Often times, they are not focused on what might please the parties or what will cause the least amount of havoc. The Solomons are simply trying to get to the bottom line—the right result, or at least what they perceive is the right result. Like King Solomon who knew that the real mother would not allow him to "split the baby," the Solomonesque judge will work with the parties to achieve the right moral result. This approach is particularly important in child custody disputes.

The "Hammers": Wear your toughest armor because this judge rarely shows any mercy for those who do not follow court orders. Like the Technocrat, this judge is skilled in the rules and the procedures. Highly respected for their familiarity with all the family law statutes—new and old—the Hammers will strictly enforce each code. Low on patience, they are high on authority and not afraid to wield it. The Hammer often reaches a conclusion on the merits, i.e., decides the outcome he/she wants and then strives to reach that result through rulings and/or pressure on the parties. Hammers are particularly dangerous if they are not well versed in the facts or the relevant legal issues. The nuances of the facts, and the applicability of the law to those facts, are often the last two lines of defense in preventing an outcome being sought by the Hammer. In this regard, the Hammer is very similar to the Lazy Judge described below, except the Hammer may be more predictable. You never want to get on the bad side of Hammers because they can pound you right into the courtroom floor. Good for you if the Hammer rules in your favor, but it could go the other way next time!

The "Judge's Judge": This Judge combines the best traits and skills of each of the judges described above. He/she is very experienced and probably has seen it all. This is not to say that a new judge cannot be a "judge's judge." This judge is thoroughly well versed in all aspects of the law and is not afraid to make the tough call or lean hard on the parties when necessary. This judge does not mind hardball, but insists on fair play. The Judge's Judge can be Solomonesque when appropriate, or address issues with diplomacy. Their goal: To get the "right" result. A Judge's Judge is clearly the type of judge everyone going through a divorce or custody battle desires. This is the judge who will take all the time necessary to hear the case! A Judge's Judge takes each case individually and listens to all the facts before making a decision. These judges are typically compassionate types who make both parties feel as though they were well heard and their requests considered. This judge wants to arrive at an equitable solution, while striving to see that both parties leave the courtroom feeling that they had a fair hearing. A Judge's Judge does not guarantee the parties will get a warm and fuzzy judge.

The "Lazy Judge": They combine the worst traits of the various judges described above (except, of course, the Judge's Judge). This is the judge who doesn't read the papers and simply goes through the motions of performing his/her judicial duties. The Lazy Judge may fall back on hyper technicalities, "split the baby," or do anything else necessary to get the matter off his/her docket. This judge is a real crap shoot for both parties. With the other judges—for better or for worse—you can plan. With the Lazy Judge, the outcome is truly unpredictable.

Though there are many other variations of the court types, the above is a summary and representation of the basic groups. Of course, your judge can be a mixture or a melding of these various them. Do not underestimate the impact of any one of them. As you go before them, know that they can have tremendous control over your marital circumstances. Again, this can bode well for you or it can be difficult, depending on how the court's rulings come down, and it can affect you for years to come!

The following is a short list of questions to help you determine how much control the court has (or has had) over your circumstances:

1. To what extent is your daily routine based on the court's rulings (i.e., spousal or child custody support payments, visitation, division of property, etc.), as opposed to a resolution/agreement that you and your ex have reached without the court's involvement?
   A lot _____
   A little _____
   Some _____
   Not at all _____

2. Did a court ruling go the way you wanted it to?
   Yes _____
   No _____

3. Did you lose rights, privileges, or financial assets as a result of a court appearance?
   Yes _____
   No _____

4. Did you gain rights, privileges, or financial assets as a result of a court appearance?
   Yes _____
   No _____

5. Is your child custody arrangement based on an agreement between you and your ex (or through your attorneys), or as a result of a court decision?
   Between me and my ex _____
   Due to a court ruling _____

Now that you have answered all the questions in this chapter geared to have you examine "Who's in Control," it is time to tally up your scores to see if any of the types in each group have a control stake in your life!

Your "Attorney": If you answered "yes" to questions one, three, four and five, I would say you have ample control in the Attorney Department. Also, if you answered "well in advance of the hearing," that too is a positive. If you answered "yes" to question two, I have legitimate concern for you, if it is control you want—for *imposing* his or her strategies is quite different from discussing and agreeing upon them. If you scored two with a "yes," make a conscious decision as to whether you are willing to hand over control of your case to your attorney. Naturally, I would like to think most people would wind up with a Partner type (that is me!), for I think we do a great job all the way around. Again, however, it is a matter of preference and what works for you!

The "Ex Type": Answers to these questions may have provided positive reinforcement or a gentle reminder that you have work to do "changing the numbers" on the Control Board. Naturally, if you answered yes to either question you need to get to work with those trusted individuals in your divorce platoon! Dealing with an ex and issues with the children are two of the most difficult areas to master when it comes to control. Do not get discouraged. In later chapters I will help you find solutions to gaining or regaining control!

The "Therapist": If you answered "yes" to all but number three, then you are truly heading up your own parade! A "yes" on number three would leave me with concern. If your therapist is talking "shoulds and coulds" you may want to switch shrinks! It is wonderful to have a great mental health professional on board during this transition, and you can benefit from one that allows you to stay in control. After all, the future is your destiny, not theirs!

The "Children": If you scored a 100 percent in the "yes" department then I want you to find a good candidate in the above category—the therapist! Given my druthers, I would have you answer "no" to each question, because even one yes tells you that you have subjugated some control to the children. Children should be guarded and protected, but they should never be allowed to control either parent.

If you have work to do in this department, do not despair. Often this is the hardest group to deal with. But one small win here and there can translate into a major victory over time. Be patient with yourself on this one. This is the group you deal with typically on a daily basis.

The "Influences": If you have "no's" to all questions that required a "yes" or "no," you are home free! If, however, you answered even one "yes" on your scorecard, stand back and see who you want to have some control in your affairs and who you do not. I would prefer that you remain at the helm on all fronts, but these questions are very subjective and the ultimate choice is up to you. Also, if you checked Neutral or Supporter, that will put my mind at ease. Any of the other three could cause you grief, and that is exactly what you do not need!

The "Court": Most people would answer number one with "at least some," and that is standard in divorce. Few divorces are processed without some court jurisdiction over the terms and settlement of divorce. If your answer is "a lot," that can be hard to live with! If you responded "a little" or "not at all," you will have more freedom and certainly more control. If a court ruling did go the way you wanted ("yes" to number two and four), that is a good thing. However, if those answers came up "no," you will have to make adjustments to regain some control. That is something to cover with your attorney! If child custody applies to you and arrangements were based on a decision by you and your ex, you probably had more control in the outcome—not always, but most times. If the court has been the decision maker in your case, only you can answer whether it worked to your benefit or not. I am hopeful you are a reader who gained in the courtroom, and if not, that you find reasonable ways to maintain control in those areas where you most want and need it.

Now that we have thoroughly covered those individuals likely to have some control in your life, let's move forward and see how they fit into the Three Typical Wars. We will start with the Emotional Wars.

Meet Johnny's new pitching coach, Trixie.

Chapter Five

THE EMOTIONAL WARS

The bracelet was 24-karat gold.

"Where did you get that?" asked a distraught father.

"Oh, mom said I could have it for dress up. She said she didn't want it anymore," answered a confident teen.

"I don't believe it..." the father muttered.

"What?" she asked innocently.

"Nothing. Never mind." The father was shattered. The bracelet had been his ten-year anniversary gift to his daughter's mother, his former wife.

◆   ◆   ◆

"You think I'm kidding, Roz?" The self-pity in his desperate voice cut through the phone line like the whine of a country western refrain.

"I will kill myself if you go through with this divorce!"

"That's not the answer, Sheldon," Roz tried calmly.

"Well, it's the only answer, the way I see it."

Roz slumped in her chair and rolled her eyes.

◆   ◆   ◆

"Send another fax, Arlene," Stan ordered his secretary through lips that barely parted.

"What do you want me to say this time, Mr. Doyle?"

"Write a note to Monica telling her I want to switch dinner with the kids from Wednesday night to Thursday night." He gave a sly Bruce Willis grin. "Explain that Stephanie and I have an appointment to get our wedding rings sized. Send it to her office fax."

Arlene started to speak...

"Tell... her... Arlene," his delivery staccato, and now cavalier, "that Wednesday night is the only night Stephanie is available to do this."

Before Arlene could resist her boss' wish to blast his ex with another hurtful and embarrassing fax, she found herself staring at his back. He had spun his black leather chair around. She scurried away as his right arm flew up as the signal for her to depart—her cue to carry out his order.

These three scenes that just drew you in were fabrications like something out of a movie; but those clips are not far-fetched from real-life events that depict real-life moments taking place in real-life Emotional Wars. There are literally thousands of such scenes being played out in real-time—scenes just like them—everywhere, as people engage in pummeling each other to the emotional ground, all in the name of "I am in control and I refuse to let you be!"

You may be one of those readers who does not want to engage in any type of war, especially an emotional one. But, like many who get battered and bruised in them, you may feel you may not be able to help it. You may think you cannot receive the emotional rounds fired at you without firing back. Or, you may be so caught up in the turmoil of feelings it seems only natural that you initiate such war games. Or, you may just be forced by your ex to be in them.

Whether they start it or not, some people participate with gusto while others do so reluctantly. In either case, folks do what most normal human beings do as they go through a divorce, they launch an attack or they have to defend against one.

Like in any other war, there are always losses and certainly casualties and collateral damage. No one walks off the Emotional War battlefield uninjured. And the goal of those who enlist for this type of war is to hurt another person. The rounds that are fired are not accidental or incidental—they are intentional!

Danny DeVito's character said it best in "War of the Roses," explaining the emotional slams of the Roses to a potential client: "There's never a winner, only degrees of losing." My advice: Think twice about waging an Emotional War; and if you are the one trying to fend one off, do whatever you can to call a ceasefire.

Emotional wars are ugly.

There is the ever-popular "emotional blackmail" maneuver as depicted in Scene Two. It is far more common than you may think, since people are often at the bottom of "how low one can feel" as a result of divorce. Many think about suicide, and some attempt to or actually do take their lives, or the lives of their ex, or even their children. It is horribly sad. And looking at it through the binoculars of the emotional war, the threat of suicide is a heavy piece of artillery to roll onto the battlefield.

In Scene One, we have the "hit 'em below the emotional belt" by a classic Passive Aggressor. She uses her teenage daughter to get to her ex-husband. Nothing screams "Charge!" more than one party downgrading a gift from better times into a piece of junk. And to use an innocent victim to carry out the attack only adds to the emotional pain, for rather than the dad being able to scream in anguish, he had to stuff down his grief. Though the ex-wife could not witness the attack, she may very well have relished the time until the missile finally hit its mark. Ah, the sense of control on her end, knowing that she had kicked her husband in the emotional groin. Real painful stuff!

In Scene Three, we see the vintage emotional warmonger who uses his fax machine as weapon of mass destruction for "shock and awe." The former Mrs. Doyle was probably not only hurt, but also embarrassed, since most office fax machines are like the coffee pots—people tend to congregate around them out of curiosity to come upon or share the latest scuttlebutt. So, add to Mrs. Doyle's pain the public reality that her ex is shopping for wedding rings on the night she should have been free from child-care responsibilities. Couple that with the fact that she has to maintain her professional demeanor while metaphorically being bent over in excruciating hurt feelings. Now, you have the potential for an emotional hemorrhage. And again, who is controlling whom? Mr. Doyle was probably spinning gleeful circles in his black-leather chair upon hearing the document feeder grab Arlene's typed message.

Don't forget, each of the above scenes are just that—scenes—*pieces* of war stories. You can only imagine what it is like when these scenes are fleshed out into full-length plays—when the wars go on for months and sometimes years. I had one friend who was a formidable opponent in a fax war that lasted eighteen years. Talk about emotional deficit! And I have actually gone to court over how many faxes each spouse was allowed to send each day. Wow!

You are probably the perpetrator in an emotional war or someone who is desperately trying to avoid one. In either case, this chapter is meant to help you identify whether you are an attacker or defender (or at times both) and make decisions about what to do about it!

Before I ask you to answer a handful of questions to determine if you are at Emotional War, and whether you are the attacker or the victim, allow me to provide a glimpse of the Emotional Attacker and the Emotional Defender.

PROFILES IN SCOURGE

The Attacker looks for opportunities to get in digs, jabs, humiliating moments, embarrassing events and takes great pleasure in backstabbing. This person can plan every attack for the day over a quiet cup of coffee, or fire one off spontaneously. A given in the psychology of this emotional perpetrator is that he or she tends to be obsessed with ways to get back at his or her ex. Not always, but most of the time, the Attacker is the Dumpee in the divorce or breakup and, as they say, "Hell hath no fury like a woman (or man) scorned." The Attacker can also be the Dumper. The act of initiating the breakup and/or filing for divorce could be his or her Atomic Bomb, and the rest of the Emotional Attacks merely residual fallout.

The Attacker can be in a state of constant combat readiness, or as cool as a stealth bomber, similar to the character Michael Corleone, portrayed by Al Pacino, in the original *Godfather*. We saw this behavior when his former wife, played by Diane Keaton, came to the door to see her children, and he just coldly slammed it in her face.

The Attacker will usually use every means possible to hurt the *feelings* of the other party—meaning you!

THE OTHER SIDE

The Defender can be just as offensive as the Attacker, if he or she has a knee-jerk reaction to every attack and engages in return fire. Unfortunately, this is what I see most often. Since both parties usually sustain some deep, personal injury from the breakup, they find it almost impossible not to get drawn into retaliation in an Emotional War. As an aside, I want to mention that I do not want you to think I have lost sight of the hard and cold fact that in any breakup the feelings run deep—so deep that the intensity alone creates an energy force to be reckoned with. In my analysis, this is what creates, perpetrates, stimulates, and sustains an Emotional War. All that energy…it simply has to be dissipated in some way. Therefore, it is very common to jump right into an Emotional War. The Defender can hardly resist engaging in a firestorm of Emotional Rounds.

The profile of the Defender is usually the self-righteous individual who claims there was no choice but to counterattack, someone who feels justified leveling the war-playing field by tossing a few emotional grenades, even after some of the smoke has cleared. Although they may feel justified, they are almost as guilty as the Attacker, because they allow themselves to become involved in the antics.

NEITHER SIDE

There is one other profile, that of the Neutral. Granted, this person is rare. Few people can keep a stance of objectivity when emotional bombs are falling on them, but Neutrals do exist. Many of them are simply well-grounded individuals who have come to terms with the divorce and chosen to resist any temptation to play petty games. They are individuals who have a great sense of self. They can clearly recognize how such war-games will minimize their self-image, so they rise above it all. They may also be able to maintain their neutrality because they are simply no longer vulnerable or emotionally attached to the Attacker. The latter is a big key to wearing the Neutral badge! It takes a pious countenance to walk through the sprays of emotional bullets with grace. Do not forget what I said a moment ago: Most people who were once intimate have some degree of hurt and sadness. These feelings are the real perpetrators behind any Emotional War. Remember the song with the lyric that simply states, *"feelings/nothing left but feelings"*? Ah, yes, emotions are indeed the ammunition! When you bear your soul to your mate—sharing your innermost fears, desires and sensitivities—your mate can, and often does, use such personal information against you during an Emotional War. Also, for those who bring emotional scar tissue from prior relationships and share that information with your new mate, the vulnerability factor is exacerbated. Those who know your history and your soft spots tend to use *that* information as well against you in an Emotional War. They know exactly where the hit will hurt the most. It is akin to a real war, where those who attack hit strategic targets—targets they know will either economically cripple or shut down a region. In any war the intent is to wipe out the opponent. So goes the game plan of ardent participants in an Emotional War.

MARCHING OFF TO WAR

It is important to determine whether you are an Attacker, a Defender, or a Neutral. The following questions are geared to help you assess whether you are in an Emotional War and what profile type you are. There are no specific judgments attached to your answers on this quiz. They are merely designed to enable you to take back control. Be candid and truthful. I believe this is a great first step in sparing you a good deal of long-term emotional damage and providing a means to help yourself move on productively. Here they are:

1. Would you describe yourself as:
   An Attacker? ____
   A Defender? ____
   Both? ____
   A Neutral? ____

2. If you are an Attacker, do you spend time:
   Plotting ways to get back at your ex? ____
   Seizing opportunities as they spontaneously arise ____?
   Both? ____

3. If you are a Defender, do you:
   Eagerly return "fire"? ____
   Relish the next attack so you can engage in it? ____
   Dread the possibility of another attack? ____

4. As either an Attacker or a Defender, do you obsess about the "War"?
   Yes ____
   No ____

5. If you do obsess, do you obsess on the battle at hand?
   Yes ____
   No ____

6. Do you spend a good deal of time anticipating the next volley?
   Yes ____
   No ____

7. If you are involved in an Emotional War as a Defender or Attacker, have you sought help from a mental health professional to deal with your Emotional War obsession?
   Yes ____
   No ____

8. Are you willing to sacrifice your emotional well-being at any cost just to win the Emotional War?
   Yes ____
   No ____

9. If you are currently engaged in an Emotional War, who do you think is winning?

Me _____

My ex _____

Another party _____ (If so, identify this party, i.e., your mother-in-law, the children, etc.) _____

10. Do you fight your own Emotional War battles, or do you drag others into them, i.e., allies, enemies, Neutrals, etc?

Fight my own battles _____

Drag others into them _____

If you "drag others into them," please identify these individuals:

_____

_____

_____

11. Do you ever feel guilty, angry, empty, annoyed, hopeless, or experience any other negative emotions after a down-and-dirty Emotional War fight?

Yes _____

No _____

12. Do you ever feel totally satisfied and victorious after an Emotional War skirmish or battle?

Yes _____

No _____

READY, AIM, DON'T FIRE

If you identified yourself primarily as an Attacker, here is another short round of questions I would like you to answer:

1. Are your attacks:

Daily? _____

Weekly? _____

Monthly? _____

Whenever I have the opportunity? _____

About once a year? _____

2. Has the need to attack become incessant or habitual?
   Yes ____
   No ____

3. Do you dwell on the damage caused by the attacks you have perpetrated?
   Yes ____
   No ____

4. What percentage, roughly, of your energy do you devote on a daily basis to Emotional War attacks (whether you are plotting them or engaging in them)?
   75 to 100% _____
   50 to 75% _____
   25 to 50% _____
    0 to 25% _____

5. Are you aware of the personal toll your attacks have taken on you?
   Yes ____
   No ____

6. Are you aware of the personal toll your attacks have taken on others?
   Yes ____
   No ____

7. Are you concerned about the personal toll your attacks have taken on you?
   Yes ____
   No ____

8. Are you concerned about the personal toll your attacks have taken on others?
   Yes ____
   No ____

We will evaluate your answers to these questions in a moment, but for now I want you to read the following suggestions that point out why you may not want to continue your Attack behavior. Next, I want you to list five additional reasons (your own choices)—perhaps more personalized ones—that help convince you that the Attacker role is not an appropriate or meaningful one for you to take on.

1. I will think less of myself by stooping to such negative behavior.
2. My children will not respect or admire me.
3. It robs me of using the same time and energy to do more productive things.
4. It precludes me from moving on and finding a more satisfying, intimate relationship.
5. It clearly demonstrates that I am out of control!!

Now make your list:

1. _____
2. _____
3. _____
4. _____
5. _____

As we move on, I have made a substitutions list—ways to use your time and energy as alternatives to setting off Emotional missiles when you feel the urge to launch them. After looking over my suggestions, you might want to make a list of your own recommendations, ones that are highly personal and practical— suggestions just for you!

Here are mine:

1. **Change your focus:** Immediately put your attention on doing something positive with that energy. For instance, rather than leaving a nasty message on your ex's voice mail, pick up the phone and leave a positive message for someone who needs your support and encouragement. If you really think about it, there is someone in your circle of family and friends who could use a kind word.

2. **Put yourself in the other person's shoes:** Now as difficult as I know this is, please ask yourself: Would I want to be attacked that way? Of course not. Empathy goes a long way in correcting the behavior of the Attacker.

3. **Do something constructive with the same amount of energy and effort:** I have a friend who ran to her computer and picked up where she left off on her latest book project every time she was tempted to fire off an emotional bomb to damage her ex. She is a writer and she chose to put the energy and effort into doing something constructive for herself rather than destructively bombarding her ex and feeling bad later. She claimed it gave her a wonderful sense of dignity to be able to resist her tendency to attack. I have another friend who joined a board of directors for a women's shelter. She claimed helping make a difference to women and children who were physically abused gave her some sense of purpose.

4. **Picture yourself in the same role with everyone you know:** Would you want to be known as an Attacker by others around you who you love and cherish? Would you treat others around you (your parents, children, friends) the same way you do your ex—drop emotional bombs on them? I am guessing, no! This exercise enables you to see the person you *do not* want to be, even in relations with your ex (even if you feel he/she deserves emotional strikes).

5. **Reward yourself in some meaningful way for resisting the urge to attack and for maintaining self-control:** Do something fun or gratifying for yourself with the same time and energy you would spend attacking. It could be something as simple as going out for an ice cream cone or taking up a new hobby like swing dancing.

I believe it is all about changing or shifting focus and the ability to discipline yourself to do that.

Now make a list of your behaviors as alternatives to engaging in the unproductive actions of the Emotional War Attacker. Keep your eye on suggestions that foster self-esteem and offer a heaping measure of gratification. Give yourself a minimum of five:

1. _____
2. _____
3. _____
4. _____
5. _____

Keep in mind, it is always all about control! If you continue to play the role of the Emotional War Attacker, there is no question that you have lost control. Emotional attacks, while tempting, are only temporarily gratifying. If, for instance, you, like the mother who handed over her 24-karat bracelet to her daughter, decide to engage in a similar Emotional War attack, you will one day regret it. I do not know when or where, but I am certain it will come back to haunt you. How do I know? I base it on countless interviews with clients, colleagues and others, where I have learned that those who chose to be an Emotional Attacker eventually suffered in some way. Either they felt horrible about their behavior on their own, or they were reminded of it by their children or another observer. Either way, they were forced to remember a mean and hurtful attack. The conscience is a funny thing—it can catch up with you! Another reason to give up the Attacker role is that it can become habitual, and the last thing you want to do is take the same behavior into a new relationship. The idea is to learn and gain from the last one!

AS THE SAYING GOES

Here is a list of sayings to keep in mind—ones that I think speak volumes. While they are not meant to frighten you, they are frequently used to describe the payback for those who do not behave well. All of them have been quoted for a long time, so there must be some merit in each philosophical tidbit. See if any of them sound familiar, resonate with you, or reinforce the lists of positives the two of us have made.

- What goes around comes around.
- He who is laughed at laughs last.
- There is no free lunch.

- What's good for the goose is good for the gander.
- It's time for the chicken to come home to roost.

Some may argue they have a right to defend themselves in an Emotional War. Well, I would agree that you certainly have the right, but in the end, you have to ask yourself: Why? What did it get me? Most likely the only thing it got you was more aggravation, and who needs that. We live in a difficult world already!

Though both had fueled the fire in "War of the Roses," the couple could not have sustained or escalated their Wars without an exchange of emotional rounds. While it may be just a movie, the theme is well taken—no Emotional War can be sustained for long unless it is ramped up in intensity, and that is what we often see. The strikes become more and more severe, more and more hurtful.

If you are a Defender, you may want to take a good look at your willingness to take part in the War and at what you do as you return emotional fire.

When you step back and assess your behavior you may come to the realization that you are just as guilty as the Attacker—the Defender is the party that keeps the War going. For instance, you may play the role of the Defender one day, only to be so carried away at the machine gun—like return fire—that you cannot resist firing off an extra set of munitions, which puts the Attacker on the defensive and then encourages yet another attack. As you can see, this War begins to take on a life of its own. It goes like this: Attack, defend. Attack, defend. Attack, defend. One more pot shot on the Defend side, and suddenly a Defender is transformed into an Attacker.

If you are merely the Defender-type that only fires back when fired upon—shoots off nothing extra, no matter how tempting it can be—I think you have a better chance of winding down an Emotional War. Very often the Attacker runs out of steam or finds another target on which to aim his/her gun when the opponent is not as energetic with volleys.

I have found that in the Emotional Wars, it is best to do nothing. A deafening silence can make a lot more noise than bombs galore! Ignoring someone is a very powerful way to win an Emotional War. Why? Because you have to fight against someone in order to be at war. Well, you might say, that sounds ideal but it's not very practical. It can be. That is the role of the Neutral, but before we get to some solid recommendations on how to become a Neutral, answer the following questions to get a good footing on where you really stand as a Defender:

1. Do you readily return "shots" when fired upon by an emotional Attacker?
   Yes_____
   No_____
   Somewhat hesitant_____

2. Do you feel justified in defending yourself?
   Yes_____
   No_____

3. Are you anxious and uncomfortable about the potential of a new attack coming your way?
   Yes_____
   No_____

4. Do you find yourself wanting to assume the Attacker role?
   Occasionally _____
   Sometimes _____
   Never _____

5. Have your Defense maneuvers taken a personal toll on you?
   Yes _____
   No _____

6. Have your Defense maneuvers taken a person toll on others?
   Yes _____
   No _____

READY, FIRE, AIM?

For those Defenders who shoot before you aim—who return reckless fire, here is another set of questions that will help you get more clarity on where you stand in this department:

1. How often do you return attacks?
   Daily _____
   Weekly _____
   Monthly _____
   Whenever he/she shoots at me _____

2. Has the need or desire to counterattack become:
   A habit? _____
   A temptation? _____
   A must? _____

3. Do you dwell on the damage your knee-jerk response has had?
   Yes _____
   No _____

4. What percentage of your time do you spend returning fire?
   75-100% _____
   50-75% _____
   25-50% _____

5. Is it stimulating and exciting to await the next attack?
   Yes _____
   No _____

As with the Attacker, I want you to consider the following suggestions as to why you may not want to participate as a Defender:

1. He or she will know they pushed my buttons.
2. My children will model my behavior.
3. It makes me stoop to a level beneath me.
4. It interferes with my focus on nurturing a new and positive personal relationship.
5. It clearly demonstrates I am out of control!

Now make your own list, but do not feel as though you need to restrict yourself to only five:

1. _____

2. _____

3. _____

4. _____

5. _____

As provided in the Attacker section, I have made a list of "substitutions" you can do in exchange for spending your valuable time engaging in answering an Emotional Attack. Once again, I want you to itemize your own suggestions, all of which should serve to inspire you to stay out of the Emotional Wars to the extent you are able.

1. **Ignore the attack:** If you find yourself gearing up for a "now watch this" reply to your Attacker, divert yourself. Instead of sounding off by saying "you're stupid," if he or she calls you "stupid" or something worse, just start humming your favorite song to yourself. Shut him or her out, hang up the phone, or turn and walk away!

2. **Kill your ex with kindness:** Though you probably will not feel like it, be pleasant and behave maturely. You can reflect back on it before you go to sleep at night, knowing you were the victor, after all—not the victim.

3. **Feel sorry for your ex:** When you stop to consider what the Attacker must be feeling, it may be easier for you to refrain from returning fire. Remember that an Attacker will only attack if and when feeling threatened or hurt, whether such attacks are real or imagined. If you can stand back and remain objective, I am rather certain you will feel a genuine sense of compassion or sympathy for this person.

4. **Do something that reinstates your sense of self or redistributes your energy:** Maybe you should run around the block, clean out the garage or take up mountain climbing. You can also put the energy into something mental like playing bridge, doing a crossword puzzle,

or helping your child with math homework. This could mean doing a favor for a friend or neighbor, taking up a new hobby, or donating time to a worthy cause, rather than getting sucked into the Emotional War dance. Doing so only serves to reaffirm the positive qualities about you and what you are all about! When you contrast the latter behavior with that of engaging in a Defense maneuver, i.e., returning fire on some emotional warfront, you get a very clear picture of what is truly worthy of your time and energy. So help that neighbor plant those rose bushes, or join that committee on your child's soccer team. Each time you are tempted to return fire, opt for a positive action that betters you or those around you.

5. **Make a list of what you do not like about your ex:** If this list mirrors *your* behavior, you know that engaging in Emotional Defense tactics is changing you into someone you do not want to be. It is very common to criticize the very things in other people we do not like in ourselves. So, stand back: Are you projecting? This can become a dangerous habit, so doing this assignment is a must! It will bring clarity. You certainly do not want to become what you most dislike. Better to leave the battlefield with your pride intact, head held high, and a good sense of self.

All this takes discipline I know, but you can master it. Know that as you make progress by not getting caught up as a chronic Defender, you stand a much better chance of ending that Emotional War. Your foe needs an opponent in order to keep this emotional chaos going!

Just as the Attacker was asked to do, make your own list that offers alternatives to sliding into the Defender role. Do not limit yourself to five suggestions. You may have a good many more. If so, terrific! You want as many reminders and tasks to keep you as busy as possible. Each is meant to divert you from the Emotional War battlefield.

1. _____
2. _____
3. _____
4. _____
5. _____

Once again, in the Defender role, as in the Attacker role, you subjugate control if you engage in Emotional War games. Absolutely, it is all about control! So if you have an ex who plays the fax war game like Mr. Doyle, for example, do not let it get to you. Instead, send the message to your attorney, or let someone else run interference for you.

Unlike the Legal War, you are never *required* to become involved in an Emotional War. And when you refuse to engage in one, the Attacker will soon come to realize you are no longer a Defender, but a Neutral. You just cannot fight a Neutral (like Switzerland), for it is the custom in that country never to get involved or to engage in war. Tell yourself, metaphorically, you choose to live in Switzerland!

I offered a handful of sayings meant to wake up the Attacker! I have also gathered a few well-known aphorisms along the same lines that apply to the Defender—thoughts that should get you thinking twice about your participation in the Emotional War.

- It takes one to know one.
- Stupid is as stupid does.
- If you can't stand the heat, stay out of the kitchen.
- Fools rush in where angels dare to tread.
- Don't bite off more than you can chew.
- Don't cut off your nose to spite your face.

STRIKES

This chapter helped you determine whether you are an Attacker, a Defender or a Neutral. Let's finish up now by taking a look at how actively you Attack or Defend and what you can do to correct such behavior. Before you add up your scores for each of the questions, take your time to fill in the following because this set of queries is the most important part of this chapter. Here goes:

1. If you are an Attacker, when did your last strike take place?
   Today ____
   Yesterday ____
   Last week ____
   Last month ____
   Within the past year ____
   Last year or before ____

2. If you are an Attacker, is there any one theme to your Attacks (i.e., using the children, showing up with your new significant other to irritate your ex, etc)?
   Yes ____
   No ____

3. If you are an Attacker, describe the nature of your last Attack:

   _____

   _____

   _____

   _____

4. If you are a Defender, do you notice a theme in your reactions or responses to your Attacker?
   Yes ____
   No ____

5. If your answer was yes, list the theme (for example: When he/she attacks me I always start yelling obscenities at him/her).

   _____

   _____

   _____

   _____

6. As the Defender, describe how you handled your last Attack, i.e., your reaction or your response.

_____

_____

_____

_____

7. If you are a Defender, how often do you find the need to defend yourself?
Daily _____
Weekly _____
Monthly _____
Occasionally _____

8. As an Attacker or a Defender, what gets you most riled up emotionally?

_____

_____

_____

_____

TALLY UP

As you sum up your answers, know that whether you are an Attacker or a Defender, you can never win the Emotional War. You can only prevail from battle to battle. Even so, that is exhausting and unrewarding in the long run. There are no medals for injuries sustained in an Emotional War. Medals are only given to the Neutrals. So then, your goal should be to wear neither label (Attacker or Defender), but to avoid the traps altogether that draw you into wanting to instigate a War or react to one in progress.

As you gather your answers for "Marching Off to War," if you identified yourself as an Attacker, you have work to do! Having a need to attack your ex or others within your close-knit circle, estranged or not (especially your children), will bring you more heartache and grief. As promised, I am not judging you. Instead I am urging you to seek help to get you off this manic track. Your attack train is a runaway one and what is worse: It leads nowhere! If you are an Attacker and you plot your attacks or obsess about them and have not enlisted help from a mental health practitioner, it is time now to reach out for one! If you found yourself admitting you were willing to sacrifice your emotional well-being at any cost to win the war, that spells big trouble, because your acts will begin to affect every area of your life: Your job, your social activities, and your need for rest and relaxation. If you gave a checkmark to the "Me" on question 9 on who is winning the Emotional War, do not kid yourself. As I already mentioned, no one wins. Not really.

If you answered "yes" to question 11 (the one about feeling guilty, angry, empty, etc.), and most sensible people do, you are on your way to walking off the battlefield. If not, and if you also answered "yes" to question 12, the one about feeling satisfied and victorious after a skirmish, then head back to the therapist. This mindset is not directing you down a productive path. While it may feel good to win in the moment, it will catch up with you ultimately.

If you are a notable Defender and answered "eagerly return fire" to question 3, get in line at the therapist's office behind your ex. This means you are one step away from becoming an Attacker! If you also said "yes" to being obsessed, (number 4), and/or "yes" to number 10 (bringing others in to help with your defense, like the children or your mother), you have exacerbated your problem and given yourself one more reason to reach out for some sound mental health assistance. If you, too, are willing to trade emotional well-being in exchange for winning the Emotional War, like the Attacker, or feel good after a battle, back up—you are going down the wrong trail. In fact, you are hand-in-hand with the Attacker, the very person you want to distance yourself from! Also, in the "Ready, Fire, Aim?" segment, if you fire away whenever your ex shoots at you, that spells trouble. If you do so occasionally, there is hope that you are resisting getting sucked into a destructive dynamic. If your need or desire to counterattack has become either a habit or a must, then back you go to square one. If you are only tempted, again you may be well on your way to hanging up your emotional bayonet. If you dwell on the damage your impulsive reactions have had, or find it stimulating or entertaining to fight back, then look in the mirror and ask yourself: Am I behaving just like my ex? Also, if you spent more than 25% of your time not thinking before you respond, it is back to the Emotional War drawing board.

The above summaries are not meant to serve as judgments, just observations on my part and suggestions of what you need to work on. My goal is for you to get yourself back in control! As I said, being an Attacker or a Defender places you in a front row seat of the Out of Control grandstand!!! If in "Ready, Aim, Don't Fire" or "The Right to Defend" categories, you find yourself engaged in an Emotional War (if you answered any of the questions in either of those sections you have already admitted to being an Attacker or Defender) and are engaged in an Emotional War with your ex more than once a year, you have a problem. If you stated that you do so on a weekly or daily basis and your therapist has a 911 hookup: Dial it! If you dwell on the damage, or marked that any percentage of your energy is devoted to the travails of strategizing games in the Emotional War, then step backward, because you are headed for Emotional Disaster! If, on the other hand, you spend little or none of your time on the Emotional Wars, you are well on your way to being truly in control. If you indicated you spend more than 50 percent in that arena, bunk down in your therapist's office, for you really need some serious help! If you now recognize your themes, you just took the first step to packing up your tent and heading home from the War. After re-reading your answers to what you did in your most recent Attack or Defense, if they disgust you, or you have come to grips with the reality that these Emotional Wars have taken a personal toll on you or others, then you are on your way to real glory! If you have taken your sayings and posted them nearby as reminders as to why you should not engage in an Emotional War, big points for you on your "moving forward into the control zone" scorecard. Also, if your list of productive substitutions for avoiding or diverting you from Attack or Defend behavior rings of positive stuff, post more points on that "I am in Control" scoreboard! You truly deserve them and are now well on your way to filling your time and life with meaningful things.

REACT OR RESPOND

Though I have cautioned you not to engage in the Emotional Wars and to now relinquish your need to hang on to the Attacker or Defender role and the behavior of that profile, I also realize there are those instances where you will need to be in direct contact with your ex or someone in your ex's camp, and the circumstances or events may not be pleasant. In those instances, the goal is not to *react*, but instead to *respond*. To react is to act on a stimulus; to respond is to reply to it. There is a huge difference! Reacting demonstrates that you are personally and *emotionally* invested—buttons are being pushed! Replying simply means you are taking care of business by handling, coolly and confidently, what needs to be taken care of. This knowledge is important as you latch onto an approach that will steer you away from engaging in any Emotional War that seems tempting. This is especially pertinent if you find yourself in the Defender role. And remember what I have pointed out in this chapter: The role of the Attacker/Defender can switch rapidly! You want to get in the habit of replying rather than reacting. It is a far more powerful position to be in, and one that broadcasts loudly: I am in control!

I have many clients who go through this lesson with me and tell me it is virtually impossible to stay out of an Emotional War while going through a breakup. I will not argue with that, yet I still think it is possible, if you arm yourself with helpful knowledge and a good team of professionals, such as your attorney and therapist. But I will share with you an old Spanish proverb—one that says it all: "Living well is the best revenge." Yes, indeed, nothing says "I win" more! So then, dig deep, and ask yourself whether participating in an Emotional War, either as an Attacker or Defender, is part of your definition of really "living well." I didn't think so! It may take time to live out this proverb, but if you heed my admonishments and stay the course, you will do exactly that. I am certain!

Now it is time to move forward for a discussion on the Psychological Wars!

Is it not true sir, that you made
your wife's life a living hell?

Chapter Six

THE PSYCHOLOGICAL WARS

"I thought you said you put the money in my account." The sweat began to drip down Blake's neck, dampening his heavily-starched white collar. He put the cell phone to his other ear and pushed harder on the gas pedal.

"I did," she said, almost too sweetly.

"Margaret, I just called the bank and they have no record of the payment. You promised you would take care of this. Furthermore," his temper started to flare, "the court ordered you to make these payments on time."

Innocently: "Gee, I don't know what could have happened."

"Margaret, you know what this will do to my credit if that loan payment is late one more time! Look, I'm trying to get financing for the new shop, and..."

"Call them, Blake. I'm sure there is some mistake on their end."

Blake started to respond, and though he attempted several retorts, he could only sputter.

"Gotta go Blake, I'm late for yoga."

Quickly hanging up, Blake punched the bank's number on his speed dial. After being shuffled to four different departments and spending twenty minutes trying to get some answers, Blake learned that Margaret had deposited the money all right, but into the wrong account. His mind began racing. Had she made an honest mistake or had the bank screwed up? He finally got the branch manager who had helped her.

"When did she make the deposit?" Blake was playing detective again.

"Oh, just a few minutes ago. Maybe ten minutes, I'd say."

With that Blake offered a curt thanks, hung up, threw his cell phone on the passenger's seat, then slammed his open palm hard against the steering wheel.

◆　　　　　◆　　　　　◆

"Though we disagree, I'm glad we could meet over dinner to discuss this calmly," said the expensively-dressed, handsome venture capitalist.

"As am I," replied the well-coiffed socialite.

"So then, even though I know you want to send him to Fremont, I suggest we send Bradley to Wintersberg. It's ranked in the top 20 of college prep institutions." This remark came across as dark and formal as his navy Giorgio Armani suit.

"Were we going to order first, Dan?"

"Oh, sure, Bonnie."

The server who was standing nearby stepped forward.

"She'll have a Manhattan."

"What?"

"Oh, I mean a Vodka Martini. Dry. I'll have a Chivas. Rocks."

"What's with the Manhattan?" Bonnie was visibly disturbed.

"Did I say that? Oh, I'm sorry."

Sorry? Bonnie knew that Cassandra, Dan's secretary of the past five years, drank Manhattans. She and Dan had been separated for only four months. Her mind ran a quick scan of the possibilities. Like a computer that had been shut down improperly, it began to rapidly check all files before booting up again.

◆　　　　　◆　　　　　◆

"Madison indicated she thought it would be fun to spend Thanksgiving in the snow," reported a cheerful soccer mom.

"Oh, did she?" a virile, weight-lifter dad asked.

"Yes, and I know how much you love to go to the desert for Thanksgiving, but..." the mom continued.

The dad replied nastily, "Madison said she wanted to learn how to play golf there this Thanksgiving. Alice (his new wife) and I told her we would love to have her join us."

"Why would she say she wanted to go to Vail skiing then?" Cheryl tried to feign annoyance.

"I don't know. I can't imagine Madison saying she wanted to be two different places at the same time."

"Nor can I."

Long silence.

"Well, I guess we'll have to ask her what she really wants."

"Now, Victor, you know what we agreed upon when she turned nineteen and went off to college. We agreed that neither of us would press Madison about her holiday plans, but instead allow her to make her own decisions. So asking her would be grossly unfair to her."

Victor started to protest, but decided against it. "Yeah, I guess that's what we will do. We'll wait and see what she wants to do. And actually, Cheryl..."

"Yes?"

"It doesn't really matter. Whatever Madison chooses is fine with me."

"Well, of course, it's fine with me, too."

Before they had even put down the receiver, Cheryl and Victor had begun plotting ways to manipulate their daughter into choosing their respective sides.

These three classic scenes of psychological war games are only a small sampling of the type of head-trips that take place in this genre of warfare. In emotional wars, feelings are always the main target, but in psychological war the mind and the soul are the objects of ruin.

Also, remember what I pointed out in Chapter Three as I delineated the three types of wars that typically take place: Psychological wars are meant to mess with one's mind. I stated that very often Psychological Wars include incidents where one party tries to make the other question his or her sanity, or attempts to persuade others that "the ex" is mentally unfit. Well, I also pointed out that psychological warfare can extend beyond those parameters to include attacks that play havoc with one's peace of mind or mental well-being or make a person question his or her core: The soul.

Another characteristic of the Psychological War is that the strikes are usually subtle or covert, whereas emotional attacks are more blatant "hits" meant to make a huge "noise" as their bombs meet their intended target. In an Emotional War, one might say, "Our daughter is fat just like you!" In a Psychological War, he or she might say, "I'm taking our daughter to the doctor to inquire about a weight loss program."

In any event, Psychological Wars, just like the Emotional and Legal Wars, are all about control!

I once had a client ask me to help him understand the difference between the Emotional and Psychological Wars more definitively. I broke it down as I said, "With an emotional attack, you feel it when it hits. It is obvious; you know you have been hit. In a Psychological War, you are sometimes unsure you have been hit, or even shot at! In other words, you are often left to *wonder*. In a Psychological War, the Defender is often left trying to figure out the meaning of a particular comment, or left to speculate as to what his Attacker will do next to annoy, disturb or mentally harass him or her. Also the Defender is usually walking around with a chronic sense of discomfort in anticipation of how he or she will be hit next, from what direction, and to what extent."

In a Psychological War, the goal of the Attacker is to make the other person's mind churn, falter, and/or question his or her very fiber.

The Psychological War is sinister.

Psychological warfare is all about messing with or controlling your mind or chipping away or profoundly wounding your soul.

In the Psychological War, the emphasis is less on "feelings" and more on "business."

Psychological Warfare can last for years.

Usually, though not always, this war is played on a two-way street. Those who engage in these types of wars can only wage one *successfully* if they can manipulate their opponent into joining in. Often the wrestling for control in this war becomes an obsession for both parties. It can become a vice—an addiction. On one day a person can be the so-called victor, the next, the big loser. So, once begun, the Psychological War perpetuates itself. The struggle for triumph can go on for years, and with many couples it usually does!

My deep inner belief: No one can possibly prevail in a Psychological War—everyone loses. Messing with one's mind is a dangerous undertaking that always has dastardly consequences. Nowhere is the adage "What goes around comes around" more apt, for I have yet to see anyone get away unscathed from a psychological attack. There just seems to be a boomerang effect or some type of unpleasant payback for both combatants.

What is worse is that those who throw their hat into the ring of Psychological War find it hard to get it out. My colleagues in the mental health profession tell me the need to seek retribution through psychological attacks is a very hard behavior to correct. They say feelings in emotional warfare, and the desire to rectify them with some type of emotional retaliation, seem to pass, to dissipate, somehow run their course. Thoughts, however, can wedge deeply into one's psyche and remain there forever! Hence the term "baggage." It is the sum of all the experiences that have been etched in the mind. Baggage is what creates and stimulates most of our neuroses.

STEER CLEAR

Certainly, you can steer clear of a Psychological War, if you see an attack coming. You can just refuse to let it bother you. But do not forget that when a person is emotionally vulnerable, he or she has a mind that is impressionable, delicate and suggestible. A person determined to win this kind of war will attempt to chisel away at the other's mental status until it is disrupted—or at least, send the other person into a self-questioning, soul-searching abyss!

The Psychological Attacker lies in wait for the perfect opportunity. The psychological Defender is just as devious because his or her participation only fuels an already inflamed dynamic.

VIEW FROM THE TOP

Let's revisit our scenarios in this chapter for a deeper understanding of how each illustrates a psychological attack.

In scene number one Blake and Margaret had a line of credit of $200,000. It was free and clear when Blake moved out of the couple's home. A few days after that move, Blake learned that Margaret had borrowed against the couple's credit line to pay off debts on her flower shop.

Margaret's act marked the first attack in the Psychological War since she knew this would catch her soon-to-be ex off guard, leave him financially vulnerable, and generally drive him crazy. Plus, she got the money, at least for the time being!

In a court hearing four months later, Margaret was ordered to repay the credit line and to make the payments on time. But Blake lay awake nights wondering if Margaret would taunt him by defaulting on the payments. His fears were realized when Margaret was late with two payments. She was well aware her actions would chip away at Blake's mental solidarity, especially since she knew he had a fear of being in debt. Quite likely Margaret was on the phone to Blake, standing in the bank line to make the credit line payment as the conversation between them (in Scene One) took place. After speaking to the bank manager, Blake figured that out. And although Margaret was not in Blake's presence when she knew he would catch on to her antics, all she had to do was look at her watch to anticipate the exact moment her strike would hit. She knew her ex-husband and how he would react. She didn't need to be face-to-face to feel victorious. She, like many I know, probably threw back her head and let out a hearty, "Hah, gotcha!" Then again, perhaps she was more discreet in her reaction: Maybe she tried to hide a steely sneer as she maneuvered her way through the grocery check-out line. In any event, this psychological hit was all part of her baleful campaign.

In Scene Two, Bonnie was left to *wonder* whether her estranged husband had been or was having an affair with his secretary. Dropping the "Manhattan" bomb certainly gave Bonnie pause. While she had agreed to a ceasefire to discuss the best interests of the couple's son, Bradley, and what school he ought to attend, she felt deceived. Though Blake played innocent, he knew full well he would symbolically pin a large medal to his chest even before salad was served! Naturally, Bonnie not only speculated over dinner about a possible affair, she ruminated over it for weeks. She became so distraught that she hired a private investigator to find out if Cassandra and Dan were an item. As you can see, Psychological Wars can get expensive, just like the Legal Wars. And, by the way, during Bonnie's search she learned her husband was not having an affair with his secretary, but with Bonnie's best friend, and had been for three years! Ah, the torment, for you can only imagine how long Bonnie cogitated over and suffered after getting that information! That psychological hit probably left a hole as large as a crater! The most insidious part of the strike was that Dan knew his ex-wife would snoop and that the trail would lead to the real affair. Sick, you might say, but effective methodology for the Attacker who wants to engage in such a ruthless war, one with no "rules of engagement." It could also have been, however, that Dan did not anticipate she would find out about his affair with Bonnie's best friend and if that was the case, he had opened a Pandora's Box! That psychological hit may well have just come back to smack him. Psychological hits are like firecrackers, you do not know which ones will make a huge bang and which ones may just fizzle out or spin out of control to burn you.

The players in Scene Three, as you probably guessed, had been engaged in a Psychological War for years. Their daughter was four when the couple divorced, so you can only imagine what psychological battles had been fought over the years, and how many! Here they were, Cheryl and Victor, still locked in a struggle for control long after the visitation order had expired. And just ponder for a minute, how it must have impacted their daughter, Madison. She had spent nineteen years trying to please both parents and was constantly being made to feel guilty by both. She had been in counseling for ten of her nineteen years trying to come to grips with how to handle her guilt and remorse, for no matter which parent she was with, she always felt as though she was betraying the other. Madison was certainly a classic case of an innocent bystander and one made to absorb unnecessary psychological shrapnel. She probably found it too painful to spend the holiday with either parent, but preferred to spend the time with a friend.

CHILD'S PLAY

As I plan this portion of the war trilogy for my "Divorce: It's All About Control" workshops, I urge my attendees to think of the many competitive children's games that symbolically align themselves with the concept of Psychological War—where one takes great joy in trying to beat the other. I ask them to focus on an imaginary game called "Musical Chairs for Two." Both Cheryl and Victor sought to push the other out of the power seat. Only one of them would get the coveted chair in the end— Thanksgiving with daughter Madison.

"Tug 'o War": Here is another game where there is struggle for control. In this game opponents drag one another through the mud as they apply their strength to prevail. This extreme is seen in "War of the Roses." Interestingly, in tug 'o war, if one person lets go of the rope, there *is* no contest. You cannot compete unless you have an opponent. So how this translates, I tell my charges, is that if someone refuses to engage in a response to a psychological attack, the Attacker is left with a limp rope. For all intents and purposes, the war is over!

"Hide and Seek": In this scenario, we have one person trying not to get caught; but when played in twos, participants go back and forth, so in the end there is no clear winner, just two people tit-for-tatting! Can you think of other children's games that are analogous to what goes on during the Control Wars? I will not go into my interpretation as to how this analogy concept applies to "Pin the Tail on the Donkey" or "See Saw."

I tell my students the point is: Some of the games you are playing are just as childish as the ones you played as a youngster. Is that what you want, I ask? Most say, absolutely not! When they stand back and catch an objective view of the foolishness of such psychological games, it is often the first step in correcting the insidious cycle.

HE/SHE STARTED IT

Very often my clients will complain that they could not help getting caught up in the volleys of such a war and that they were simply defending themselves. Well, my answer to that is, "Do not engage in one, no matter how tempting." The only war you may have to enlist in is the Legal War. You must respond to a legal proceeding, (like when your ex is asking for a modification of child support) or if you need to wage one (like your ex wants to move out of state and you need to file a motion to prevent him/her from taking the children). Or, in a more informal instance, you may need to respond to a letter or fax sent to you by your ex in an attempt to take care of some important business. This might include a request by your ex to switch weekends because he/she is having a special family gathering and wants the children during that time. If you do not respond to that letter, fax or email, this may be construed as you being inflexible and could land you in some legal hot water.

But Psychological Wars should be avoided, period.

We often discover that a client unwittingly started the Psychological War with no evil intent. For example, maybe you planned a lavish New Year's Eve party at your home one year and your children fussed so much about missing it (even though it was not your year to have the children on that holiday), that your spouse relented and allowed the children to go. Perhaps you never meant to start the Psychological War, it just sort of happened. Maybe this particular year, family was flying in from around the country and your brothers or sisters decided to do New Year's at your house rather than their in-laws. There are so many variables that can create a Psychological Strike quite by accident. But still, in the end, innocent or not, the damage these incidents can cause is horrendous, and most often the other party feels compelled to get even. Once the ball in a Psychological War starts rolling, it is almost impossible to stop. My advice to those who have been hit by a strike: Let it go. Move on. If you counter-attack, you only perpetuate it.

It is time now to assess your involvement, if any, in a Psychological War, and see if you can list yourself as an Attacker, Defender, or both. Naturally, you can also wear the uniform of a Neutral in such a war, though I realize that it is difficult to do.

The following is my first round of questions. As I requested in the Emotional War questionnaire, please be candid and truthful. By so doing, you may be able to ward off years of unneeded misery.

1. How would you describe yourself?
   An Attacker ____
   A Defender ____
   Both ____
   A Neutral ____

2. If you are an Attacker, how do you spend your time?
   Planning attacks well in advance or orchestrating
      them ____
   Jumping on an opportunity when one presents
      itself ____
   Getting others to do the attacking for you ____

3. How do you behave if you are the Defender?
   Eagerly return "fire"____
   Coyly wait for the next attack so you can hit back ____
   Dread the possibility of another attack ____
   Get others to conduct the attack for you ____

4. As either an Attacker or Defender, do you obsess about the "War"?
   Yes _____
   No _____

5. If you do obsess, do you:
   Obsess about the battle at hand? _____
   Subsequent battles to come? _____
   Both? _____

6. As either an Attacker or Defender do you find a certain amount of enjoyment in the process, or a feeling of euphoria in getting even?
   Yes _____
   No _____

7. Whether you are an Attacker or Defender in the Psychological War, have you sought help from a mental health professional to deal with your need to engage in psychological skirmishes?
   Yes _____
   No _____

8. Are you willing to give up your mental well-being at any cost to "win" the battles in a Psychological War?
   Yes _____
   No _____

9. If you are currently involved in a Psychological War, how long has it been raging? (List exact days, months and/or years)
   _____ days
   _____ months
   _____ years

10. If you are a participant in a Psychological War, who do you think is winning?
    Me _____
    My ex _____
    Another party _____ (If so, identify this party, i.e., mother-in-law, the children, etc.) _____

11. Do you fight your own Psychological War battles?
    Yes _____
    No _____

    If you answered no, please identify the individuals you
    drag into the battles with you:

    _____

    _____

    _____

    _____

12. Do you suffer remorse, self-loathing, shame, angst, or
    regret when you Attack or Defend in a Psychological War?
    Yes _____
    No _____

13. Do you ever feel totally satisfied and victorious after a
    Psychological battle?
    Yes _____
    No _____

14. Do you ever feel regret or remorse when others get
    "shot" by accident?
    Yes _____
    No _____

GUNS A BLAZIN'

If you categorized yourself as an Attacker, here is another
short round of questions I would like you to answer. Be
honest, for candid answers are a first great step in turning in
your armor:

1. How often do you attack?
   Daily _____
   Weekly _____
   Monthly _____
   Whenever I find a suitable opportunity _____
   About once a year _____
   On special occasions just to wreck them _____

2. Has the need to attack become incessant and habitual?
   Yes _____
   No _____

3. If you answered yes to the last question, what is it that triggers your need to attack?

   _____

   _____

   _____

   _____

   _____

   _____

4. Do you dwell on the damage caused by the attacks you have perpetrated?
   Yes _____
   No _____

5. Do you dwell on the damage caused to others by the attack?
   Yes _____
   No _____

6. What percentage of your energy do you devote on a daily basis to Psychological War attacks (whether you are planning or engaging in them)?
   75 to 100% _____
   50 to 75% _____
   25 to 50% _____
    0 to 25% _____

7. Are you aware of the personal toll your attacks have taken on you?
   Yes _____
   No _____

8. Are you at all concerned about the personal toll your attacks have taken on others?
   Yes _____
   No _____

As we did in the last chapter, we will evaluate your answers to these questions shortly, but for the present I would like to ask you to glance over the following recommendations that point to why you may not want to continue your Attack behavior:

1. Expending the mental energy it takes to participate in a Psychological War is clearly wasted energy.
2. Reducing myself to such juvenile and negative behavior patterns brings out the very worst in me.
3. If anyone catches me engaging in this ridiculous War, they will think less of me.
4. I could spend the same amount of mental creativity doing something I can be proud of.
5. Life is just too short to waste on such nonsense.
6. Instigating and perpetuating a Psychological War clearly demonstrates I am virtually out of control!

Now make your own list:

1. _____
2. _____
3. _____
4. _____
5. _____

Moving forward, I have provided a suggested list of "substitutions" that utilize the same amount of time and energy that can be spent on Psychological War antics, all of which will make better use of your mental faculties. Similar to other requests, I am asking you to make your own list of "alternatives"—ones that are very personal, and ones that will prove very productive to you!

Here are mine:

1. **Distract yourself:** It is perfectly normal for destructive thoughts to creep into one's mind—thoughts that center around ways in which to get back at one's ex (or peripheral others). Such thoughts are the underpinnings of the Psychological War, for these ideas pull a person

toward an urge to act out his or her worst behavior. When such thoughts occur, derail them with other choices. For example, rather than concocting a plan to make your ex think you are going to hit on his or her best friend, devise a plan that will move you forward. Here's an example: A woman traded the time and energy she would have spent gathering her ex's financial records (for the IRS!), in exchange for gathering her own "Personal Board of Directors." This board was comprised of a dozen friends and business colleagues who agreed to attend a board meeting to help this woman make a five-year plan for both her personal and professional goals. She was so busy sorting through their suggestions, and then implementing them, that she had no time to spend on game playing with her ex. Instead, she used the same mental energy on herself for productive purposes.

2. **Fantasize about other things:** When your mind begins to wander as you are driving down the street—drifting toward ideas that might make for a hard-hitting psychological attack—quickly shift your focus to daydreams about deep-seated wishes. Spend time pretending what it would be like to accept an Academy Award instead of fantasizing about sharing your ex's shortcomings with his/her new lover! Your mind can get immersed in only one fantasy at a time. Put yours to good use. It is a wonderful way to prevail in a Psychological War!

3. **Make a list of all the people you know who play such childish games:** We have all heard stories about couples who split, and as they did, who did what to whom. As you recall them, these incidents will help you remember how you felt and thought about the person or persons who instigated psychological attacks. These feelings and thoughts may range from embarrassment for them, to pity, to disgust. Make three columns: One for the name of the person, the second for what they did in Psychological War attempts to injure their opponent, and the third for your true reaction to such deranged mental craziness.

4. **Do some soul searching:** When you get a yearning to crush the soul of someone who has hurt you or made you angry, pull back and look within. I find the irony is this: When going through a difficult breakup, people unknowingly hand over their heart and soul once they instigate or enter a Psychological War. Do you really want anyone to have that kind of power over you? I am guessing not! Besides, when you do some soul searching you get a wonderful opportunity to reacquaint yourself with who you really are, or who you aspire to be, as both a human and spiritual being.

5. **Reward yourself lavishly for resisting the yen to wreak mental havoc on your ex or his or her circle of friends and family:** Such gifts might include buying something special for yourself within your budget or taking time to read that new best-selling novel. I am big on incentives, because I believe that choosing to do something pleasurable for yourself in exchange for engaging in mentally destructive behavior is a wonderful way of reinstating and bolstering your self-worth. When you spend time thinking about how you will reward yourself for keeping your sense of class and dignity, you certainly cannot be plotting ways to strike a psychological blow or two.

6. **Try the buddy system:** Call friends and colleagues who might be going through the same situation (a breakup) and support one another with *positives,* not negatives. Go out to a movie or a play together, or hook up with other friends you and your buddy can enjoy being with.

7. **Go ahead and write that letter:** Make sure to tear it up when you are done. Venting your anger and frustrations, or just pretending to do something damaging, can be a positive outlet, just so it is only that—a way to blow off steam.

Just as I mentioned in Chapter Five, The Emotional Wars, changing or shifting your focus when a misguided thought enters is a terrific way to maintain control.

Though the above may be all you need to stave off the desire to attack, I would still like to ask that you itemize suggestions of your own. List at least five:

1. _____
2. _____
3. _____
4. _____
5. _____

The list you just made is one that reinstates your reasons for steering clear of falling into the Psychological War Attacker trap. When you get a sudden urge to launch an attack, for I know many are extremely tempting and you are only human, remember that if you do go forward with one, you have suddenly said yes to handing over control. That is the last thing you want to do!

In my discussion about the Emotional Wars, I mentioned that I was certain you would regret becoming an Emotional Attacker. Well, the same holds true with regard to taking on the role of the Psychological Attacker.

Bad behavior does not go unpunished.

I say this with authority because I have witnessed many a client take the Psychological War gauntlet into his or her own hands. The payback for their deeds can be catastrophic. The last point I wish to make about this part of the chapter is that when you are totally immersed in a Psychological War, it is virtually impossible to look ahead and beyond the chaos to better days. You are simply too busy mired in the muck! My advice is to move forward, and do so with a mindset that is constructive. Do not allow circumstances or people to lure you into becoming a Psychological Attacker. If you really find yourself teetering on the edge, get a friend to play "Psychological Cop," a friend who will know when you are about to sabotage yourself, a friend who can act as a safety net.

STICKS AND STONES AND NAMES CAN REALLY HURT YOU

Psychological Attackers are not spoken about kindly. I can think of no better way to ruin a reputation than to be known as a person who tries to play with another's mind. People not only dislike Psychological Attackers, they fear them, and they usually tag them with unflattering labels like

- Bruiser
- Bully
- Sicko
- Psycho
- Headcase
- Drama King/Queen
- Loser
- Backstabber
- Phony
- Liar
- Cheat

I rather doubt that you would want to be referred to in these terms, especially by those who can be objective about you or those you care most what they think. Most of us have reputations we don't want tainted. Perhaps you are one of those Psycho Attackers who lets the whole office know your next sinister ploy—the one geared to mess with your ex's mind; or maybe you spread the word of your upcoming mind game to those sitting next to you in the Little League bleachers. I once heard a bitter divorcee belt a snide remark across the field to the volunteer coach (the man she had lived with for two years) with Bette Midler-like verve, right in the middle of his son's game, "The Pregnancy test came back positive!" she screamed. Then she promptly tore off in her car. Naturally he was embarrassed and befuddled. Talk about having to keep your game face on! You can only imagine the pain this caused the son as well. And, of course, this outburst did nothing for her reputation!

This guy showed up in my office fearful she would file a paternity suit against him. He spent considerable time (and money) with me only to find out six weeks later that she was not pregnant. He suffered severe anxiety during that period, however, running every possibility through his exhausted mind. He also used up a good deal of mental energy anticipating what he could or should do. The six weeks were hell. I know that because he came to see me each week and I could see the toll it was taking on him. Beware, no one wants to be around or associated with those who wear the negative labels. So then, think twice before you decide to serve as Commander-in-Chief of a Psychological Attack!

WORDS OF WISDOM

I have compiled a list of sayings that are simple, yet profound. All of them are meant to help you re-orient your thinking when you are tempted to kick off a Psychological Attack.

You may want to keep these posted nearby, like by your phone on your desk, on your dashboard, or in your day planner, just in case the temptation starts to gnaw away at you. Think about them before you thrust yourself onto the Psychological battlefield.

1. You reap what you sow.
2. An idle mind is the devil's playground.
3. I think, therefore I am.
4. Thoughts are things.
5. Think outside the box.
6. Mind your own business.
7. Mind over matter.

Each of the above should sound familiar to you. Do some have new meaning? Study them. Then take them to heart and think about the message or double meaning that each conveys. They should serve as daily reminders to help you keep Psychological Wars at bay.

THE RIGHT TO BEAR HARM

Just as in the Emotional War, you may feel justified in returning fire in a Psychological War.

Well, that is certainly understandable, but it is foolish. Getting sucked into a Psychological War is like swimming in the Niagara River. Once you take to the water, it is only a matter of time before you tumble down those deadly falls. So, although you may think you have no recourse but to combat a Psychological Attack, think again, because you do not need to partake in such insanity.

I have clients who argue that if they can just get in one good psychological jab against the Attacker, the bully in them may stop. When someone steps up and meets the bully on his or her turf and strikes a blow of equivalent force, it may stop the bully from continuing, but more often it only spurs him or her on. My experience: It simply makes the bully hit that much harder.

What is also extremely ominous about fueling an Attacker is that the Psychological Wars (as I pointed out earlier) seem to last a great deal longer than the Emotional Wars, especially for those folks who have children together. I happen to believe Psychological Wars are also far more intense than the Emotional variety. Consider this harsh reality: The warring couple with children will always have to deal with one another, just like Madison's parents, even long after the child leaves the nest. There are holidays and special events like weddings, the birth of grandchildren, christenings, graduations and other important moments when both parents are typically expected to participate. Other reasons a couple stays obscurely tethered to one another are due to crises. Tragedies and emergencies happen in every family, and families typically come together at such times. For some unknown reason, I have many a client who thinks the psychological nonsense will stop when the children are grown. In truth, some parents feel even more compelled to play Psychological War when there is no court order to go by. For instance, when Madison was suddenly given the choice of where to spend Thanksgiving, her parents could declare "open season" on war strategies—they had to become even more devious, deceptive and psychologically treacherous in order to prevail. Remember, such individuals will try even harder because the last thing they ever want is to lose control.

Often I find another reason the Psychological War has tenure is because once such a dynamic is set in place, it is hard to change. Indeed, bad habits are hard to break. Also, once a couple begins the Psychological War Dance it builds on itself. Maybe you cannot forgive or forget your ex's titillating "better set-up for the summer," causing your child to beg to spend the summer with your ex. Rack up enough deep-seated psychological injuries like this, and when the perfect opportunity presents itself, the psychological "victim" may be unable to resist lashing out.

I had one client who constantly badgered her ex with psychological ploys like setting parent/teacher conferences at times when he couldn't attend (she had physical custody), and pretending to be extremely sorry when she told her ex to show up for the child's doctor appointment the day after it had been scheduled. So, when this woman several years later was severely injured in an accident, not only did her ex refuse to help her, he used the opportunity to get back at her, having not forgotten the mental anguish he had been put through. He filed for custody of their child and got it. He convinced the court she would be laid up for nearly a year, and when she could not produce evidence of reliable care (since her family lived in the East), the court decided in his favor. In fact, the court thought it would be doing her a favor to allow her to recuperate with as little responsibility as necessary. Talk about a double whammy! If only she could have taken on the role of a Neutral from day one of the split, perhaps her ex would have shown some compassion and handled the situation differently. But like so many others in this woman's shoes, it is impossible to predict the future.

I have a friend who has been divorced three times and who is also very aware of the mistakes she has made. It has been her custom through each divorce to jump into the Psychological War trenches. Recently I overheard her say through a rueful laugh, "I've never met a bridge I didn't burn." She admitted she has lived to regret many of her antics.

JUST SAY NO

To be a successful Defender in a Psychological War, do not engage. It is just that simple. Remember, a Psycho Attacker has to penetrate his or her target in order to wage a war. No target, no war. No war, no game. No game, the Attacker eventually spins his or her warped ploys in circles, messing up their own minds. To use my analogy once again: If someone lets go of the rope in the tug 'o war there is no more contest. In fact, the person left holding the rope usually goes flying, and as a result, tumbles to the ground!

As a Defender in a Psychological War you have a greater advantage over being a victim than in an Emotional War. Why is that? Because often it is hard to fend off an Emotional Attack since most people going through a breakup do suffer some emotional pain. So you are naturally vulnerable. If you can get a solid grip on your emotions and work through them, however, you ultimately win the Emotional War. In a Psychological War, no Attacker can make you engage if you choose not to. But there lies the rub: Choosing not to return fire, or finding safe haven so the Psychological Attacks simply ricochet—they do not penetrate. I realize not letting your ex (or others connected to your breakup) get to you mentally—finding the wherewithal to avoid having them chisel away at your peace of mind or mental status-quo—takes a Herculean effort. Yes, I know it is sometimes next to impossible. However, you just might be able to tiptoe around the Psychological landmines, if you can seek help from a mental health professional, surround yourself with mental health allies, friends and other supporters, and find ways to boost your self-esteem and center yourself.

There is no sense trying to defend yourself in a Psychological War. By playing into the hands of the perpetrator—by trying to defend your sanity or engaging in a mental game of tit-for-tat—you suddenly become just as guilty as the Attacker. Think about it: If both of you are heavily engaged in Psychological fire, you are equal in status. You can only become a victim if you allow yourself to participate. In the end, you lose even if you only play Defender because that is exactly what the Attacker wants—for you to stoop to his or her level. It is the old "gotcha" game!

Psychological Attackers want a reaction from you. It is the only means by which they feel powerful: To know that they penetrated your mental stability. Nothing makes them happier!

Perhaps you are one of those readers who is lamenting that while it is easy at first to stay clear of a Psychological Attack, when the Attacker keeps firing away, there comes a time when you just can't take it anymore; you feel the need to strike back. Ah, but there are ways to cleverly divert the Attacker. I had one client who feigned dramatic and histrionic reactions to his Attacker (he was a great actor!). Yet, all the while and deep inside he was laughing at his ex's antics. She felt she was effective at upsetting his mental stability. One day she finally caught on. He tells me she eventually whimpered helplessly off the battlefield. That is one way to call off the Psychological War.

My suggestion is to avoid displaying any responses whatsoever, for I have seen many an Attacker in this War finally give up. For those who do not though, it is better to just stand back and watch them spin like metaphorical dreidels. Eventually they will just wear themselves out and spin out of control. You want no part in that movie! Talk about maintaining a sense of control! Ignoring as best you can any Psychological War games is truly a winning approach in my playbook.

The following are a few questions to help you get your head on straight, assess whether you fit the Defender profile, or are currently successfully gaining on this warfront.

1. Do you consider yourself a "Defender"? In other words, do you offer up a knee-jerk, negative counterattack in response to the Psychological attacks perpetrated on you?
   Yes _____
   No _____

2. If you answered "yes", do you feel justified in doing so?
   Yes _____
   No _____

3. Do you wait in fear of the next attack?
   Yes _____
   No _____

4. Would you say the Psychological attacks against you are aimed more at:
   Your mind? _____
   Your soul? _____
   Both? _____

5. Do you find yourself conjuring up ways to conduct a pre-emptive strike?
   Yes _____
   No _____

6. Are you successful at ignoring a Psychological Attack?
   Yes _____
   No _____
   Sometimes _____

7. If you play the role of Defender, has your participation taken a toll on you?
   Yes _____
   No _____

8. Have your Defense reactions taken a toll on others?
   Yes _____
   No _____

9. If you play Defender, do you have moments of regret and remorse for doing so?
   Yes _____
   No _____

As I listed a handful of very good reasons *not* to be an Attacker, here is my list of reasons to resist the Defender role:

1. I will get sucked into a negative mental vortex of which I will not be able to extract myself.
2. There is no victory in playing the Defender role.
3. If anyone can regulate my thoughts and get me to question my inner core, I have lost my self.
4. I will have allowed another person to completely run my life.
5. Playing Defender clearly indicates I am out of control!

Now, of course, it is time to make your own list, and do not think you must limit your number of answers. As far as I am concerned, you can grab another piece of paper, or pop open that laptop and jot down as many that come to mind.

1. _____

2. _____

3. _____

4. _____

5. _____

For the sake of getting you off on the right foot, I will share with you a short list of alternatives to falling into the trap of engaging in a Psychological War as the Defender. Hopefully they will help trigger other suggestions—ones that will keep you squarely on track to maintaining a stable and comfortable sense of mental well-being.

1. **Blow it off:** That is right! If someone is trying to get you into trouble by nudging you into taking part in a Psychological volley, just turn your attention elsewhere and give yourself a "So, whatever" attitude. Soon you will recognize an incoming attack long before it lands, and you'll be able to simply step aside. Sure, you may have to practice this one, but once you are successful, you will build on that success.

2. **Take the same amount of time and energy it would take to return "fire," and spend it on something more meaningful and gratifying:** For example, occupy your mental muscles with a good crossword puzzle, invite some friends over for bridge, teach your children how to play chess, or make up riddles! There is no end to what you can create with that wonderful mind of yours when you put your creativity to good use. Remember, it does take creativity to Attack or Defend in a Psychological War, so why not re-direct that talent. Here is an illustrative example of how to do

just that. I had one client who had a backwards birthday party for her six-year-old daughter, because she did not have custody of her daughter on or near her birthday! The guests were instructed to wear their clothes backward or inside out, the name on her cake was spelled right to left, and the piñata was upside down. She claims the children loved it! She also made up backward games like blindfolding the kids and having them take the tails off the donkey! It also served to stimulate lots of laughs with the parents who attended, and it provided great conversation in my client's circle of friends.

3. **Take up a new hobby or sport you had only thought about:** One idea might be to get a college degree, if you do not already have one. Or, obtain a Masters in that subject that has always intrigued you. When you are busy using your mind for homework, rather than devising ways to counterattack in a Psychological War, you will have something substantial to show for it. Or, you can tackle that new project at work you have been putting off. Choosing any of these ideas will serve as a newfound sense of pride!

4. **Occupy your mind with things of interest:** Movies are a great way to remove yourself from the aim and the stress of an attack. Rent a new movie from the video store, or grab your coat and make a beeline for the movie theater. Visit a museum. Turn on the television. Read a new book. Call a friend you have not spoken to for some time. Write some poetry. There is no end to what you can do with your mind when you summon up creativity.

5. **Get yourself some "soul" food:** Head for your special spiritual retreat like church, your synagogue, that self-help class, or the sacred rock you sit on overlooking the ocean. Read some inpiring affirmations. Talk to your priest, your rabbi, or your minister about your spiritual needs. That is why they are there!

As you can well imagine (and I know you can!), there are so many choices in terms of what you can do to put your powerful mind to good use.

Now make a list that is very personal, one that helps you stimulate those mental muscles with positives, all of which are geared to eliminate the negatives. Feel free to make a lengthy list this time, for once you get started firing up that diverse mind, there is no reason to stop! Give yourself at least five suggestions that you will truly look forward to.

1. _____

2. _____

3. _____

4. _____

5. _____

Always remember: No one but you should have control of your own mind. That is certainly the single most important part of this lesson and the underlying theme of this book!

THE NAME GAME

In addition to having feelings of frustration and angst while falling into the role of the Defender, you may also have people labeling you in not-so-complimentary ways! I made a list of terms often used to refer to the Attacker. This next list is what most people draw from when dishing with friends and family over the latest goings-on with someone in the role of Defender:

- Sucker
- Wuss
- Puppet
- Patsy
- Pawn
- Airhead
- Fool
- Wimp

Can you think of others? My goal for you through your difficult breakup is to hold on to your sense of self. I also want you to walk with your head held high. To that end, I certainly would not want anyone to refer to you with such a derogatory moniker. So as you ponder whether or not it would be worth it to fire back when attacked in a Psychological War, give that thought careful consideration, for I am certain you will find that playing such a volatile and onerous game will simply not be worth it. Do not forget that list of alternatives I proposed, or the one you made for yourself. They will serve as your Red Cross station should you find yourself being pummeled by a Psychological strike.

EATING YOUR WORDS

I have put together a list of a few famous sayings that may make you think twice before signing up for the Defender draft! They are not unlike all those admonishments your mother drilled into you. Latch on to all of them and take time out to muse over their inherent meanings. They may just keep you from regretting your involvement in a Psychological War.

1. It takes one to know one.
2. It serves you right.
3. There is more than one way to skin a cat.
4. Mind over matter.
5. Don't let him/her get your goat.

You, no doubt, have your own "pearls of wisdom"—ones that resonate with you. Make a list of them and let them provide you comfort and guidance.

RANK AND STYLE

To sum up a clearer definition of where you stand, it is time now to do an assessment—a critique of how active you are as an Attacker or Defender in the Psychological War. Prior to adding up your scores to the answers of these questions, read over the following questions more than once or twice, because the answers are very revealing and may also provide the first step—awareness—that will help you sidestep the lure of the Psychological War Game. Here goes:

1. If you are an Attacker, when did your last strike occur?
   Today _____
   Yesterday _____
   Last Week _____
   Last month _____
   Last year _____

2. If you are an Attacker, is there a particular theme to your Attacks (i.e., plot, aim, attack; using the children or in-laws to carry out your missions)?
   Yes _____
   No _____

3. If you are an Attacker, describe your last "hit":

   _____
   _____
   _____
   _____

4. If you are a Defender, is there a specific theme in your responses or reactions to your Attacker?
   Yes _____
   No _____

5. If your answer was "yes", list the "theme" (for instance, "I make sure my counterattack packs more punch," or "I always use the children as 'shields' when I hit back.")

   _____
   _____
   _____
   _____

6. As the Defender, describe how you handled your last attack. (Did you ignore it? Hit back harder? Wait for a ripe opportunity?)

_____

_____

_____

_____

7. As a Defender, how often do you find the need to defend yourself?
Daily _____
Weekly _____
Monthly _____
Occasionally _____

8. As an Attacker or Defender, what is it that most pushes your buttons psychologically?

_____

_____

_____

_____

SCORECARD

Now that you have answered all the questions, it is time to look at what a summarization of them means.

In the first round of questions I asked you to identify whether you are an Attacker, Defender or a Neutral. If you are typically the Attacker and spend a good deal of time devising strategies to strike, you have some serious work to do in the area of redirecting your energies. If instead you simply seize opportunities as they present themselves to orchestrate a Psychological Attack, at least you are in a much better position of stopping such nonproductive behavior.

If you are Defender in this type of war and you answered "yes" to finding enjoyment in striking back, or if you obsess about the battle at hand or those you anticipate are on the horizon, you are not far from setting up headquarters in the Attacker's camp. Remember what I have said all along, when you become a Defender you are just as active as an Attacker. If you fight on either of these sides—the Attacker or the Defender—and you are in some type of therapy, that is a wonderful start to ending the War. If, on the other hand, you are not in counseling, or if you do not seem to care what toll it is taking on you or others—if you cannot see beyond what you conceive is a victory to the carnage you are leaving behind—then you are in trouble! It is time to get help. In addition, if you have been involved in a Psychological War beyond the date of the divorce settlement and/or your decree being final, you have substantial work to do in order to get on with a more productive life.

If you think you are winning any of these wars and it gives you a sense of joy, pride or satisfaction, stand back and truly assess that observation. It is a no-win proposition, and this holds true no matter what side you are on.

If you experience any sort of shame or remorse, that is actually a positive; for "not liking yourself" may be a great first step in making viable changes to behavior patterns. We all need to feel good about ourselves!

If you are involving the children, friends, family, business associates and others, double up on therapy, because you really need it! It is one thing to fight your battles, yet quite another to cause collateral damage.

Finally, if you are a Neutral, you get the Medal of Honor, for that is a very hard stance to take when a Psychological War is raging.

ATTACKER TALLY

If you answered question 1 saying your attacks are about once a year, it is still too often; but at least the problem is not chronic, and I am hopeful your urge to attack will dissipate with time. If you stated that your attacks are habitual, that is another reason to cry out for help. Recognizing what it is that triggers your need to fire away is another good beginning to resolving your Psychological Warmonger issues. If you dwell on the damage at all (questions number 4 and 5), then, once again, head off to the therapy sofa. And, finally, it is never acceptable to involve anyone else in your War; in fact, it is cruel and vicious to do so. Though I do not want to judge you or make you feel bad, I do want you to examine what impact you have had on others. After you have done that, I want you to ask your self, "Is this the person I want to be?"

Lastly, if you are heavily into your role as a Psychological Attacker, double up on the homework assignments—increase your lists of reasons why you should not play this part and how you can redirect such energy.

DEFENDER SCORE

If you answered "yes" to question 2, saying you feel justified in striking back at your Attacker, or "yes" to question 5, finding ways to conduct a pre-emptive strike, then you are just as guilty as your ex for taking part in such a ridiculous pastime.

If you wait in fear, stewing over the next potential strike (yes to question 3), you need to get help from a mental health professional who can allay your fears.

If you find that the attacks perpetrated against you are aimed at both your mind and your soul, you have a serious threat if you let your Attacker's actions get to you. If your mind is at risk, just know it is a powerful instrument that can work through this craziness and eventually find an even keel. If your soul is hampered in any way, make a dash for a therapist or spiritual mentor you can trust, for no one should ever be allowed to tamper with your inner core; and I mean no one!

If you realize that you are hurting others by countering the Psychological attacks that come your way, that is an excellent start in getting mentally fit. If like your perpetrator, you cannot see the damage you are causing, or if you really do not care, then back you go to square one to reorient your thinking and your behavior. I am making the same request to you as a Defender as I made to the Attacker: I would like you to add reasons to your list of why it is futile to stay lodged in a Defender role, and also beef up your substitutions list. This will aid you tremendously—go back and review these lists whenever you are on the verge of wanting to strike back at your Attacker.

FINAL THOUGHTS

If you are an Attacker, Defender or Neutral, I would like to ask that you do one additional assignment: I want to ask that you add to the list of sayings and labels. I think you will find that when you scratch down some of the names people call those who take part in a Psychological War (and on your own private list you can use expletives!), your pride will get the better of you! And, that is a good thing! No one enjoys being referred to in a negative way! Also, as you do your addendum to your sayings, call friends, family and others to get some interesting input. This will keep your mind productively occupied!

As you review this chapter and all the assignments in it, just know that earnestly doing them is a superb way not only to move your life forward, but also to serve as a means to reprogram your thought processes. Think about it: You cannot possibly be wasting time devising negative strategies to Attack or Defend when your mind is busy with other thoughts. Yes, it is virtually impossible, because most of us can only have one thought at a time.

Do not forget what I also mentioned when addressing the Emotional Wars. In my closing remarks, I requested that you not *react*, but simply *respond*. Same holds true for the Psychological Wars. And, if a response is not required, nothing screams, "I am the victor" louder in a Psychological War than if no one can get a rise out of you! That is pure power. And power is control. Stay focused on that thought!

I leave you with a couple of final notes: The late Dr. Alex Kappas, reputed to have been one of the brightest and most innovative psychotherapists, always told his patients: "For every negative thought or negative mental suggestion, think two positives." He claimed that by doubling up on the positives, it would automatically nullify the negatives. I happen to think he is right. Since I left you with a song lyric to consider in the Emotional Wars chapter, here is another that fits this war category: *And I think I'm goin' out of my head over you, over you...*

Let's move forward now to address the final War in our trilogy: The Legal Wars—the category that can be tremendously costly all the way around!

Chapter Seven

THE LEGAL WARS

"What the (bleep) is a deposition?" yelled the heavy-metal rocker, his voice noticeably gruff, skipping a few syllables as a result of the hoarseness caused by his recent 23-city tour.

"Well, it's a statement given under oath, and it takes place..."

Cutting me off, "Fine, then you (bleepin') go!" he ordered. I wasn't fooled by his machismo, detecting a hint of fear in his tone. He started to mutter under his breath.

Working to get his attention, I said, "Rod...Rod, listen, of course I will go, but you must be there, too."

"What the (bleep) for? I'm due in the studio on the tenth of December. I can't go to no (bleepin') disposition."

"Deposition," I gently corrected.

"Yeah, well, whatever. You go."

"You have to go, Rod. Your wife's lawyer is taking sworn testimony." I attempted a slight laugh, "Yours!"

"Why? Oh (bleep)! That bleached-blonde (bleep) has cost me fifty thousand (bleepin') dollars in just the last four (bleepin') months!"

It was true—she had. Marta's attorney had filed a number of motions, most of them ridiculous, but nonetheless legal.

Underneath his crusty and profane exterior this rock star really was a nice guy. He had even warned me the day he signed his Retainer Agreement that when he became upset he was prone to uncontrollable swearing. While I am not a fan of such language, I told him I would cut him some slack in that department, so long as he helped his case by behaving gentlemanly in court—by not swearing there—and at all other legal proceedings, including depositions. I also told him he could not swear at me, ever, and if he did, our legal "concert" would be over.

So far, he had kept his promise. I knew that as tough as he appeared on stage and during media interviews, he crumbled inside each time his ex-wife's attorney shot another series of legal bullets at him. Such hits were like machine-gun fire; they came rapidly and often. In fact, there had been little let-up, since she filed divorce proceedings eleven months earlier.

◆　　　　　◆　　　　　◆

"Yes, he probably is stretching the legal aspects of your divorce because he knows it will hit you where it really hurts," I explained.

"Yeah, he knows how I hate to spend money on what I consider frivolous things," the petite redhead in her mid-forties said.

"Remember what you told your therapist last week, Gwen." I knew my reminder would give her strength.

"Oh yes, Rocco would love to see me lose everything, including all three of my boutiques, fighting this child support thing."

"That's right," I affirmed. "But according to California guidelines, Rocco will have to pay a hefty amount of child support. You do not have to, nor should you, accept what he has offered."

Between clenched teeth: "I refuse to allow him to intimidate me! I did that for fourteen years. I am entitled to a reasonable amount of child support, and I need to fight for it."

"Absolutely. You're right." I could not believe how Gwen's ex had toyed with her sanity. Filing motion after motion, he alleged he had evidence to prove he could not afford the support we proposed. So he kept the Legal War going for sixteen months, causing my client tremendous duress and a good deal of money. Her stamina was wearing thin—exactly what Rocco had in mind.

◆　　　　　◆　　　　　◆

"I'll say it again, Harold," bordering on no-more-patience, *"Why not just let her have the condominium in Palm Springs, and you keep the Aspen lot?"*

"No!"

"Look, Harold, I know that the Palm Springs retreat has sentimental value to you, but I want you to consider what it is you have spent in legal fees trying to hold on to it."

"I don't care, Janine is not getting it. Period."

Hoping this would sober him up, *"You know, Harold, between the audits, the hearings, the investigators, the appraisals, the continuances and the interrogatories, you have spent, to date, nearly $750,000."*

"Money is no object. She is not getting that condominium."

Every conversation with Harold was too familiar—as the great *"philosopher"* and Hall of Fame catcher Yogi Berra once said, *'It's déjà vu all over again!'* We had been haggling over this last piece of property for more than a year.

Janine and Harold were like two bargain basement shoppers trying to buy the same overcoat. They each had a hand on it, yanking it back and forth, and neither was about to let go.

"I saw it first," they both decreed.

"It's mine," Harold would say.

"No, it's mine. Give it to me," Janine would demand.

I felt like a parent trying to separate two squabbling siblings.

PRISONERS OF WAR

Marta and Rod, Gwen and Rocco, and Janine and Harold were three couples all embroiled in complicated and tedious legal proceedings—battles, whether prudent or not, that were costing them thousands of dollars. Though it may sound odd, those of us who practice divorce law are absolutely amazed at how many legal battles have little to do with real legal *necessities*. Too often, they are simply based on keeping the Legal Wars going, all for the sake of control. Do not misunderstand me: The legal battles I fight on behalf of my clients are the appropriate means to get to resolution when other means of getting to the bottom line have failed. But I will tell you what I tell all my clients: Keeping the Legal Wars going is not going to be cheap! And the impact on your bank account and your peace of mind may continue for many years.

When you combine the financial deficit that only a Legal War can render with the raging Emotional and Psychological Wars that seem to loom over the whole Legal War process, you have what can be a back-breaking experience—a burden that can take a hefty toll.

COMPULSIVE LITIGANTS

Many of those who engage in the Legal Wars cannot help themselves. A large handful of Legal Warriors are obsessive and compulsive about the need not only to declare a Legal War, but to keep one going. Often, those who have the most gold actually get a kick out of grinding down the one who has less. It becomes a way of torturing them. In a Legal War, it is not uncommon for the party who possesses less financially (material means) to finally buckle under the pressure and settle for less than what they wanted (or what they were rightfully entitled to), just to end the Legal War.

On the flip side, those who have less gold use the Legal War as a means of reducing the "Most Gold" opponent to a lesser status. Usually in that case, the "Lesser Gold" party is hopeful that he or she will bring the other to his or her financial knees. Sometimes—but not as often as you think —that happens.

I say, God have mercy on those who play the Legal War as a game—a means to get more, or to hassle an opponent for the sake of gouging them where it might hurt most. For more often than not, both parties hobble off the Legal War battleground bloodied, bruised and on financial crutches for a very long time. There is no financial toll like the Legal War toll, especially for those who try to use this form of dangerous combat to get back at an ex.

I have talked to many couples (other than just my clients) in the throes of a Legal War who told me they were determined to see the War through (those who were either the "Gold-Havers" or "Gold-Wanters"), because they simply had to win in the divorce, and at any cost. Well, that mindset certainly gives a whole new meaning to the term "D-Day"!

NECESSITIES OF WAR

Some people who engage in the Legal Wars are in them for practical reasons. They have no recourse but to go through the courts to resolve their property settlement, spousal and child support issues, and child custody issues. I mentioned earlier in Chapter Three that the court is usually the vehicle of choice when the divorcing couple cannot find any other way to settle their differences. Still, it is a hard decision to make and an even more difficult task to sustain, once a person makes the choice to launch into a Legal War.

Then again, I have spoken also to those who admitted—and know others who would not cop to the truth—that they used the Legal War as a means to hide behind what they purported to be were legitimate battles (i.e. "the kids would be better off with me," "You *will* pay me more support," "I am entitled to half your business") just to feel a sense of power and to secure what they perceived to be the highest ranking in the realm of control sovereignty. Yes, many people use it just for that!

Those I have spoken with—who had been through the Legal Wars—confided that they had no idea that the scope of the damage such a War would render would be so devastating. They also stated that given an opportunity to redo that event—that part of their lives—they would have opted for another tactic in settling their disputes. And of course, there are others who believed they were too passive in their divorce process and wished they had used the Legal Wars to get more (or give less) than what they did. They opted not to use the Legal Wars out of emotional, psychological or financial fear, or just because they thought they were doing the right thing! All too often, the Legal War is the means to fight the Psychological or Emotional War, as we discussed in Chapters 5 and 6. The Legal War is not the intended end in itself; it is merely the means to implement the Psychological and Emotional War.

You may think that those who have been through the Legal Wars would learn their lesson. But no, many veterans do not sign on for a prenuptial agreement (or any other protection) the second or third time around, and then engage in some of the same legal skirmishes in the second and third divorce as they did with the first.

One of the primary reasons more prenuptial agreements are not written is that many attorneys are not willing to subject themselves to the liability or the potential exposure often associated with authoring such contracts. When many of these contracts are disputed, it can often be the attorney who is named in a lawsuit; thus it has discouraged many of my colleagues from drafting them. There may come a time when the family law attorney is better protected, and therefore, willing to take on such assignments; but for now many are reluctant to do so.

WAR TORN

In any case, whether a Legal War is kicked off to make the other person crazy or a pragmatic way to get to the finish line, it can cost a bundle! I mentioned before that when I am referring to cost, the legal fees and court costs are only part of it. What one will spend in the way of time and energy—both emotional and psychological—is also extremely expensive and draining.

Many people's incomes dip considerably due to the time away from work to help prepare for a case—time they could be using to make money or increasing their financial status. Others lose more precious non-monetary valuables, such as heart and peace of mind as they skirmish in the Legal War. They forego what they would otherwise do with more pleasant forms of emotional and mental stimulation and relaxation. Adding up those losses can be staggering.

If you are suiting up and getting ready to fight on the Legal War battlefront, or strategizing to conduct a Legal War, be ready for a rough ride. No Legal War is easy, even if in the end you consider yourself the victor. Attaining victory can be an experience from which you need a long period of recovery. Recouping your losses can take years. Remember, you can win the battle and lose the war.

PRISONER OF WAR

Do not assume that a Legal War means you are going to court. A Legal War, can be fought outside the courtroom vis-à-vis volumes of paperwork—letters, interrogatories, requests for admission, subpoenas, depositions, document production and the like—sent back and forth between attorneys or you and your ex, much of which can be accumulated over months or years.

Many of my clients have the misconception that if they decide to launch a Legal War, it means they are going from filing the appropriate paperwork to their perceived next step: Standing before a judge to be heard. Not so quick! Most Legal Wars move at a snail's pace. And the pace is what often does someone in.

For example, the Legal War can start just like any other war—with an "incident." This "incident" would not be a major issue in an intact family, but in a separated or divorced couple, it can bring major warfare. Let's take a hypothetical case: Say your ex sends you a letter in January, announcing that he will be taking the children for a month during the summer rather than the two weeks allotted in your court order, because, well, your ex has simply made a unilateral decision to do so. He has not *asked* if you would be willing to move your summer vacation around to accommodate his wishes, but rather simply made his intentions known. Unless, you are willing to acquiesce, (a sign for many that you have relinquished control), this one incident will no doubt lead to another incident: Your response. Let's say you write back and refuse to allow him to take the children for a month during summer vacation because you have already made plans. Next, your ex may ask his attorney to send your attorney a letter requesting the change more formally. Your attorney confers with you and you say "no." Now your attorney writes to his attorney to convey that information. Your ex now has his attorney file a request with the court to ask for a change in visitation to accommodate his wishes. (Yes, the cash register is ringing: Cah-ching, cah-ching!) Pretty soon, both of you have spent a bundle over who gets the children, for a certain period of time during the summer. By the time you get to court, you may have spent several thousand dollars over one issue. So you need to closely examine similar such incidents to determine whether the hard cost of fighting such legal battles is worth it in the end.

You may feel that standing up for yourself is a means to keep control and to buckle would only leave the door open for your ex to exert more control over you. Those answers have to come from within. My advice: choose your Legal Battles wisely.

You can only imagine what happens when "incidents" escalate, or when there are several disputes (thus multiple "incidents") that need resolving. This process is not unlike any other war: Once it begins with one simple event, it can perpetuate itself—take off from there and suddenly you are a few years down the road still in the "conflict" with your War deficit mounting. What I find most people do not bargain for is the time involved from the initial "incident," to the time it takes to prepare for the Legal War, to the time it takes to hit the real war theater, the courtroom, and the time for the court to handle the case. And, of course, there are the post-trial (or hearing) procedures, the piles of paperwork, *and* appeals! There are delays, the need for new War Strategies, roadblocks, and unexpected attacks along the way. The speed with which the Legal War can plod along can be as lumbering as a huge tank crossing the desert in a sandstorm. So do not expect that just because you have decided to enter into a Legal Battle that it is going to be on a timetable you can predict, or within a budget you planned; it will not.

It is not unusual for those who decided to declare war or return fire to realize that the War may have been a big mistake, because the process can be tedious, slow, and of course, expensive. In fact, the price-point on the Legal War can be staggering. In dollars and cents, it is like building a house; it virtually always costs far more than expected. The primary reason: You never know what the other side will do, what they will fire back with in response to your action (or continuing reaction), and what will transpire as a result. Therefore, what you may have to cough up financially can be surprising and frustrating.

Compounding the tension is the reality that the Legal War is not always your action or your ex's reaction type of warfare. If the court gets involved, and that happens quite often in a

Legal War, you never know what the court will decide. So even if you have a solid position and are feeling righteous about your cause, it will be (if you take it that far) the court that decides who prevails. I have seen many cases where no one won or each party gained so little that it was certainly not worth the tariff.

But forget the court for a minute: What you can spend on attorneys in the goings-on back and forth between you, your ex and the courts, can cost a fortune. Some people spend thousands and never get to court; or when they do, they are ordered to pay not only their own fees, but the bulk of their spouse's fees as well! I have a colleague who half jokingly referred to the expansion at her upscale family law firm as the "McLeod Wing." McLeod had been a client for seven years who refused to let up on his ex. Though they never went to court, they conducted a Legal War through their respective attorneys. He was a wealthy oil baron in Texas, she a prominent heiress; so to them money was no object. My friend's office wing was mostly financed by the McLeods, because they had spent thousands and thousands of dollars in attorney's fees to keep the strife going. Granted, the McLeods are not the norm, and most people cannot handle the high stakes to either launch or stay in a Legal War for a long duration. But then many do, just for the sake of taking back control.

You may not have realized it, but once you play the high-stakes Legal Wars game, you are throwing caution and control to the wind! Though we family law attorneys work extremely hard as advocates for our clients, we do not control the courtroom. So think twice about the Legal War. Is there some other way to resolve your differences or disputes? Can you give up something in exchange for peace of mind and the money you may lose? Is the Legal War you are about to enter into worth it? That is the key question: Is it worth it emotionally, psychologically and personally?

BATTLE FATIGUE

In many cases, because of the tedium and the costs of the Legal War, many people break down, surrender to the other side, or even begin to lose sight of what it is they are fighting for.

I have had clients tell me they felt like their War would never end, that they felt like they had become some type of prisoner of war and feared that they would never be free. It can sure feel that way. What is odd, is that many people bring such Wars upon themselves. So my advice: Know what you are getting into and scrutinize those "incidents" carefully, so if they escalate to a full-blown Legal War, you are prepared for what lies ahead. And do not violate any court orders or give your ex legitimate reason to drag you into court. You may feel smug at first, messing with your ex, but such a cavalier attitude could eventually humble you.

GROUNDS FOR WAR

I believe in the Legal War. Actually, I believe in the Legal War process. This divorce war is what I do everyday. I do not, however, believe a Legal War should be fought if a) the party is not emotionally and financially equipped to enter into battle, or b) they are not fighting for a meaningful purpose. Fighting for the best interests of the children or long-term financial security is a worthwhile call to War; but fighting to get even, is not. I believe fervently that there should be an objective place to resolve disputes.

If you are considering enlisting in a Legal War, just know what lies ahead and be prepared for it. A good attorney is there to see that you are geared up and ready to go, but even when attorneys like me do our best, we cannot shield clients from the spray of bullets flying or ricocheting around the Legal War battlefield. Nor can we guarantee any outcome, especially when the court gets involved.

And do not forget that in a Legal War, you can also expect, on some level, to be fighting the Emotional and Psychological Wars simultaneously, for it is impossible to remain unscathed from the emotional impact such a war causes, and it is unthinkable not to feel mentally "on the edge" from the uncertainty of a Legal War. Paying for grief is partly to blame for why some people feel bitter when the Legal War is over, even if they win.

VIDEO PLAY-BACK

Let's take a look at the three scenes I depicted earlier where Marta and Rod, Gwen and Rocco, and Janine and Harold were deeply embedded in their own individual Legal Wars.

In the case of Marta and Rod, Marta knew one way to lord control over her former rocker husband, and that was to throw his schedule out of kilter (since he was in the studio recording and on the road touring constantly), with demands that he appear in court. She also knew that Rod felt very insecure about the business he was in—uncertain of how long his success would last. He had only begun to make substantial sums of money in the two years prior to their divorce (they were married for four years). She knew that he had come from humble beginnings and he had confided to her many times he was afraid of returning to such a lifestyle. Rod could not have cared less when Marta showed up with a new beau, and, remarkably, Rod was one of those people who was rarely fazed by the "headtrips" Marta tried to put on him (like making him wonder if she was sleeping with the bass player in the band). Rod was, as he put it "through with her," so Psychological Warfare was not working. The only way Marta could get to Rod was through his wallet. Though they had a Prenuptial Agreement and she received a hefty settlement (and Rod thought he was "done with her"), she would not let go. Marta's choice of warfare (and her method of getting control) was the Legal type, and according to Rod's recent barrage of expletives, she was making substantial headway.

Though my team and I were successful in stopping Marta, it took thousands of dollars and nearly two years to get her to call a ceasefire. In the end, the judge ordered Marta to pay her own attorneys fees, totaling $145,000. Also, she had gained no additional spousal support, her alleged impetus for war.

In the case of Gwen and Rocco, Gwen had asked for $8,000 per month for child support for her three children (according to Rocco's reported income, clearly within California's state guidelines). Rocco, well-off and highly paid as a designer of luxury yachts, claimed he had sudden reversals, and was not getting the contracts he once had. Gwen suspected Rocco was not being honest, and she had knowledge through one of his former colleagues that he was collecting consulting fees under the table. Indeed, when they were married, he frequently did so. Rocco continued to hide his assets and worked diligently to stall the child and spousal support hearings, asking for one continuance after another. Rocco always had plausible reasons for postponements. He would purposely plan business trips or feign illness to drag things out. During the sixteen months of back and forth paperwork, Rocco managed to have a forensic accountant audit Gwen's books from her string of boutiques, and hired a private investigative service to look into her assets and holdings.

Rocco maintained that he cared very much about paying an equitable amount for the welfare of his children, and was willing to pay spousal support, but his claims were antithetical to his actions. He took more than two years to stave off any permanent court ruling as to what he would have to pay. Two years after the court ordered Rocco to pay $8,500 in spousal support and $7,000 in child support each month (retroactive from the day of the first hearing), Rocco declared bankruptcy. Some people will do anything to remain in control! He thought that would stop his child and spousal support payments; he was wrong. Child and spousal support payments are exempt from a bankruptcy. But Gwen had to pay more legal fees to deal with the bankruptcy and its effect on the family law action. In addition, Gwen realized she must focus on growing her business, so as not to be dependent upon Rocco, who would continue to pull these stunts. And she did! For her it was a wonderful feeling to pull the control rug out from under her devious ex and subsist on her own.

Harold and Janine stayed rooted in their Legal War over the properties in question—Aspen, Colorado and Palm Springs, California—for six years. After more than half a decade, here was the bottom line: The court finally ordered that both properties be sold and the proceeds split between the couple. The numbers stacked up: The Aspen parcel sold for $450,000, the condo in Palm Springs for $550,000. Harold spent $260,000 in attorneys' fees; Janine spent $250,000. After court costs, closing costs on both properties, maintenance, repairs and upkeep, realtor's commissions and moving expenses (to clean out the Palm

Springs condo), the costs came to another $200,000. Well, you do the math! In the end, the two wound up with about $150,000 each. Money notwithstanding, you can only imagine what this cost in lost income with time that could have been spent on loftier enterprises for both Janine and Harold. Of course, you can also take into account the mental anguish they kept alive for half a dozen years by continuing this ridiculous legal slugfest. Once again, such battles have nothing to do with logic or assets; they are all about control!

As you can see, even if two people hate each other, the vying for control costs them both, big time. Dollars and cents (and common sense, too) should support an effort to resolve issues—even if you use the old-fashioned "split the baby" approach, which would have been faster, less expensive and more effective.

WHICH OUTFIT ARE YOU FROM?

What is slightly different between a Legal War and the Emotional and Psychological Wars, is that in the latter two wars, you can decide not to participate. In the former, you have no choice but to respond. You cannot ignore correspondence, if it requires a reasonable response (like a request for a change in visitation). If, however, your ex threatens you with court action over an increase in support (spousal or child) referred to as a "modification," you can choose to ignore it and see if he or she acts on that threat. Most often, it is advisable to respond to any action that may make its way to the courts, or is court-oriented, for taking a passive role can backfire.

If you are the perpetrator, do not enter into a Legal War nonchalantly, for unlike the other two Typical Wars, this one potentially involves a third party—the court system—and you cannot just call off the War one day on a whim. If you are the victim of a Legal War, make sure you have a tough attorney—one that has prevailed for other clients during litigation. This is an absolute must for being shielded and protected in a Legal War. When you have been bombarded, it is both the best defense and offense.

As we did in previous chapters, it is now time to determine whether you are an Attacker or Defender (or Neutral, if that is at all possible), and what you can do about it. Please answer the following questions with candor:

1. Are you currently in the midst of handling the issues relative to your divorce or cohabitation breakup, and are you doing so through your attorneys?
   Yes _____
   No _____

2. If you answered "no," are you fighting it out for viable and practical reasons or as a means to keep control?
   Viable reasons _____
   To keep control _____

3. If you have finalized your original "Settlement," in terms of property, spousal, and child support, do you frequently send your ex letters, faxes, or emails that could result in legal action?
   Yes _____
   No _____

4. Have you recently initiated any court proceedings against your ex?
   Yes _____
   No _____

5. If you have not initiated any court proceedings against your ex, but are attempting to engage in a Legal War, are you doing so through letters, faxes, or emails?
   Yes _____
   No _____

6. If you answered, "yes," to the above, consider the action you are taking (be brutally honest). It is:
   Legitimate _____
   It is a means by which to irritate and harass my ex _____

7. Other than the original papers for the dissolution of your marriage and those forms *required* to process your matter, how many court proceedings have you *initiated* since the two of you broke up (despite the amount of time you have been separated)?
   1-5 _____
   5-10 _____
   10-20 _____
   20 or more _____

8. Other than the original papers for the dissolution of your marriage and those forms *required* to process your matter, how many court proceedings have you *responded* to since the two of you broke up (despite the amount of time you have been separated)?
   1-5 _____
   5-10 _____
   10-20 _____
   20 or more _____

9. How would you characterize yourself?
   Defender _____
   Attacker _____

10. Between you and your ex, who currently has the greater financial means to fight the Legal War?
    Me _____
    My ex _____

11. How many times have you instigated action that has led to a court appearance?
    _____ times
    Never _____

If you have identified yourself as an "Attacker," answer the following question:

1. As you engage in the Legal War, what is your primary reason (be honest now) for doing so?
   Out of sheer necessity _____
   Somewhat necessary, but my issue could be resolved through other means _____
   Out of spite _____

If you answered anything other than "out of sheer necessity," know that this Legal War has more to do with bolstering the Emotional and Psychological Wars than it does with resolving an important legal issue that cannot be resolved by any other means except legal action.

If you are a Legal War Attacker, and again, are playing this role for any reason other than a practical one, go over the following punch list that points out why it might not be wise for you to play the perpetrator in a Legal War.

1. It will forever affect my children and other loved ones.
2. It costs too much money.
3. Whether I can or cannot afford to wage a Legal War, I could certainly do better things with the same funds.
4. I may very well lose.
5. I will waste not only money, but also valuable time and energy.
6. I run the risk of relinquishing control to a neutral party (the court) who may not see things my way.
7. If I take on the role of the Legal War Attacker, I may find out I have bitten off more than I can financially (or emotionally or psychologically) chew!

Now make your list, and get a giant pad of paper for this one. Five reasons will be your minimum.

1. _____
2. _____
3. _____
4. _____
5. _____

As in previous chapters, I now offer a list of "substitutions" to serve as alternatives and diversions to behaving as the Attacker in a Legal War:

1. **Make a spreadsheet:** This ledger should include two columns: One for what you would spend on a Legal War, the other, using the same funds and what you would

spend them on (i.e., items you would like to purchase). For those with lesser means, these can include something as minimal as a new set of bed sheets. For those with greater means, this money could be used to purchase a new piece of property, a collectible (like a car or antique), or something as basic as college education or private school tuition for your children. Money is relative to all of us. We all have pleasures in which we like to indulge, and we all have necessities that drive us to earn income. On your spreadsheet, list all of the items you could use the *same* Legal War war chest on that will help take care of things you need and things that will give you pleasure.

2. **Take the same strategy and put it to better use:** Are you angry? Do you want to go to war? Do you feel like having a good fight? If you were planning a major attack against your ex just for the sake of an attack, see if you can take the same strategy to wage war on something that might offer up more gratifying and productive results. One example might be to fight to get your local Congressman out of office in order to get a better one. Maybe you want to put the same effort into lobbying for a better position at work. Or, how about tackling your weight issue head on—the one that has been plaguing you? Perhaps you can join a task force that helps go after the abusers of children. There are so many choices and so many other ways to use the same bellicose strategies.

3. **Find alternative ways to resolve disputes:** If you are going to pay an attorney, ask for help to find alternate means to resolve your legal dispute, ones that are cost-conscious and take a lesser toll on your peace of mind. Mediation is one way, a four-way conference between you, your attorney, your ex and his/her attorney is another. One other option is a hearing before a retired judge. Ask for suggestions for viable means to get your legal business handled with as little legal haggling as possible. Again, ask your lawyer to provide a number of alternatives.

4. **Put the money in a splurge account:** I had one client who calculated how much she would have been spending on attorney's fees and court costs and put those funds in what

she called her "splurge" account. Though she was tempted to spend a fortune on her ex-husband to get additional child support (which she knew he could pay), she realized she might not get it at all. By socking the same money away, she felt she had won the Legal War. She used a hefty portion of it to tour Europe with a friend several years after her divorce issues had settled down. She also put some toward a college account for one or her children.

5. **Boost that retirement account or start a new business:** Legal Wars, as I have already mentioned, can cost a fortune. Why not take the same money and ask your stockbroker to add to your stock portfolio, invest in long-term bonds, or even find a small piece of income property or a timeshare? If you are really adventurous, you may wish to start your own company. I know of many clients who took what they would have spent on a court battle and started a business venture. One used her projected Legal War funds to go to film school. (Three years after she finished film school, she became an associate producer for a major motion picture studio.)

It is time now for you to make a list of "substitutions." These will be very personal, I'm sure, for each of us has certain things on which we like to spend our time and money. Again, do not limit yourself to a handful.

1. _____
2. _____
3. _____
4. _____
5. _____

NAME CALLING

Just as I did in the previous two chapters, I will now present a list of adjectives—the most common ones used to describe those who launch a Legal War.

Adjectives:

- Ruthless
- Avaricious
- Greedy
- Vicious
- Heartless
- Calculating
- Materialistic
- Litigious
- Manipulating

The following are a few "labels" you might be called:

- Leech
- Sue-happy
- Money-monger
- Money-grubber
- Gold Digger
- Opportunist
- Gouger

DEFENDER'S CHOICE

If you find yourself being pelted with Legal War missiles, it is time to ask your current attorney (or hire a new one), to assist you. It would be prudent for you, as a Defender, to have a legal expert in your corner to both guide and instruct you on how to either stay clear of a Legal War, or how best to minimize the damage a Legal War can render. Of course, the other reason you want a capable divorce attorney is to fight the Legal War if you are forced to do so, or at least resolve your matter in a manner that is advantageous to you.

The following are a few suggestions on how to stave off the Legal War if one is brewing:

1. **Let your Attacker know:** In the early stages—when the threatening correspondence is coming your way—make it clear that you are not interested in fighting. If possible, share the reasons legal action might be detrimental to both of you. Be firm, however, and explain that if attacks persist, you will vigorously defend yourself.
2. **Get your attorney on the phone or set up a meeting:** Keep your attorney apprised of all goings-on between you and your ex—especially those that indicate your ex might be planning a Legal Attack. It could be that your attorney can head off such an ugly War before it even gets started.

3. **Investigate what a Legal War entails:** Often just knowing what to expect can be helpful in paving the way for major decisions. For example, rather than fight over a piece of property, as in the case of Janine and Harold, it might be wiser to calculate your losses and opt to trade a piece of property for peace of mind. If you recall, this couple had fought for six years, and in the end, the toll was devastating. Knowledge is power, as you know; so bone up on what is to come, because this may help you decide what strategies to put into place—i.e., try to settle your differences outside the realm of legal action, or gear up for the big war. Learn as much as you can about the legal processes you are about to go through, for many people get sideswiped with frustration and anxiety when they do not know what the process is or how it works. Study up!

4. **Get in shape:** If it appears you will have to defend yourself, spend time with your therapist, your attorney, family members, or anyone who can offer moral support. Even look into joining a support group. A Legal War is overwhelming to most, so make sure you are emotionally, physically, psychologically and spiritually fit to handle the stress such a war will produce.

5. **Reward yourself:** Promise yourself when this Legal War is all over, that you will do something self-gratifying. Actually, to sustain yourself (keep your sanity) throughout the process, you need to take time off or give yourself rewards. If you wait until the end, you may not make it. Planning a payoff of some kind for yourself for all the trouble and stress you have had to endure in the Legal War can give you something to look forward to. We all need a respite or a payoff to balance out the trials we go through. A Legal War is no exception. Start making your list and keep in mind that such rewards do not have to be simply monetary ones. You can promise yourself a bubble bath every night for three weeks, time to putter around in that rose garden you have sorely neglected, or the treat of three movies in one day! These rewards do not have to cost a lot. They should simply be rich in gratification.

TAKING COVER

If you are the Defender type who takes pleasure in fighting back in a Legal War, I ask that you redirect that energy. It is one thing to fight when it is the appropriate thing to do and a necessity to resolve some complicated issue (like a move-away in the child custody arena), but it is another to revel in the thought that you will be duking it out in court.

The following is a list of questions to help you determine whether playing Legal War reciprocator is beneficial to you, or if you can find another means to settle your differences outside of court.

1. Have you tried to reason with your ex in order to stay out of any legal action?
   Yes _____
   No _____

2. Have you participated in fueling "incidents" that exacerbate the Legal War probability?
   Yes _____
   No _____

3. Is the pending Legal War a result of your initial divorce proceedings, or is it due to the ongoing battles—issues that are either new or that you have been unable to resolve?
   Initial divorce issues _____
   Issues we have been unable to resolve _____
   New disputes _____

4. Has your attorney advised you and prepared you for the Legal War?
   Yes _____
   No _____

5. If a Legal War is imminent, do you feel you are fully prepared and equipped to engage in such a battle?
   Yes _____
   No _____
   Somewhat _____

I will interpret the various answers of both query sections for the Attacker and the Defender in a moment; but for now, I would like to comment on the role of the Neutral in the Legal War.

Unlike the Neutral in the Emotional and Psychological Wars, a person cannot really become or stay Neutral in a Legal War. The only Neutral party in the Legal War is the court system. Now this may take form in the way of a court-appointed or privately hired mediator, a "rent-a-judge," an arbitrator, or most often, a courtroom judge. As I pointed out in Chapter Four in my discussion about the Three Typical Wars, the Legal War is the one where you lose or relinquish the most control. This is true whether you are an Attacker or a Defender. Granted, if you can resolve your dispute(s) through your attorneys, you have a modicum of control over the "legal" outcome. But if you find it necessary to have your issues resolved by the court, there is no telling how each dispute will be resolved. While in most cases I have seen judges rule fairly—like in issues dealing with child support and property matters—I have seen judges revoke physical custody from one parent and give it to another. I have also seen judges who became so fed up (the "Heard-It-Alls," and the "Hammers") that they used their *discretion* (discretion being a key word here) to make a decision. Such was the case with Janine and Harold when the judge ordered they sell both properties and split the difference. Depending upon the judge, the case's outcome could have gone several ways. Remember, in court you lose control; your fight is determined by a third party—the judge, the ultimate decision maker—who will undoubtedly be one of the judge "types" we discussed in Chapter Four. Do you really want the judge to decide your fate?

Keep in mind that once the court does make a decision, it sticks. Unless, of course, you want to start that Legal War ball rolling all over again to try and change that ruling. If that is the case, just sit back and watch that cash register drawer get drained all over again; that is, if you even have any cash left! And even if you do start from square one again, it does not mean the court decision will be reversed or that this time you will win. Quite often you will not. Having said that and since there are there are changes in financial circumstances that could be mitigating factors in reducing or increasing child or spousal support payments, there are also many gray areas in Legal Wars. A youngster might even prefer to change residences to live with the other parent. So then, going to court just once is not how it often goes. Some people spend years in and out of court, using the system as a means to retain or opt for control.

Legal Wars can be "iffy" and unpredictable; that is the most important thing to keep in mind. Also, they can be expensive. Just because your spouse makes more money than you, it does not always mean that the courts will order him or her to pay your attorney's fees and costs. Remember what I have said all along: The courts are the Neutral party that can decide however, or whatever, they see fit.

My esteemed colleague in New York, an excellent family law attorney, Patricia Ferrari, who has been with the Phillips Nizer firm since 1979, has seen a variety of cases during her career. She cautions her clients to think doubly hard about whether the Legal War is worth the fight. Some time ago, she encouraged one of her clients (who walked out of a settlement conference in exchange for fighting it out in a courtroom), to take another stab at settlement with a court-appointed mediator to prove to her client that her expectations were unrealistic and the offer on the table was not a bad one. "Some people just get it in their heads that they can do better if they take their case to trial," Ferrari says, "When more often than not, it can be the opposite." Ferrari urges her clients to take a good hard look at what they hope to gain and what they will *probably* gain if they go before the person in the black robe, control notwithstanding.

I know of some divorced couples who said they were fully aware of the downsides of going to trial. However, when they did not get what they thought they would or should during a court hearing, they were mortified. Some feel so angry and humiliated with what they perceive as such a public defeat, that they insist on returning to court in an attempt to try to get the judge to look at it again, and hopefully, this time see it their way! The Legal War can become as addictive as gambling in a casino: Some just want to try another hand. However, when you compound your losses, such a gamble can be ridiculously costly. And just like in a casino, sometimes you win, and sometimes you lose! And if and when you do finally win, when you total what you spent to get that jackpot, you may find (just like in a casino) you spent three times the jackpot just to say you won.

AS THE SAYING GOES

No matter what side you fight on in the Legal War, there are a number of "philosophies" that may sound familiar to you—ones that may make you think twice before you take to the Legal Battlefield! Just as in other chapters, I have prepared a list of "isms" I thought you should consider. Here they are:

- A penny saved, is a penny earned
- Penny wise and pound foolish
- Throwing good money after bad
- Pigs get fat, hogs get slaughtered
- You pay 'yur money, ya take 'yur chances
- A bird in the hand is worth two in the bush

Can you think of others? Sometimes recalling some of those "pearls of wisdom" your mother or father instilled in you can have tremendous impact when deciding what stance you will take in a Legal War. List them now:

1. _____
2. _____
3. _____
4. _____
5. _____

FREE ADVICE

If you are one of the readers considering (or already embroiled in) a Legal War, the following are some sound suggestions for making this War easier to manage:

1. **Do not use your attorney as a "hand-holder":** Many people engaged in a Legal War tend to call their attorney constantly for reassurance, for support, or to vent. Just remember that every phone call and every meeting costs money. Try to keep those legal costs to a minimum.

2. **Do some of the groundwork:** Gather records, documents, income tax returns, bills, bank statements and any other materials your attorney will need. Ask ahead of time how many copies will be needed for your file. You can make them yourself to save money and time. Attorney Ferrari also insists (as I do) that her clients take all important documents out of the house and place them in a safety deposit box or vault so they do not mysteriously disappear. We both have had clients who suddenly could not find automobile pink slips, jewelry appraisals, and prenuptial agreements, let alone bank statements, or credit card statements, etc. Make those copies, but put those originals in an indestructible place!

3. **Reveal all:** *Do not hold anything back from your lawyers.* Do not be one of those warriors that neglects to tell your attorney important facts—information that could come out during your Legal War that could harm you. *Always* be truthful. *Always* be forthright. Do not forget that you and your attorney are a team. As such, you need to work closely together to attempt to get the result you want. If you have "phantom" income that suddenly emerges as a result of an investigation from the opponent, or you say something counter-productive in a deposition that could come back to haunt you, you may be defeating your own purpose. Your lawyer can only assist you with the information that is available. *Hide nothing!* No matter how good an attorney is, he or she can become as defenseless as you are, if caught off guard because you didn't reveal an important fact. A lawyer without data is more dangerous to you than no lawyer at all.

4. **Be organized:** When you meet with your attorney, have all paperwork and answers to his or her questions ready. Also have those questions you wish to ask jotted down and in front of you. You do not want to pay for an attorney visit, be billed for phone time or a second meeting only to ask questions you *forgot* to ask at the prior meeting.

5. **Get equipped:** When a Legal War is in progress you may want to consider having an email address, voicemail, and a fax machine installed at both your home and office. You should also have a cell phone on which you can be easily reached. Smartphones, Blackberries, iPads, and other devices are also beneficial if that is how your attorney prefers communicating with you outside the office. Are you one of those who prefer to check your email every hour or just once a day? Find out what other equipment you need to have on hand to stay in contact with your attorney. Also, let your attorney know if you are traveling, taking a vacation, or won't be available for an extended period of time. Provide information about where you will be, just in case he or she needs to reach you. Chasing you down could cost a bundle, and you certainly do not want your attorney to bill hours for anything but Legal War necessities.

6. **Be a clever negotiator:** If you find yourself going through a series of negotiations—either with a retired judge, a mediator, or in a four-way conference with your attorney —be smart and keep a few aces up your sleeve. A client of mine, after thirty-two years of marriage and a cheating husband, decided to handle her dissolution as coolly as a business deal. She purposely held her tongue in asking for certain items she desperately wanted, until her ex, exhausted after twelve days of haggling before a mediator, finally agreed to give her a prized antique music box that had been a wedding gift from her ex's grandmother. So hold a few things back—bargaining chips—for use at just the right time. It's a shrewd way to win on a few battlefronts. But be sure your lawyer knows what you are holding back and what your real intentions are.

READY OR NOT? HERE YOU GO!

Here is a list of questions that may help you determine whether or not you are ready to be deployed to the Legal War battlefield:

1. Do you have an excellent attorney—one you can trust and that you feel is solidly in your corner?
   Yes _____
   No _____
   Not sure _____

2. Do you have all your documents in hand and copies made?
   Yes _____
   No _____
   Not sure what I should gather _____

3. Have you carefully assessed the win-to-cost ratio of the Legal War?
   Yes _____
   No _____

4. Do you have the patience to endure in this Legal War?
   Yes _____
   No _____
   Hope so _____

5. Have you diligently tried other means by which to settle your marital disputes?
   Yes _____
   No _____

6. Have you accounted for the time you may need to take off work to engage in this war?
   Yes _____
   No _____

7. Can you afford to lose?
   Yes _____
   No _____
   Not sure _____

8. Can you handle the emotional impact of the Legal War?
   Yes ____
   No ____
   Not sure ____

9. Can you handle the psychological impact of the Legal War?
   Yes ____
   No ____
   Not sure ____

10. Are you in good health?
    Yes ____
    No ____
    Sort of ____

11. How long are you willing to stay in the Legal War?
    Six months ____
    One year ____
    Eighteen months ____
    Two years ____
    For as long as it takes ____

12. If there are others who are affected by this Legal War (i.e., the children, in-laws, business partners), can you handle the impact this war will have on them?
    Yes ____
    No ____
    Not sure ____

13. Are you willing to hand over control to a higher power (in this case, the judge)?
    Yes ____
    No ____
    Not sure ____

SUMMING UP

Whether you are an Attacker or a Defender, it is time now to look at the significance of your answers. They are critical, for if there is any hesitation at all on your part, or if the pieces are not properly in place to fight in this War, it is time to go back to the War Room and redesign your strategy. My point is this: If the answers reveal a different intention than you thought, then discuss a different strategy with your lawyer. If you have lots of "not sure" answers, then it is time to reassess your approach and possibly your attorney.

Let's begin with the section "Which Outfit Are You From." If you answered "yes" to handling your issues between your ex via your attorneys, that is a good thing, because most reputable attorneys attempt to arrive at equitable settlements. If you stated that you are fighting it out for good reasons, well, then fine, go forward. If on the other hand, it is all about control or spite, step back and regroup. You may want to surrender such grandiose thoughts of going to a War you might not win, one that could leave you angry, frustrated and broke.

If you are, for the most part, done with your divorce or breakup and are still taunting your ex with communications that could create an "incident" that could lead to a Legal War, back off; you may be venturing into dangerous territory. If you recently filed a court action against your ex, ask yourself if your reasons are legitimate. Are you really up to this fight? If fighting is worth the risk, then by all means go for it. If not, see if you can find other less damaging ways to settle your disputes.

If you have filed court actions more than three times, you may want to take a close look at why this is your preferred method of resolving issues. If you are the Defender in this instance, get resourceful and clever and see if you can find ways to work out what needs attention, without getting "legal" about it.

If you are the Attacker, you need to ask yourself if you can afford this war in every way—emotionally, psychologically and financially. If you are the Defender, be brutally honest as to whether you can find a route around this dangerous tact, or if you have no choice but to meet it head on. Compromise might be a concept that would have a more beneficial result.

If you have the lesser financial means to go to Legal War, once again, see if you can manage another way to stave off this fight. It does not mean you need to cave in to demands, but do think creatively about how you might avoid this major altercation. If you have the greater means financially, be prepared to pick up the tab for you *and* your opponent. Often, the court orders the person that has the most means to pick up the other's check, or at least part of it.

If you are one of those who passively or actively incites anger in your ex—such anger that he or she drags you into a Legal War and forces a court appearance on you—look inward and ask if the instigator role is a wise one to take on. You just might want to place that energy into more productive enterprises.

Once again, if you answer anything other than "out of sheer necessity" as a reason for going to court, you are headed down the dark alley of uncertainty and you better be wearing a bulletproof vest and carrying a large flashlight! You also better have a good attorney leading you into battle and a support team covering your back!

In "Taking Cover," I asked if you have tried to stave off the Legal War by trying to reason with your ex, or if you had inflamed an "incident." If you said "yes," then you are almost as guilty as the Attacker. Redirect your thinking and your actions.

If the pending Legal War is a result of ongoing battles, then look for new ways to handle these differences. Confer with your attorney to see if you can be more inventive in calling a peace summit to end the discord.

If your attorney has prepared you for the Legal War, terrific; for you just may have to defend yourself in one. But if the answer to this question is "no," then you better get busy and recruit an army of help, for you are going to need it. The Legal War is one you cannot fight alone!

In "Ready Or Not? Here You Go!" where I asked if you were ready to go to war as either an Attacker or Defender, I mentioned you must have an excellent attorney to do so. You also must be practical and handle this event in a businesslike fashion. So get your head on straight and methodically collect all the paperwork you need to pass on to your legal counsel. If this is too much of a headache, you certainly are not a good candidate for the Legal

War. Talk to your attorney and see if you can discharge yourself from it honorably. If you do decide to go ahead, you will need a spreadsheet to determine whether or not you can afford the price tag of the Legal War. Even if you can, you should lay out a budget for all its expenditures. (Heavy artillery needed here!) If you are not patient, pull out. You may be one of those Attackers or Defenders that shoots yourself in more than the foot when all is said and done.

If you cannot afford to lose, in any way, emotionally, psychologically or financially, get a grip, and then recruit a neutral party to assist you with mediation or settlement as your solution. Clearly, a Legal War is not for you.

If you are not in good health, see if you can throw up a white flag that does not demonstrate defeat or weakness but good sense, since your health is more important than anything else. Without your health, how can you possibly go about your life tending to other things of great importance such as making a living or raising your children? Yes, you are needed on the home front! So then, health is a fundamental requirement in enlisting and enduring in a Legal War.

If you have the fortitude to endure in a Legal War that may go on indefinitely, or end in defeat, then you are one of the chosen few. Most people reach a point when enough is enough. Can you take it? Really? Only you can decide. Or stated differently, are you willing to roll the dice with the judge? As Clint Eastwood, as the main character in "Dirty Harry" once said, "Do you feel lucky? Well, do you?" Only you can decide.

If your Legal War is affecting others and you are a Defender, then see what you can do to side-step this major conflict. The last thing you want to do is have those around you and those you care about suffer. Wasn't the divorce itself hard enough on everyone? A real soul-searcher, this question!

Last, but certainly not least, if you said you were willing to subjugate control to a higher power, you are one tough cookie, and I wish you the best! Many family law attorneys will tell you, this one included, that we often hear people say they can handle giving control to the court. In truth, however, it is a horribly helpless and frightening feeling when you are (once and for all) standing before a person in a black robe you have never met—a person who is deciding your fate and your future. It can be a roll of the dice; do not forget this. My last note: If you do find yourself handing over control, make sure you hire the best family law attorney you can get, one who has an impressive and enviable track record both in court and in resolving matters. That is an absolute, for there is no margin for error when choosing a General/Admiral to lead you into the Legal War. Also, make certain you have a good rapport with this attorney. In the Legal War, you are a team, a partnership, and you do not want to be squabbling within your own camp. This often happens!

I would like to leave you with a few famous adages to mull over—sayings that may bolster you, if in fact you are marching off to Legal War:

- Patience is a virtue
- Nothing ventured, nothing gained
- Good things come to those who wait
- There is light at the end of the tunnel
- Easy does it
- No pain, no gain
- Keep your nose to the grindstone
- Hang in there
- This too shall pass

A contemporary adage perhaps sums up this chapter best of all: "God grant me the strength to accept the things I cannot change, the courage to change the things I can, and the wisdom to know the difference."

You may have others, and if so, I suggest you write them down and post a new one every day in front of you (where you can easily see it), in order to reinforce your resolve and keep you strong. Sometimes, those who venture into a Legal War need to be bolstered and coached. For instance, you may want to post that song lyric: *Money/money/money/money/money...*from the song of the same title, all over the place! Whatever it takes, for this is the perfect time to be your own best friend!

Now let's move on to a discussion of the Miscellaneous Wars, those hard-to-identify hidden enemies that can sneak up on you!

*"Affected by my divorce!?! Do I LOOK like
I'm affected by my divorce!?!?"*

Chapter Eight

THE INTERNAL WARS:
The Enemies Within

Anne Marie staggered up the stairs, trailing the contents of her purse behind her as she searched for her keys. "Damn," she muttered. Then she fell, breaking the left heel of her new Jimmy Choo's.

"Mommy, is that you?" a soft voice forced itself through a crack in the apartment door.

"Yes, it's me," Anne Marie said, too loudly and ruefully.

The soft voice began to cry.

"Danielle, calm down. I'm fine, honey."

"But I heard you fall down again."

"Well, I got up again," Anne Marie laughed, though she tried to stave off tears as she pushed open the door, "I'm just fine."

"You don't look fine, Mommy," the frightened thirteen-year-old said.

"I'm fine," the mother replied. "I just need a drink."

Danielle returned to the sofa, curled up on it, fixed her eyes on the TV, and pulled the blanket up around her neck. Her mother headed for the kitchen to pour herself a stiff drink.

♦   ♦   ♦

"Does the suit come in brown, too?" the well-groomed thirty-seven-year old computer programmer asked.

"Yes, it does. Not just the gray, but brown and black as well," replied the attentive salesman.

"Hey, then I'll take it in all three colors."

Unsure of how to say it, the salesman finally managed: "I'm afraid that will put you over your credit limit."

"Well, then, here, put it on my new Visa card."

◆   ◆   ◆

"Look, she's my attorney, and I need to know exactly what she has planned in response to this last letter," Dominique's voice trailed off as she muttered, "...how dare he threaten me with a modification."

"I'm sorry Dominique, I can't answer that question for you," said the polite paralegal. "Though I assure you Ms. Stanton is handling your case to the best of her ability, and in a manner that is both appropriate and beneficial to your case."

"I hear that, but that's not enough. I need to know every detail," Dominique's jaws were beginning to clinch. "Make sure she calls me before the end of the day."

◆   ◆   ◆

"I'm sorry, but we have to let you go," said the Human Resources Director, looking the tragically sad young woman directly in the eye.

"I am truly sorry, Mr. Bennett. I didn't mean to fall asleep at my desk again, and I know you were kind enough to overlook this on two other occasions, but..."

"I understand your marital problems have been an issue," Bennett was quick to interject, "however, we have a business, a very busy accounting firm, to run."

Fighting back the tears in eyes that were noticeably tired and swollen, the young woman took her pink slip and made her exit.

THE ENEMIES WITHIN

While many of the wars you will fight during your marital demise are closely connected with the dealings between you and your ex, in the emotional, psychological and legal sense, you can become involved in many other types of war. Some of these wars are the ones in which you will be fighting with, and against, yourself!

These Internal Wars can wage just as viciously against you as the Three Typical Wars: That is, if you let them. In fact, the Enemies Within can be even more pervasive since they can sometimes start the divorce ball rolling or exacerbate any one of the Three Typical Wars already in progress. These Enemies Within can also outfit the other side with ammunition to use against you. And quite often, these Enemies Within can serve as the catalyst for self-inflicted injury. In other words, as a result of declaring war upon yourself!

With that in mind, this chapter is dedicated to profiling the Enemies Within and offering sound reasons why it is in your best interest not to let them control you.

Consider this age-old concept: In conflict there is man against man, man against nature, and man against himself. The latter is the subject of discussion here.

I have broken these "Internal" wars into two categories. I refer to them as the "Way Too Much" or "Far Too Little" Wars.

With either the "Way Too Much War" or the "Far Too Little War," keep in mind, neither of them is any different in concept than the Three Typical Wars. What's in sharp contrast is that these Internal Wars attack from the inside, while the others usually strike from the outside.

The "Way Too Much" War can set up a dynamic whereby you are battling for control against your impulses to overdo; while the "Far Too Little" War-genre presents struggles to "under do." The former may include *too much* alcohol, while the latter may have to do with *too little* sleep. In either case, control of yourself and defeating the enemies within is the heart of this chapter. As you can probably tell, the Internal Wars can be just as devastating as the other Wars; and, of course, engaging in them or fighting them is also all about control. For after all—war is war, no matter who or *what* is waging it.

Often when a person is going through the many ups and downs that only a marital breakup will produce, he or she can spin out of control and begin a self-abuse process, one that is always the result of some type of internal struggle. It could be drugs, alcohol, compulsive shopping, gambling, over-eating, under-eating, over-working, under-working, too much sex, drastic weight gain or weight loss, minimal focus, sleep deprivation, driving too fast, mood swings, physical vanity, or the abuse of others.

I have not overlooked the possibility that you may be one of the readers who is in fine shape—one who is not fighting any demons. But if you are going through a breakup, I am willing to bet that you have at least one thing that may be getting the best of you: That *thing* with which you are at war. For if you are engaged in an Emotional, Psychological or Legal War, generally you are fighting an Enemy Within at the same time. Most people, as they fight one of the Typical Three, tend to either over or under indulge in some way. So they wind up fighting both External and Internal Wars simultaneously.

It is important to identify the Enemy Within to determine what is robbing you of self-control and to find ways of getting you back in control. Do not forget, that is what this book is all about: Control. Remember?

If you are not in control of your *issues*, you are not in a strategic position to deal with the many difficulties the Typical Three Wars can present—those Wars you may be currently engaged in or about to be engaged in. So, first things first. Ask yourself this: In *addition* to the Typical Three Wars, or in lieu of any one of them, are you at war with yourself? And if so, what type of war (or wars) are you fighting?

REAR VIEW MIRROR

My first request of you is to go back and take another peek at the opening scenes in this chapter to see if any one of the four of them looks familiar to you. In Scene One, Anne Marie, the mother of a teenage daughter, was drinking to excess. In Scene Two, our computer programmer was spending more than he could afford. In Scene Three, the client was trying to micro-manage his attorney. In Scene Four, the pathetic young lady was obviously not sleeping enough—she was "under doing," and in the end it cost her her job.

WAY TOO MUCH

When one is not feeling mentally or emotionally well, he or she may lunge for a tonic of sorts, something to alter the state and medicate against emotional pain much the same way one would take medicine to alleviate physical pain. Alcohol and drugs are certainly the most popular and common elixirs in the "Way Too Much" War. Food is another remedy. In any case, those who begin to overdo with regard to the things they ingest, well, they are clearly at war with themselves. You may argue that this "Way Too Much" War problem—this issue you have identified—may have preceded the divorce. Quite possibly, that could be true. In the case of Anne Marie, for example, it is possible she had a drinking problem before her divorce—perhaps it was a contributing factor. That being the case, it could have easily become exacerbated during the divorce process, for most Enemies Within seem to heavily infiltrate during or after the relationship breakup. It appears that most people who have a previous "issue" find that issue amplified when under great duress. I do not want that to happen to you!

GETTING BOMBED

Even those who have never had a "Way Too Much" issue may find themselves smack dab in the middle of some damaging behavior. Another note—those who have a penchant for obsessive or "Way Too Much" behavior, now faced with divorce, sometimes add something to the existing neurotic mix. For example, someone who may have been a heavy drinker may now also turn to drugs. For those who had two credit cards, it may mean they now have six; and those who micro-managed their office staff, perhaps now also try to micro-manage their attorney, therapist or accountant.

Typically, those who have had a tendency toward some destructive behavior soon become even more destructive in that behavior, or again, compound the destruction by adding a new addiction to the pile of "just can't help myself!" behaviors.

BREAKDOWN

Looking more closely at the "Way Too Much" War, let's round up the "usual suspects"—those Enemies Within that can pit us against ourselves. Though you may not have realized it, the "Way Too Much" Wars can be the deadliest of all the Wars, for if you are fighting against yourself, it is hard to remove yourself from battle and walk away. The War is waging within, and you cannot get away from it. Sometimes it seems, and is, never ending. I know some clients who, long after the divorce and all the details of it were completed, remained at war with themselves.

Let's first identify the most common Enemies Within. As you begin to identify them, you can then begin to take control of what might be controlling you. After the identification process, you can start to personalize and recognize why it is so important to defeat these combatants. Although there may be many on any person's list, the following single out the most common Enemy Within culprits. They include alcohol and drugs. Drinking socially at any time in your life is acceptable. Having the need to rely on alcohol every day, of course, is not. If you are the type of person who has teetered on the brink of a drinking issue, know that your *urge* (the real Enemy Within) to up the ante and belly up to the bar more frequently (or to consume more quantity) is a war in which you will need to vigorously defend yourself. If you can closely identify with Anne Marie, be aware that your drinking or drug abuse is horrifically painful for others to witness. (For instance, I am certain you must have felt compassion for Anne Marie's daughter, Danielle.) Over-indulgence in drugs and alcohol also diminishes your self-esteem to a level that can become a bottomless pit, one that is hard to pull out of. If you are going through a divorce or a relationship breakup, the last thing you need is low self-esteem. As hard as it may be, my advice is to forego both alcohol and drugs, if it appears you cannot be in control of *them*. To convince you further, here is a partial list of reasons why alcohol and drug abuse can be detrimental to you. You might say...

1. I will deeply hurt my children, parents, friends and others close to me by allowing them to witness the effects of what such excesses can do to me.
2. I may lose custody or visitation with my children.
3. I will set a bad example for my children.
4. I will not be able to function as productively in my profession.
5. I may lose my job.
6. I may get busted for drunk driving or arrested for possession of illegal drugs.
7. My physical well-being could be at stake.
8. I may embarrass myself in public.
9. People will talk badly about me behind my back.
10. I'll miss out on the better things in life.
11. I will look foolish and disgusting to those whose opinions mean a great deal to me.
12. Alcohol and drug abuse will age me.
13. I will continuously live in an "Out of Control" state.

As you did in previous chapters, make your own list of reasons why overindulging in drugs and alcohol can become detrimental to you. There is no limit, so feel free to list more than five.

1. _____
2. _____
3. _____
4. _____
5. _____

Compulsive Spending: Most people who go through a breakup suffer financially in some fashion. Losing income (if both parties were income-earning), having to pay attorneys' fees, putting up new funds to set up housekeeping, and splitting assets are only a few financial realities/drawbacks most face when the relationship is over. As such, the last thing you need is to find yourself heavily in debt because of a compulsive need to buy things you may not need or cannot afford. Overspending is certainly the remedy of choice for many, because it tends to ward off depression, and, if only temporarily, makes people feel they are being bolstered or soothed as they surround themselves with nice things—from gadgets to garb.

I think it is perfectly fine to spend lavishly, if you have the means to do so! There is nothing wrong with enjoying what you have. However, when your spending exceeds your financial means or limits, then you definitely have a major war to fight: The urge to buy, buy, buy!

In Scene Three, the gentleman did not care that he was over his limit at the clothing store. He did what many people do in this war; he simply pulled out a new credit card. One, I am sure, that would probably be maxed out soon enough as well.

Another problem with overspending is that it often depletes the resources you could be using for more long lasting financial gains. With what you have been throwing away on clothes through your marital breakup, perhaps you could have purchased mutual funds, or put a down payment on a house. I have a dear friend who received the proceeds from the sale of her house (community property split), and through her rage and anger (two of the Most Wanted Enemies Within), and spent the entire amount on clothes. Though it was only $25,000, it could have been a good start in building a base for an eventual down payment on a condo or house. This woman had two small children, three years and ten months old, and it took her ten years to be able to finally save enough to buy a permanent place. How about you? Are you throwing your money away or spending more than you should? The following are a few good reasons why you may want to change that behavior:

1. You could ruin your credit.
2. Overspending will keep you in debt.
3. You may grow tired of what you purchased and want another new "one" (whether it is a car, a dress, etc.) sooner than when you can afford.

4. You may find yourself constantly needing to borrow more money just to stay afloat.
5. Those whose opinions mean something to you could find you shallow.
6. You can use the money for more gratifying things that may have staying power or a longer shelf-life in terms of your future, such as a home, a college fund for the children, or an IRA.
7. If you are overspending in one area, another area that needs your financial resources may suffer. For instance, do you skate on the dental bill because you have to make a minimum payment to that department store bill instead?
8. You are creating a dangerous pattern, one that may be hard to stop once the divorce is over and the rest of your life settles down.
9. You are setting an example for your children that tells them material things are a priority.
10. You will find yourself being controlled by the Enemy Within—"Compulsive Spender."

Gambling: It is not a theory but a known fact that most of those who gamble will eventually lose. If that were not the case, resorts such as Las Vegas, Monte Carlo and Atlantic City would soon be out of business. Bookmakers would have to find another way to make a living, and the people who manufacture poker chips would have to start making potato chips instead! Fighting the Gambling War can be as arduous as fighting any of the other "Way Too Much" Wars, because once you dig a deep enough hole, it can take years of payback and rehabilitation to recover. Gambling is a drug of sorts. At first, those who engage in it think they will just "try it," yet soon they find themselves deeply addicted. There is the allure of thinking you can get something for nothing.

Think of the gentleman who took a $200,000 property settlement to Vegas (the wife got the house) and threw it down on the Roulette table. On his first pass on red, he won and doubled his money! But he became greedy, and it took less than an hour for him to lose the entire amount. Those who have gambling addictions are typically fighting other wars simultaneously. For instance, many of those who gamble also drink, overspend, or eat too much. These types are headed down a dark trail. If you find yourself counted among the troops who are at war with this Enemy, glance over the following. Hopefully, you will find some alternate ways to assuage your cravings. If you are in the grip of the Gambling Enemy, you may want to recite the following out loud:

1. I will never get ahead.
2. I work too hard for my money to lose it so easily.
3. I will sink deeper into this addiction if I allow it to perpetuate.
4. I may find myself hanging out with unsavory types.
5. I will set a negative example for my children.
6. I may discover it is a behavior I need to hide from others.
7. I could blow the same money on other things that are far more rewarding.
8. I may lose sleep over my losses.
9. I really cannot afford such an expensive habit.
10. By gambling, I surrender control to an Enemy Within.

Now make your list, and by all means do not be chintzy with your reasons, as they may be very personal ones, and ones that will convince you to walk off this battlefield.

1. _____
2. _____
3. _____
4. _____
5. _____

Overeating: This might very well be one of the most harmful of all Enemies Within and one of the most common Internal Wars. It is a natural reaction to want to soothe and comfort yourself when you feel the battle fatigue from the effects of the Three Typical Wars; but in the end, you may be trading one war for another. Overeating can take a heavy toll on your body and your spirit. Self-esteem is an important commodity when you are going through a breakup. If you go from a (women) size 6 to a size 12, or you go from a (men) 38 waist to a 44 (with a beer belly), chances are you will walk around in a deeper sense of despair. Nothing says "you win" louder to your ex than to show him or her that you have let yourself go. As with the other "Way Too Much" Wars, it could be that overeating was a problem before the divorce, but now that you are on your own, wouldn't it be nice to feel that you are a brand new you—an attractive you—that you can flaunt if you feel like it?

Besides alcohol and drugs, overeating ranks next on the top of the Enemy Within list. Now, it is quite possible you will have your own list without my even having to prod you; but for starters, here are a few considerations:

1. I will risk my physical health.
2. My children will become ashamed of me.
3. My children may follow my example.
4. I will not be able to fit into my clothes; I will have to keep buying a brand new wardrobe.
5. I will be unattractive to the opposite sex.
6. My ex will smirk at my misfortune.
7. More groceries cost more money.
8. I will not like what I see in the mirror.
9. My mental well-being will suffer tremendously.
10. I will have less energy.
11. I will have lost control.

Now go ahead and add to this list. The point is to make sure that if this war is one you are fighting, that you face it head-on and do something about it.

1. _____
2. _____
3. _____
4. _____
5. _____

Overworking: Though some people find that throwing themselves into work is a wonderful and constructive remedy to stave off the divorce blues, it can also be damaging if it becomes "Way Too Much." Naturally, I would rather see my clients put in too many hours at the office than to drink or overeat, but I am also fully aware that working *too much* can wreak havoc in one's life.

Overworking robs you of achieving balance, which is the most important goal any of us should have by far! If you find, for example, overworking means that you are neglecting the children and others close to you, or it precludes you from an active social life, or if you are using work to escape (yes, it can be a drug!) or avoid work that you need to do on yourself in the emotional or spiritual realms, then you have a war on your hands. Work may have been a major factor in your breakup, and if so, you certainly do not want to repeat this behavior—an isolating one—that will be off-putting to anyone new who may want to enter your life.

How can you tell if you are overworking? If your mantra is "I don't have time for…" then you know you are overworking. This addiction can be just as bothersome as the others I mentioned, for spending *too much* time on the job can become an obsession and a habit that is hard to break. Just as I have done before, I have put together a list of why you may want to take some of that energy used "Way Too Much" on the job and divvy it up elsewhere. Here are my suggestions for why you may want to consider a change:

1. I will miss out on a good portion of my children's growing up.
2. I will find it difficult to meet a potential new mate.
3. I will not have time to work out at the gym.
4. I may get tired of my job—burned out.
5. I will miss out on "smelling the roses."
6. I will lose my creativity or passion for my work.
7. I will not be able to play golf, see that new movie, or engage in some other enjoyable hobby or pastime.
8. I may not be able to watch the sun come up or the sun go down.

9. All work and no play, makes _____
   (your name here) a very dull boy/girl.
10. My job will be in control of my life and me.

The Sexaholic: Another internal war concerns that of the Sexaholic. Many of those going through a breakup find their salve in sex. Many of those who have not been intimate in a marriage or relationship for some time, find they need to "reinstate" their sexuality or to make up for lost time in that sexless marriage. Becoming sexually active after a breakup is certainly not wrong, but more often than not, I find people using sexual activity to mend a broken heart or as a means to prove their viability as a sexual being. When sex becomes a chronic remedy, one that gives you instant gratification or acts as a "bromo" for what ails you, you know you are on your way to marching into an ominous war. Do not overlook the prospect of contracting AIDS or HIV because of your erratic sexual obsession—two wars over which you can never prevail. So, just because your ex makes an unflattering remark about your figure that is no reason to hit on your gardener (even though he has been eyeing you for years). And just because your ex shows up with her new beau at your child's holiday school pageant, that does not mean you should bed down with every colleague in the office. But this often happens. Rather than overeating or working *too much*, there are those who get caught up in the "Way Too Much" sex wars. They spend every waking moment figuring out how to prove their prowess or satisfy their need for pleasure. Again, I am not suggesting that sex is wrong between two consenting adults; but if your need for or use of sex becomes habitual or creates an obsessive need, then there is no question that you are allowing a very specific Enemy Within to win.

I am sure you will find an assortment of reasons why becoming a Sexaholic could be a detriment to your well-being, physically, emotionally and spiritually. But before you make your list, here is one to get you thinking:

1. I may lose self-esteem, if I am promiscuous.
2. I may lose the prospect of making sex something special

and meaningful with a very significant other.

3. I could easily contract a sexually transmitted disease (including AIDS and/or HIV).
4. I will hate myself "in the morning."
5. I could become pregnant (woman), or (man) set myself up for a paternity suit.
6. Chronic and/or deviant sex can become affiliated with other perverse behaviors, such as illicit drug and alcohol use.
7. If my children, parents, business associates, or friends find out about my sexaholic tendencies, they may look down on me. Worse yet, they may shun me!
8. I may wind up with shame, regret and remorse—feelings that will be hard to shake.
9. I could be putting myself in some dangerous circumstances, other than those presented by possible diseases.
10. I will be ruled by physical urges and most definitely remain out of control!

Just as you have done in the prior sections, if this is a war that you may be about to engage in, or one in which you are heavily ensconced, make your own list of reasons you need to get this issue under control:

1. _____
2. _____
3. _____
4. _____
5. _____

Makeovers: Blindly plunging into a Makeover War is another very common conflict from within. Some believe that by altering their physical appearance, they will change their lives. I will not argue with that. In fact, I think a physical makeover is a great idea: New look, new attitude. But when a person goes nuts with altering his or her appearance, does so radically, or finds the need to continuously opt for some new vanity "addendum," he or she can also become out of control! I know both men and women who have had several cosmetic procedures in just a few months. What constitutes a full-on Makeover War is when someone is not satisfied with a makeover but keeps opting for one more physical change. This might include liposuction one day, two months later a face lift, three months after that a brow lift, and, well…the list of procedures can be endless. Same goes for those who have red hair one week, blonde the next—people who feel the constant need to "upgrade" their appearance because they are seemingly never satisfied. They are clearly at war with the "Image"—a perception of what they *think* will be attractive to the opposite sex and will elevate their sense self worth.

Do not think I am restricting Makeovers to just one's physical appearance. Makeover Mania can extend to all things physical, such as one's home or office. I know of one divorcee who changed the color of her Mercedes from beige to fire engine red, another who ripped out all her rose bushes to plunk in a pool.

Again, I make no judgments on anyone's need or desire to change his/her physical look or the motif of his/her possessions. My concern becomes legitimate when people become overly-obsessive about how they look or how their belongings appear and when they are constantly finding excuses to do something new to make themselves look or feel better. When the need overtakes practicality, I suggest you step back and take a good look (not just in visual terms) at what you are doing, and more importantly, why. Makeovers are fast becoming big winners in the "Way Too Much" War within.

The following is a list of reasons why you may want to sit yourself down for a heart-to-heart talk on whether the Makeover War is taking over:

1. If I keep on this mission, I may never be satisfied with how I look or what I have.
2. I do not want my ex to think I am trying to prove how desirable I am to others.
3. Constant makeovers could get terribly expensive.
4. I, or my surroundings, may begin to look a little "overdone."
5. I may be spending money that should be spent on other things.

6. I may not be unable to "undo" what I have done (if I find I do not like the results).

7. The constant change in my looks or physical surroundings may disturb my children. They may not think I am the same person I was, or they may feel insecure with yet another change in their lives.

8. Focusing on makeover issues may preclude me from dealing with my real issues.

9. My outward appearances will be in control; I will not.

Now make your own list. It may be only a few reasons and that is all right.

1. _____

2. _____

3. _____

4. _____

5. _____

Mood Du Jour: While this may seem an odd inclusion on our list of "Way Too Much" War skirmishes, it is not. This category covers a lot of ground! For instance, when moods are swinging, those affected by such changes can react and overreact in erratic ways and wind up constantly fighting nonproductive battles. Too many mood swings could become quite a problem and grounds for a "Way Too Much" War. The "over the top" moods I am referring to manifest themselves in weird and often destructive ways. For example, driving too fast is usually a symptom of *too much* anger or frustration. Crying *too much* could lead to *too much* isolation. Fantasizing *too much* in a state of bitterness may distract you from the tasks at hand and lead you to conjuring up ways to get back at your ex. Sounding off due to profound desperation could culminate in blurting out things you will later wish you had not said. Yes, all these are just a few samples of other Little Enemies that can grow to be big ones. And here are a few life circumstances that fuel the "Mood Du Jour" Enemy Within—egg that Enemy on—that may or may not apply to you: Menopause,

Midlife Crisis, Unexpected/Unwanted Pregnancy, Postpartum Blues, Realization of One's Own Mortality, Physical Handicaps. Can you think of other *conditions* that affect mood? Those who undergo constant mood fluctuations find themselves behaving in ways they come to regret. Do you snap at those you love? Do you spout off at the wrong person and do you so at the wrong time? Check your moods. You may find that your Enemy Within is your inability to manage your feelings appropriately. Extreme and frequent mood swings can be a formidable opponent in a "Way Too Much" War.

As we have done with the other categories, I have made a list of reasons why you may want to get your mood swings in check so they do not entice you onto the battlefield.

1. I do not want my ex to think he or she has gotten the best of me by seeing how upset and off balance I have become emotionally.
2. I do not want to regret lashing out at the people I love and care about.
3. People may not want to be around me because they never know what to expect in terms of my disposition.
4. I may hurt myself physically (get into an automobile accident, drive my fist through a wall, for instance).
5. People will begin to pity me, and that will rob me of my dignity.
6. I do not want my ex or anyone else to think this life crisis has rendered me out of control!
7. I may be creating a pattern of behavior that will stick with me.
8. Overreacting is one sure way to turn off a potential new love interest.
9. Not getting a grip on my moods may cause me to engage in some type of rash behavior, characterized in some of the other "Way Too Much" Wars, like gambling, over-eating, etc.
10. Nothing screams in neon more brightly that I am out of control than to wear my heart on my sleeve.

Now yours:

1. _____
2. _____
3. _____
4. _____
5. _____

Blabbing: Though it may sound strange and even funny to you, talking too much may also be a contentious Enemy Within (that comes "Without" at not-so-propitious times). Some people are in such dire straits they feel a constant need to unload—to talk about their divorce. They spill their guts—their fears, wants, their thoughts of retribution—and far too often they do so indiscreetly and to the wrong pair of ears! Yakking too much can get you into trouble and also cause you great remorse. So talking *too much* is not a good idea for the people you talk to (unless they are licensed professionals who are mandated to keep your conversations confidential). Yes, people talk. They tell other people what it is you have said. Do not forget you and your ex may have common friends, family members (the children!) and business associates. So one sure way for your thoughts and feelings to get back to your ex is to talk a lot. It is your attorney, your therapist, and perhaps a trusted family member or friend you can vent to, but be wary of not spilling the beans to anyone and everyone. One of my favorite sayings is, "Loose lips sink ships." If you over-dialogue, it could be that you are tipping your hand or providing your ex with ammunition that can be used to pummel you in one of the Three Typical Wars. I know it is very tempting to let this Enemy Within infiltrate your status quo because it is natural to have the need to want to discuss your pain, suffering, confusion, and disillusionment with others; but do not do it randomly. Choose your listeners wisely. Sharing too much information could lead to a disaster.

The following are only a handful of reasons why chatting it up about your divorce, your feelings about it, and perhaps your plans of attack against your ex to win either the Emotional,

Psychological or Legal War, could cause you to lose the "Way Too Much" War, as well as the former three!

1. What you say may get back to the wrong person.
2. If you are thinking "strategy," you may just well blow your cover.
3. People may perceive you as being unstable.
4. Without knowing it, you could be constantly embarrassing yourself.
5. You may say things you will live to regret.
6. The people you talk to will probably gossip.
7. You may unintentionally hurt your children, parents, friends, and others close to you by the things you say.
8. You may lose friends because you are obsessed with blabbing about everything in your divorce.
9. You may "turn off" potential new friends or alienate old ones because they just do not want to hear it anymore!
10. "Over-dialoguing" more than whispers, "I am out of control!"

If you are in a conflict with this Enemy Within, do not beat yourself up about it just become more cautious with what you say and to whom you say it. One way to impress upon you the importance of keeping mum except to those you should be talking to, is for you to make your own, very personal list as to why *too much* talk could hurt you. So, go ahead, start writing.

1. _____
2. _____
3. _____
4. _____
5. _____

Obsessing: A kissing cousin to Blabbing is Obsessing. Some people just cannot help themselves from constantly thinking and over-thinking specific feelings or events in the Three Typical Wars, and often they begin to blab about them. Sometimes they talk incessantly to others about these issues of concern, yet more often than not, they continue a running dialogue or narrative in their heads about "things." Obsessing can lead to many deviant behaviors, from stalking to angry letter writing to rash behaviors that may earn some a restraining order! Obsessing can undo a person—take them prisoner and hold them in captivity for eons. Obsessing over your ex and his/her new lover, how unfair it is that they got "this" and you got "that," or obsessing over ways to win the children's affection, or "payback" your ex with revenge, or plotting ways to ruin your ex's life, or constantly thinking about how much you miss and long for your departed partner—these are all blatant signs that indicate you are in the clutches of the Obsessive Enemy Within. Obsessing also causes a host of problems from the inability to sleep well or concentrate on work, to being distracted in the face of opportunity, like meeting a potential new significant other. If you are not functioning properly and productively, chances are you have been taken prisoner by an enemy called Obsession. Here are just a few reasons why you may want to take to the hills:

1. People will begin to think I am not "all there."
2. I will miss out on many things—from quality sleep to new business and personal opportunities.
3. I will have given my ex power he/she does not deserve.
4. Obsessing can bring out the worst in terms of my behavior.
5. My children will lose respect for me.
6. My friends will not want to spend time with me, as I hash out the same issue over and over again.
7. The impulse to find comfort from my need to Obsess could lead to over-drinking, over-eating, illicit drugs, or a host of other negative choices as a means to relieve tension.
8. People may start making fun of me.
9. I will definitely lose any semblance of balance.
10. I may as well scream from the mountain tops: "I am out of control, big time!"

Over-managing: This is another Enemy Within that can suddenly become ruler of your psyche and throw you into a war you do not want to be in. When we micro-manage our attorney, our children's nanny, and others, it demonstrates that we have no trust in the very people to whom we have pledged our trust. Not only are we being counter-productive, we are probably driving those around us nuts—ironically the very people who are so intently trying to help us. Are you too managerial—too microscopic in overseeing those key individuals around you? Think about this: You hired each of them—your attorney, your nanny, your CPA, your Financial Planner—to take care of certain specific needs that you have. Are you allowing them to do so, or are you second-guessing everything they do? And how about this: Are you too involved in your children's lives? Since the divorce are you now "overdoing" in your children's world, like volunteering to help in class, on every field trip or sports team… if they are teenagers, are you trying to hang out and be one of the guys or gals? Throwing yourself into your children's lives and becoming involved—or obsessed—in a more than healthy manner can present itself as one more combatant in the "Way Too Much" War. So then, as we talk about Over-managing, count this last problem as another potential opponent with which to go to war. Here is a collection of reasons why Over-managing may not be a good idea:

1. Over-managing the people I have asked to help me will intimidate, irritate or make them angry.
2. These trusted individuals might get fed up and leave me.
3. I cannot focus adequately on the things I should be doing if I am spending time meddling.
4. People will call me "insecure" and "obnoxious."
5. I may annoy my children or turn them off completely by smothering them with too much involvement in their lives.
6. I may easily demoralize the very people I need most to inspire.
7. Pestering or badgering the professionals I hired does not say much for trusting myself to have hired the right people.

8. People will begin to avoid me or behave distantly when I am around.
9. I will alienate the very people I need.
10. People may start making fun of me behind my back (my children included).
11. The business professionals cannot perform effectively in their jobs if I am micro-managing them.
12. *Too much* managing clearly states I need control because I feel totally out of control.

Over-exercising/Extreme sports: Another very popular pastime in the post breakup milieu is the urge to buff up to perfection, to take up some exhilarating sport that serves to use up all that adrenalin that is flowing through your system. Some people go from no exercise to working out obsessively, as if they were training for a marathon! Others go for helicopter skiing or bungee jumping as a means to prove their prowess or relieve their tension. Working out and getting into shape, or taking up a new physical hobby, can be both distracting and pleasing. But when a person overdoes it in this area, it sends signals that all is not well on the control front. If, for instance, you suddenly throw yourself on a bobsled and you have never frolicked in the snow, you just might be caught up in the Enemy Within—the one that is trying to prove you are more powerful than your ex suggested you might be. Or, if on the other hand, you are running miles when you used to get by with a brisk walk around the neighborhood block, or you went from refusing to fly in airplanes, out of fear, to skydiving, look these changes squarely in the proverbial eye, because I am certain you are heading into one more "Way Too Much" War scenario.

I know of people who appeared to have had a death wish or who blatantly risked their health and physical well-being just to show their ex a thing or two. Well, once again, this War is no different than any of the other aforementioned "Way Too Much" Wars; to overdo is to pummel. Doing things reasonably is the key to a good healthy lifestyle when it comes to exercise or choosing a physical hobby that is satisfying. But if you are one of those who is just immersing yourself too intensely in either exercise or sport, then you have a problem.

Here is a menu of thought-provoking ideas to get you to rethink whether or not your physical well-being may be at serious risk. If are one of the readers who is a victim of the "Way Too Much" physical-prove-it battle, then read on. For those of you who do not connect with this section, skip it and go to the next one.

1. I just might injure myself causing permanent physical damage.
2. I might frighten my children and make them worry about my safety.
3. Injury could interfere with my job, my social life and my sex life!
4. I could find the need to resort to constant medications to ease the stiffness and pain from *too much* exertion or strain.
5. People will think I am foolish and reckless.
6. I may be inadvertently teaching my children bad habits.
7. I could lose income if I hurt myself.
8. I may increase my physical addiction by the need to ramp up the thrill and wind up flat on my back!
9. I will be yelling in bullhorn-fashion: "Hey, look at me: I'm out of control!

The Great Escape: This enemy within has you losing yourself in some distraction, like watching TV or hanging out on the Internet; in other words, too much "get-away." There is nothing wrong with a little TV and surfing the net for interesting sites, but when you spend most of your after-work hours and weekends losing yourself in such media, then you may find yourself in a war with Escape. Often when people find the need to absorb themselves with means of escape, they can lose contact with the real world. Like it or not, the real world requires our attention in order to do important things like attend to our children and socialize with others. However, I know people who go from work to the sofa or the computer, and that is where they remain until it is bedtime. Then they do the same routine all over again, day after day. Weekends become a blur between college football and chat rooms! As a result, it is very easy to lose touch with life in general. Nothing is more tempting than to escape from the pain of a breakup, as I have pointed out all along in this chapter, by some means: Forced distraction is certainly a formidable opponent among all the others. Allow me to just mention a few reasons why you may not want to escape via this "Way Too Much" War. These reasons may echo inside your head.

1. I will become isolated.
2. I may miss those special, little moments with my children—moments I will one day want to recall.
3. I will make those who wish to interact with me feel left out.
4. I will have a one-track mind and not be very interesting.
5. I may miss out on opportunities to meet a potential significant other.
6. It may cause me to struggle or become uncomfortable conversing with others, since I have become so used to being "self-contained."
7. I will only be putting off dealing with issues that I'll have to deal with at some point.
8. I may not be taking care of other important areas in my life, like going to the gym, visiting friends and relatives, and seeking out new networking opportunities for social and business purposes.
9. I will ultimately become lonely.
10. I may be distancing myself, but the echo of "I'm out of control" will be heard for miles around.

Now make your own list of why escaping might be detrimental to your progress as a divorced person.

1. _____
2. _____
3. _____
4. _____
5. _____

WHAT HAVE YOU GOT?

I could very well have left out some specific areas that belong in this "Way Too Much" War category. Perhaps your malady is over-thinking or over-analyzing, or obsessing too much on what might be in the future. No right or wrong answers here, just another fine opportunity to take back control. I have provided plenty of spaces below for you to list those Enemies Within that are causing you to be at war, and worse yet, lose it. This is not a time to feel ashamed or discouraged. It is perfectly normal and natural for you to have a few Enemies Within during this trying time in your life. The point is to identify the Enemy and then find a way to defeat it. Go ahead, make your list, for it is the first step in gaining control, and that is what you want.

My Enemies Within in the "Way Too Much" War include the following:

1. _____
2. _____
3. _____
4. _____
5. _____

Do not feel awkward about adding more lines to this part of the "self-test." It takes introspection and courage to step forward and call it like it is! After you have taken all the time you need to examine where you stand on the battlefield in the "Way Too Much" War, take a breather before moving on to the next part of the chapter where you will be asked to look within for the perpetrators in the "Far Too Little" War.

FAR TOO LITTLE

Whether you have battles going on in the "Way Too Much" War or in the "Far Too Little" War, the problem is the same. Some issue is at the helm, something other than you is in control, and that is precisely what you do *not* want. The difference between the two wars, of course, is that in one you overdo and the other—the one I am discussing now—you "underdo."

Some of the most common perpetrators in the "Far Too Little" War can include the ones I touched on earlier, such as too much distraction, too little sleep, or too little productivity on the job. They can also be poor nutrition or puny attempts at exercise. I will cover just a handful of them for you, then ask that you itemize your own.

Self-Neglect: This Enemy is the one that is characterized by too little attention to your personal needs, like letting your hair get shaggy or foregoing that regular pedicure. Perhaps it is not allowing yourself a good listen to that music you used to love. It might also be blowing off your regular "soul feeding" ritual, like attending your place of worship. Self-Neglect can creep up on you, especially when you are in the throes of one of the Typical Three Wars or a "Way Too Much" skirmish. Self-Neglect can become a real enemy. Here's a list of reasons you might want to fight this Enemy off:

1. People will begin to say I look unkempt.
2. I will begin to lose my sense of self-worth and pride.
3. My Self-Neglect will snowball into other wars, like not enough of the right foods, no exercise, or no fun in my life.
4. The opposite sex will find me unattractive if I project an image that says, "I don't care about me."
5. My mother or father (or my children) will start lecturing me.
6. Self-neglect can lead to a sense of depression and hopelessness.
7. My ex will comment on how much I've let myself go.
8. It may cause a deep sense of resentment within, because I do not do nice things for myself.
9. If I believe I do not deserve to be treated well, others will pick up that cue and follow suit.
10. I will get in the habit of not doing nice things for myself and go forward in life with that attitude.
11. Worst of all, I will have copped to the attitude that I have no control of self.

This time, I am going to ask you to do something a little different with your lists— write down what your personal needs are. Take some quiet time to consider this section, for taking good care of yourself could be a key factor in winning every single War I have covered in this book. The sky is the limit here!

1. _____
2. _____
3. _____
4. _____
5. _____

Now make your list as to why it would be prudent for you to take good care of your personal needs and not "underdo" and lose this War.

1. _____
2. _____
3. _____
4. _____
5. _____

Minimal Focus: One of the most common "incidents" in perpetrating any war within is lack of concentration. The inability to stay on course, whether it is at work getting the job done, or helping your children with homework, "Minimal Focus" can grab you and hold you captive. The inability to sleep—or to sleep well—is among the top culprits in causing one to lose focus. When your head is foggy, it is clearly difficult to concentrate on anything for very long or very intently. The stress any one of the Marital Wars can produce can cause you to be restless and out of sync with your routine. This affects sleep, the ability to watch a movie, to follow through on that important presentation. Many clients tell me they can fall asleep, but cannot stay asleep. Others say they cannot stay immersed for very long in any one task at work that requires single-minded compartmentalization.

If Minimal Focus is an Enemy Within in this "Far Too Little" War of yours, I would strongly suggest you seek ways to manage this problem. I am not suggesting that you scan the pharmacy shelves for remedies; nor am I recommending that you ask your doctor for recommendations on herbal supplements. Often times, taking drugs can just increase the many warfronts you are thrust upon—such as throwing you into battle with one of the "Way Too Much" Wars, like alcohol or drug abuse. Some resort to sugar or caffeine highs to keep them on track, but then find themselves heavily reliant on "substances." As a result, their ability to focus is dependent on something other than themselves! The first course of action, instead, should be a chat with your therapist or physician to ask what they would suggest.

I have learned many ways to ensure that concentration can be enhanced even under stress. Some include Yoga, meditation, self-hypnosis, a good night's sleep and biofeedback. If you are one of the readers wrestling with Far Too Little focus, check out your options. The answer to staying tuned-in on that important job-related task might be something you had not thought of before.

For those of you who are at war with this Enemy Within, know that knowledge about the problem is your first step to conquering it—getting help to fight it. When you are under great duress, the mind drifts into areas of what it perceives as places of greater concern. Obsessing is another close ally to the Minimal Focus Enemy. Many of the "All Too Much" and "Far Too Little" Enemies work in tandem to create chaos, so beware! Unfortunately for the young woman we saw in Scene Four—the one who lost her job—her lack of sleep led to her inability to concentrate productively on the job. If this is happening to you, try to get a grip; for Minimal Focus can infiltrate many areas of your life and cause destruction.

I have made a list of why it is so important for you get a handle on your ability to keep focused, despite the turmoil going on around you. Do not forget how much mental energy is used up when fighting any one of the Marital Wars. You need to be able to stay tuned-in and concentrate on the task at hand! The following are some solid reasons why "Far Too Little" focus can become your enemy:

1. I will not be able to function properly, even when it comes to mundane tasks such as driving a car or shopping for groceries.
2. I may embarrass myself in an important meeting or business situation.
3. I will give the impression that I am not interested in the goings-on of the people closest to me and those who need my attention.
4. I cannot be as productive on the job.
5. I will be more susceptible to making mistakes.
6. I give my opponent the edge in any of the Three Typical Wars when my mind is not sharply focused.
7. I may lose in the Emotional, Psychological or Legal Wars.
8. Staying deeply distracted could cause me to lose much needed sleep.
9. My inability to stay tuned-in may necessitate me having to do the same task several times to get it right.
10. Nothing says, "This mind is out of control" more blatantly than when someone catches me in a "distracted" moment.

I am now asking that you write down how being taken prisoner by this "Far Too Little" enemy can disrupt your life and well being. Do not shortchange yourself with answers to this one. Staying tuned-in is an important soldier in your fight against this Enemy Within and an important ally in the Typical Three Wars, as well.

1. _____
2. _____
3. _____
4. _____
5. _____

Poor Nutrition: One of the first things to go when we are upset, anxious and out of sorts, is our appetite. This is natural; occasionally, we just do not feel like eating or we choose to only eat comfort foods. But when you extend poor nutritional habits over a period of time, it can be detrimental to your health. Not just in the short term, but in the long run. Not eating healthily can be responsible for a host of maladies. "Far Too Little" of the nationally recognized food groups might seem like a wimpy Enemy Within, but it is not. It can be the Enemy that brings you to your knees. The reason I mention (and single out) poor nutrition as an important enemy, is that relationship breakups are not an over-the-weekend situation. It is not like you will be eating poorly for just a few days—the fallout from most breakups can easily take up to a year. Eating "Far Too Little" for that long can be injurious to your health!

The following spells out more specifically just a handful of reasons you may want to play back to yourself, all of which bolster my claim that keeping to a solid eating regimen seven days a week is a must:

1. I could become anorexic (this applies to men, too!).
2. I will certainly not be setting a positive example for my children.
3. Eating *too little* robs me of the strength I should have to do much needed physical exercise.
4. If I do not eat enough, it may make me look drained and haggard.
5. Eating *too little* can lead to serious health problems and could cause everything from depression to digestive problems to hypoglycemia.
6. I will not be able to wear my clothes (they will hang on me!).
7. Eating *too little* will deplete my body of the right vitamin mix.
8. Eating *too little* could cause sleep disturbances.
9. I will not have the stamina to fight any of the Three Typical Wars or other Enemies Within.
10. I will demonstrate that I have no control over my physical well-being.

Now make your list.

1. _____
2. _____
3. _____
4. _____
5. _____

Little or no exercise: This is the sister-enemy of "Way Too Much exercise" (or sport), for it does not matter what side of the battlefield on which you find yourself fighting, you are still at war. Exercise, done regularly and properly, can help vent frustration, tune up our minds and bodies, and keep us in shape to ensure good health and face the day's challenges with more ease and energy.

In my opinion, doing *too little* is far worse than doing *too much* in this category, because it is an open door and an invitation to additional Enemies Within. Soon, you may be fighting your weight, find yourself listless and depressed (mood swings), and resort to drugs or alcohol as a "feel good" substitute. When you go through a breakup you will find yourself angry a good deal of the time, or frustrated or even down and out. Medical experts have proven that lack of exercise can adversely affect us both physically and mentally. There even seems to be a direct correlation between being sedentary and losing one's sense of humor.

The following items are on my list of why "Far Too Little" exercise can be harmful to you, not only as you go through your breakup, but also as it adversely affects you down the road:

1. I will gain weight.
2. I will get flabby.
3. I will not have the dexterity, mobility or flexibility that my physical body needs.
4. Far Too Little exercise may preclude me from sleeping well.
5. I will not be able to burn off calories from those things I like to eat so much, like chocolate, French fries, or Crème Brulee.

6. My children will follow suit.
7. I will not make a very good impression on the new potential mate in my life.
8. I could cut my life short.
9. It may become a hard habit to break.
10. Far *too little* exercise can aid and abet viruses that invade my immune system.
11. Control will beat me to the finish line every day!

Minimum Socialization: This "Far Too Little Enemy" can sneak up on you or hit you very hard, depending upon your personality. Some who go through divorce tell me that they just want to be left alone. They do not want to talk or interact with others. On the flip side, there are those who tell me they gradually had become withdrawn and anti-social. It does not really matter *how* this Enemy Within infiltrates your psyche or *when* it throws you off guard or takes over and holds you in captivity; just know it can be a covertly dangerous enemy. The last thing you need when you are going through a trying time is to shut others out and go into seclusion. When you do, other enemies can begin to present themselves, and I am sure you can guess what they are.

How about the whole list in this chapter, save one: Blabbing. If you guessed all but that one, bingo, you just hit the jackpot, because isolation paves the way to being at war with all the Way Too Much and Far Too Little Enemies. So then, just know that becoming anti-social is a dangerous undertaking. You can set yourself up for a big fight. I know of clients who have gone "underground" and when they finally decided to come out, it took months to gain back their self-confidence and social skills. No, now is not the time to let this Enemy prevail. Now is the time to make friends and stay connected with the rest of the world.

You may argue that this breakup has dismantled your "social circle"—some of your friends when you were a couple are now your ex's friends. So what? For every friend you lose or feel it is necessary to stay away from, make a new one. You can meet new friends and business contacts through other trusted friends and business contacts. Whatever you do, do not, and I stress, *do not*, lock yourself away and check out.

This Enemy Within can overtake you, I know; but do not let it win. Stay in control and stay in the social loop. I have made a list of reasons why I feel this is so important—why you will want to beat one more Enemy Within. You might be saying these to yourself! Soon, I will ask you to add to this list. For now consider these:

1. It may preclude me from having as much fun as my ex.
2. I may miss out on an opportunity to meet someone new.
3. I always feel good when I get out and about.
4. Staying locked within prevents me from stepping outside my traumatic circumstances and taking time to enjoy interesting and enjoyable people—folks that can give me back a healthy perspective on my current situation.
5. Remaining anti-social can rob me of a wonderful therapeutic opportunity to minimize and neutralize my grief.
6. Being antisocial and withdrawn can deplete my supply of hope.
7. Being antisocial may send out the wrong message. People may think I do not appreciate them or wish to be with them.
8. My children will begin to feel responsible for my well-being, which is not a fair burden to put upon them.
9. No one likes a party pooper, so how can I impress a potential mate?
10. Shutting myself out of the social loop screams: "The Enemy Within is in control."

Now make your list of very good reasons why you do not want to withdraw.

1. _____
2. _____
3. _____
4. _____
5. _____

THE ALL-IN-ONE NEUTRALIZER

For every perpetrator in the "Way Too Much" and the "Far Too Little" Wars, there is an army of combatants that can come to your rescue. One such combatant in the "Way Too Much" Wars is Moderation. For all of those items on the "Way Too Much" list—alcohol, drugs, overeating, gambling, spending, vanity, blabbing, moods, sleeping too much, over-exercising, escaping and overworking—Moderation is definitely your strongest ally. Where there is Moderation, there is balance. Where there is balance, there is control. And, once again, control is the heartbeat of the message in this book: Establish it and keep it. So if you find yourself face-to-face with any of the above listed foes, call in Moderation as a first defense.

If you are one of the readers with a heavily addictive personality and find yourself unable to control any urges that are related to compulsive behavior, call in the other defense team: Abstinence. Some people just have to say "no" to things that will get them into trouble. Some folks cannot indulge in even a moderate amount of certain things. Instead, they must forego them altogether. Let's say you like to bet on college football, but your betting has gotten out of hand. Then, do not bet at all. That's right—take the money and do something satisfying with it, but not damaging to you. How about donating a few bucks to a worthwhile charity or putting it toward that car loan. The whole idea is to feel good about yourself and to defeat all the Enemies Within. And, the main objective is to keep *you* in control.

For those of you battling the hard-hitting opponents in the "Far Too Little" Wars, take each battle and devise a game plan that will reverse the negative effects that war is having on you and your lifestyle. For instance, if you are not exercising, join a gym, hire a personal trainer (if that is within your budget), or find ways to stimulate your interests so you do not want to sleep or retreat a good deal of the time. If you are not eating properly, do a study with your youngsters on the three basic food groups, and then plan a menu to honor a healthy eating regimen. There are so many choices. Just get creative with your war strategies.

With regard to any of the previously mentioned wars, there is good news on all battlefronts. For one thing, you have the liberty of better managing any of the "Way Too Much" and "Far Too Little" Wars—they are not the same type of wars in the Typical Three, wherein you are often the target of your ex. The wars I am addressing in this chapter have to do with you, your urges, and the ways in which you neglect yourself. Knowing this, it may be easier for you to grab these Enemies Within by the proverbial throat and throttle every one of them until they surrender.

What I do not want you to do is to be at war in any one of the Three Typical Wars while simultaneously having to fight Enemies Within. I am sure you will agree that it takes a great deal of resources and strength to fight one war, let alone several at the same time. You must do this or you *will* lose to the Enemies Without!

If you can get an adequate grip on what your Internal Conflicts are, then you have a very strong chance of defeating each of them as they attack you. You also stand a very good chance of being far more victorious in any or all of the Three Typical Wars. Being able to focus on the Enemies Without is going to be very important if you wish to emerge victorious.

As you finish up your tasks in this chapter, make a list of substitutions for every "Way Too Much" and "Far Too Little" War you may be fighting. A moment ago, I offered some strategies for combating the Enemy. Now it is time to take out pencil and paper (or fire up the computer), and after each Enemy that is attacking you, write down a means to fight or neutralize that Enemy—ways that will leave no question as to who has won and who is in control. This particular exercise just may be the ticket for winning each and every war you have to fight, for if you are not at war with yourself, you can meet each challenge with a clear head and a strong constitution.

Let's move forward now for an important look at Threats— real and imagined—two other wars that can certainly cause grave concern and/or serious injury.

Chapter Nine

THREATS AND CONTROL:
Real, Implied, and Imagined

Frustrated to get Courtney's voicemail again, Dennis was seething. "Pick up the phone, Courtney. I mean it. You better pick up the phone. We have unfinished business."

Courtney had stopped answering her home phone three months earlier. Only close friends and family knew her cell phone number, and she only answered after checking the caller ID. She used her home phone for dialing out and for checking messages.

"Courtneeeeeeeeeeeeeeeyyyyyyyyyyyy! I said, pick up the phone. I-said-pick-up-the-phone!" Dennis foolishly waited, thinking she might. He waited a good ten seconds. From deep inside his throat, he finally uttered, "Okay, that's it!"

◆   ◆   ◆

Nervously twisting her Movado watchband on her left wrist, Faith began to sob. It was 8:30, Sunday night. Her children were more than two hours late. She had had a bad feeling when her ex picked them up two days earlier for a weekend visit. Something didn't feel right.

Had Fahid finally acted upon his threat to abscond with the children to the Middle East? Faith's stomach sank. Frantically she tried his cell phone. She heard the words she dreaded, "The number you have called is no longer in service. If you would like to try the number again, please hang up and dial…"

Faith hung up and called the police. Scrambling through her file drawer, she dug for her court order. The friendly police officer asked that she bring it to the station. Even with an Amber Alert (the national highway electronic bulletin alert system that notifies drivers of abducted children), Faith sensed it was too late. Her children were probably out of the country.

◆   ◆   ◆

Mort missed the turn again. It was the third time in a week. "This is nuts," he thought as he slapped his right palm against his forehead. He'd taken the same route to work for seven years in a row! Out loud, he berated himself: "What the hell am I doing?"

Thinking.

Thinking hard.

Mort was distracted—riveted to the mental picture of his newly estranged ex-wife, Laverne, who one week earlier, when he had confessed his three-year extramarital affair to her and asked for a divorce, said nothing. Instead she looked him squarely in the face. Coldly. She registered no emotion, yet her eyes sent a sinister message. Mort continued to put the incident on rewind, playing it over and over again. His imagination was working overtime. What did that look mean???

A THREAT, OR NOT A THREAT, THAT IS THE QUESTION

In my long experience as a family law attorney in many high profile divorces, I have found that one of the most difficult aspects of the divorce or breakup process is dealing with revenge, retribution and the punitive measures some will resort to out of hurt, anger and rejection.

Many such actions originate from threats.

Threats are a masterful way to assert control over others.

Some threats are Real. In other words, they are openly expressed and can manifest themselves through some type of physical violence, emotional abuse, financial control, or threats through the children. Other threats are Implied. By that I mean tossed out obliquely or indirectly. Yet, these can also result in disaster. Imagined threats leave a person thinking or wondering if a threat has been directed at them, or if one will be carried out. Sometimes the Threatener (my word) follows through, other times he/she does not.

You can probably already see how threats play an integral part in the Three Typical Wars and the Internal Wars, because they can impact an individual emotionally, psychologically and legally, as well as pit them against the Enemies Within.

Emotionally, threats can impact a person by instigating fear, trepidation and worry. While in terms of psychological stress, threats can keep a person off kilter with countless thoughts of "what if" and "how soon?" In the legal realm, a person may be afraid of being taken to court, in need of obtaining a restraining order, or, if he or she is the perpetrator, may be concerned he/she is headed for jail.

With regard to the Enemies Within, threats can spawn their fair share of troubles, too, because a person can get trapped in some of the "Way Too Much" or "Far Too Little" conflicts by engaging in an array of destructive behaviors, from obsessing to blabbing to withdrawing.

All the way around, threats are bad news.

"Real" threats can result in death.

"Implied" threats can cause unnecessary trauma (and death, too).

"Imagined" threats can cause mental chaos.

Threats can go on for years.

Threats are *always* about control.

Threats are the winds of war! Yes, they can kick up and kick off any of the Typical Three Wars (and the ones associated with the Enemies Within), or keep them going long after they should have died down. From strong breezes to heavy gales, in their wake, threats can wreak all kinds of havoc.

THE DELINEATION OF THREATS

For clarity, here is a more descriptive breakdown of the three types of threats—the ones that I have come to know in my years of practice in family law:

- **Real threats** are oral or written statements promising harm to persons or possessions. This might include everything from your ex proclaiming he/she will smash your windshield, to kidnapping the children, to beating you up. Real threats are always obvious, for as they are made, specific acts are described that clearly state what the "Threatener" intends to do. A Real threat is exact and openly expressed through dialogue, a letter, fax or email. A Real threat can also be made by raising a fist, brandishing a weapon, or stalking someone. Real threats may not only be physical: They can be emotional and psychological, as I have pointed out. An emotional Real threat might include the suggestion that your ex will offer your new lover a copy of a "sex video" the two of you made when you were together. Acted upon, this could cause great embarrassment and shame. A psychological Real threat might be one where your ex suggests he or she will report a mock-scenario to persuade Child Protection Services (or whatever the agency is called in your state) that you are molesting the children. A Legal threat, of course, is when your ex flatly states, "I'll see *you* in court!"
- **Implied threats** are inferences that a person may get hurt or harassed. Implied threats are connotations—implications and insinuations that something aggravating or disastrous may occur. Some Implied threats should be taken seriously. Others are as transient as the moment in which they are made. Implied threats may be comments like "If you start dating right away, you might get hurt," or "you will live to regret this," or "...so you think you're going to leave me, do you?"
- **Imagined threats** are fantasies of what you think your ex *may do or say*. Laverne, who said not a word in response to her husband's confession of infidelity (but instead stared

at her husband coldly), set off a firestorm of concern over what ominous course she *may take.* Imagined threats may stem from dirty looks (if looks could kill), slammed doors, cars screeching away from the curb, or items being thrown. Imagined threats are hard to manage because nothing is ever said; it is just that one is left to ponder whether a threat was inferred (and intended). Imagined threats are crazymaking, because most of them are manufactured, self-created, and become lodged inside the mind of the potential victim.

I tell all my clients to take threats seriously: Prepare for the worst and hope for the best. And I tell those clients who are making threats to cease such behavior, immediately.

Living with threats can be oppressive. Often, those who are plagued by threats live with a relentless feeling of impending doom or an anxious restlessness; for they never know if a threat will be carried out. This is certainly no way to live!

WHY THREATS?

Emotions are raw when people are profoundly injured over the breakup of their personal relationship. "He went ballistic," or "she was crazed," or "he was out of his mind," or "she flipped out," are all ways to describe what can happen at the slightest provocation for those who are under tremendous emotional or psychological duress. In such states, many people lose their cool and begin to make threats. You may have thought that only those who acted on threats could be prosecuted (some people perceive them as "crimes of passion"), but such is not the case. A threat, in and of itself, is considered a crime. Of course, there are times when a threat is actually acted upon. This often occurs when a person can no longer contain himself/herself in a state of anger or jealousy, for instance—two emotions that can trigger a moment of complete "insanity." So whether someone assaults another individual, or simply threatens, both are crimes. Making a threat against someone can carry a hefty penalty.

When people are faced with the deep hurt that accompanies seeing one's ex with a new "flame," or if they are forced to "visit" children rather than live with them, lose face in the community, or have their support checks bounce continuously, these are all motivators—provocations for people to retaliate against what they perceive as gross injustices. When such pressures mount, threats can be the norm.

Normally, the threats come first; the actualization of them follows.

The only good thing about overt threats may be that you can usually gauge them, get a sense of what may lie ahead, and prepare for them. If she swears she will marry the first guy she finds and change the children's last name to his, or he dictates that no one else will sleep in the same house with his children that the two of you lived in together, "or else," or he shoots you a menacing look when the judge orders him to pay you more child support, or she faxes you a copy of her new concealed weapon permit and signs it with an upside-down happy face, this is an indication that something sinister may be in the works. Knowing something is up may enable you to head him/her off "at the pass." Or at least be prepared to defend or protect yourself.

I often tell my clients that sometimes threats can be a positive, because at least you know what you are dealing with. There are many somber, aloof or seemingly apathetic spouses who, two hours after a court hearing, blow their ex away with a .22.

Knowing what you may be up against is always what is best in a bad situation. If you were fighting a war, it would certainly be beneficial to see the enemy coming!

Being aware of what drives the impulse to threaten can also be helpful if you are the threatener. I always tell those few clients of mine who are compulsive threateners to stop, of course. But, I also point out to them that the focus of their threat reflects the issue they need to work through in therapy. For instance, if only seeing the children when the court allows sends him/her over the edge, that issue should be worked on with the therapist or strategized over with the attorney. A note to Threateners: There is an ethical obligation of a therapist to report threats to the authorities, so be careful how you vent your frustration. If you say, "I feel like I'd like to throttle her sometimes," that may be acceptable. However, if you say, "I'm going to throttle her and

I plan to do it before the week is out," you have left yourself wide open to being turned in. [The ethical obligations of any attorney are beyond the scope of this book, however, in some states, the lawyer may have an obligation to alert the other side or authorities of the threat of possible harm; while in other states such disclosure may be discretionary (up to the lawyer to decide) or not permitted at all.] No one takes threats lightly, nor should they.

It is my custom to ferret out what positives lay within what appear to be negatives. Threats are no exception. From any point of view, threats, then, at a minimum are indicators. It is like hearing and seeing a speeding car so you can get out of its way, compared to just walking along and suddenly having a car slam into you. What you know of, you can do something about; what you do *not* know of, may wind up devastating you when you least expect it. With that in mind, try to look at threats as potential and helpful road signs.

My suggestion is that you take cover if a threat is made and anticipate danger if one is Implied. Be rational about those threats you have Imagined. Do they have credence? Potential? Are they likely to occur based on previous events—did your ex ever shove you around, point a gun at you, kick the dog? If so, let others know. The more people you tell the better. They can help keep an eye out for looming danger and in the end help keep you safe.

THREATENING PROFILE

If you are the "Threatener," it is time to stop. If you are the "Threatee," take heed and what precautions you can.

What is the profile of a "Threatener"? A "Threatener" can be defined as one who makes menacing suggestions, demonstrates blatantly dangerous behavior, or works at oppressing others. A "Threatee" is one who is the target of the ominous suggestion or act, and often referred to as the "victim." Physical abuse threats that have been acted out are commonly referred to as domestic violence.

If you fit the profile of the "Threatener" and carry out your threats, you may very well ruin your life (as well as those of many others). Regret may become your middle name! So get help. Nothing diminishes your dignity faster than to carry the red letter "T" on your chest! I have seen many distinguished and accomplished individuals go from reverence and renown, to complete degradation and shame because of their threats and/or their actions. A threat may equal a crime, one that may result in incarceration.

If you fit the profile of the "Threatee," you may first want to look within to see if you have provoked the threats against you. For instance, knowing your ex is feeling horribly rejected because you dumped her, did you agitate the situation by showing up at your son's high school graduation with your "new squeeze?" Some people are calculating, and while they use these events to launch into an Emotional or Psychological War, they fail to realize that the consequences of their choices may leave them open to a kind of retaliatory vengeance that can result in catastrophe. With that in mind, give an honest appraisal of whether you are egging-on your ex to force him or her to lose control and resort to the most desperate of all choices: *Making or acting on threats.*

As a "Threatener," know that to declare you will inflict injury or pain on a person will only get you into trouble, possibly on many fronts. If you are a "Threatener" who loses control and acts on your threats, you will have crossed a life-altering line. Headlines across the country are full of such accounts: The woman in Texas (now serving a life sentence) who ran over her dentist-husband in a hotel parking lot, not once but three times, and killed him (and remarked that she intended to do so); the man who waited outside the courtroom then shot and killed his ex-wife, five minutes after their divorce was granted; the woman in San Diego who ambushed and killed both her ex-husband and his new wife as they lay asleep (this woman had left numerous threatening and chilling threats on the couple's voice mail for months). Though you may find it hard to believe, there are hundreds of incidents each year similar to these; you just don't hear about most of them.

As a "Threatener," also know that you could be committing a misdemeanor or a felony, depending upon what state you live in and what threat you make. You may also be risking the affection and trust of your children or others close to you. You may wind up with a restraining order against you (not good if the company you work for finds out), or taken to the extreme, you may find yourself doing jail time. The consequences can just snowball (there are no voting rights for a convicted felon). There is only a short-lived sense of gratification (or perceived justice) for those who make or act out threats.

If you are the "Threatee," do not get sucked into the dance of threats. If you react strongly to your ex's threat by declaring one of your own, you are no better than he or she. Once again, "War of the Roses" illustrates how one leads to another. Though I know it is difficult, stand back and take a deep breath before you engage in retaliation.

If you are a "Threatee" and you feel as though you are in physical danger, do not take a passive stance; get to the proper authorities and secure your safety. To the extent allowed by the courts (if you have minor children) you may have to move to another town, change your phone number, not show up at your regular hangouts, and get another job. Keep as much distance and make as little contact as necessary with your ex, the "Threatener."

Do not take the bait and issue a threat against a threat. So if your ex says, "I am going to tell the Mercedes dealer you lied on your financial statement just to get that car loan," do not follow up with "Oh yeah, well I'm going to call the IRS and tell them *you* filed a bogus tax return this year." If both of you have perpetrated a fraud against a bank or government agency, and you are found out, you both go down in flames.

THREATS CAN TURN DEADLY

When threats get volleyed back and forth, they often get bigger and grander, and so it goes. For example, "I don't care what the judge says, I will tell you when you can see the kids," may result in, "Well, I'm taking the kids and leaving the country," and then, "Oh no you won't. I'll kill myself *and* the kids before you get a chance." The next response may actually be murder and suicide.

As you can see, one threat can easily evolve and mushroom into utter disaster, for such behavior usually culminates in "high-risk"/"no-win" situations. So if you are the one who is both making *and* receiving threats, stop the cycle. Though it is very tempting to react to a threat by issuing one of your own, once again, you lose on both fronts. And, what about all those around you who are counting on you to get through this nasty breakup with dignity and stability (your children, parents, and business partners? Certainly they will get caught in the crossfire. Is that what you want?

"I CANNOT BELIEVE I DID THAT!"

Understand that those who make threats are often acting on some type of irrational impulse. It is a way to mitigate hurt and anger. Just be aware that if you injure your ex in any emotional, psychological or legal way, threats may follow, and those threats may be acted upon illogically, sometimes immediately, before reason is restored.

Angry and sad people, and those who inflict Implied threats, do not always preface their unconscionable actions by giving a precise warning or by making an explicit announcement. Instead, they are subtly presented. Nonetheless, many unpleasant events can send Threateners roaring to the finish line of acting out such threats.

Impulsiveness is often the problem, because many people who immediately act on their threats say they cannot believe they did what they did. Through tearful apologies they claim they were helpless—"temporarily insane." That may be true, but who cares how the Threatener feels *after* the fact? It is safety and peace of mind that you want.

If you are the Threatener, making frivolous, violent or harassing threats, stop! It will gain you nothing. No one involved in the marital breakup should be issuing threats. Here is my rule: Never threaten, but if threatened, protect yourself by taking action if a situation is serious enough to warrant it. For example, if your ex comes at you with a fist, do not threaten to call the police, do it.

NOW HEAR THIS!

A threat in itself can be frightening enough, and though many threats are hollow, one should still pay attention to the road signs because they can help to ward off potential danger. Yes, there are a large percentage of broken-hearted people who may make threats in the heat of the moment, but sit on their impulses out of sheer sensibility. Within a short time, they come to realize they would be foolish to carry out such threats. Hooray for those folks! If you tend to threaten, know at a minimum that it is robbing you of your dignity and self-respect. I do hope you are in the group that has second thoughts about acting on your threats, whether they are minor, i.e., "I'm bringing the children back late, I don't care what the court says" or major, "I'm going to kill you, and this time I mean it!"

Something else you should know: If you threaten your attorney, your therapist, the psych evaluator, the mediator or the judge or frankly, anyone, you are also leaving yourself open to legal action. Threats can certainly extend beyond one's ex, family and friends. They are often made against those who are closely related to a case. So, if you have a hair-trigger temper, get help. You certainly do not want to lose your freedom and all that goes with it and do prison time. It can happen. This is serious stuff!

CONTROL

What is most important, whether you are the Threatener/ Threatee/or both, is that threats tip the hand of the person making them, revealing a huge loss of control. I find the people caught up in this desperate game to be those I most pity. Persons who are centered, reasonable, rational and appropriate are the ones who power through the breakup process, and though it may be painful, they emerge with no regrets. You do not want the people around you to feel sorry for you because you have demonstrated less than first-class behavior (or have them remind you as the months and years go by about how badly you behaved). When it comes to the children, for example, your ability to control your impulses sends a strong message to them. If they see you act on a threat, it will have long-lasting consequences. Case in point: The woman dentist who ran over her husband three times in a hotel parking lot was not alone when she did it. Her stepdaughter, his daughter, was seated next to her on the passenger side of the car. It was this teenage girl who sealed her stepmother's fate by testifying that her stepmother had lost complete control and began yelling threatening remarks inside the car. As she circled the lot, she began acting on her "terrorist" threats. She was subsequently sentenced to a life term. This child, of course, will carry this trauma for the rest of her life. I am sure you can see how a moment of rage can translate into a lifetime of misery.

I am guessing that one of the main reasons you are reading this book is to find ways to keep control, both of yourself and your environment. With that in mind, realize that threat-making is like screaming to the world, "Hey, look at me, I'm completely and utterly out of control."

THREAT MENU

Although there is not enough room in this text to do so, there are plenty of typical threats to fill every page of this book and then some! I have culled from lists of threats in each of the three categories: Real, Implied and Imagined—those that I have actually found to be the most common.

REAL: The majority of Real threats that are *physical* in nature fall within the realm of domestic violence. There is one thing I know: During the first year of a breakup, the chances of death due to a domestic violence incident are greater than at any other time. This is not to suggest that you forego taking a physical threat seriously after a 12-month period. In 1994, I coauthored a bill in the state legislature in California that expanded the statute of limitations for victims of domestic violence for the right to sue their abusers in civil court. This was an important step to help victims of domestic violence seek justice and one that allows them ample time to do so. While I realize that going through a marital breakup is traumatizing, it is still no excuse to terrorize a person, or for a person to be subject to such abuse. Therefore, those who are victims should have more vindication than just criminal penalties against their perpetrators; they also should be able to receive monetary compensation.

If you are on the receiving end of a threat, take action. If you are the party making them, once again, cease and desist. Here are some of the classic Real threats, all of which can become intertwined in the emotional, psychological and legal wars:

1. "I'm going to kill you."
2. "You will never work in this town again."
3. "I'm taking the kids away from you."
4. "I'm turning you in to the IRS."
5. "I'll ruin your reputation."
6. "I'll take the children and leave the country."
7. "I'll get you fired."
8. "I'm declaring bankruptcy so you'll get nothing."
9. "I'll kill your new boyfriend/girlfriend."
10. "I'll take you to the cleaners."

IMPLIED: These threats are more "veiled" in nature, but nonetheless can be just as catastrophic as "Real" threats, because they can also be acted upon with dire consequences. Sometimes those on the receiving end of Implied threats are not certain what the "Threatener" means, since the threats are often vague or subtle in nature. For your reference, I've selected a handful of those that seem to be made most often.

1. "You'll be sorry."
2. "You just wait."
3. "I wouldn't do that if I were you."
4. "You'll see what I mean."
5. "Oh, you think *that* was bad?"
6. "You're going to wish you hadn't said that."
7. "You will *not* get away with this."
8. "You made a *big* mistake, _____ (your name here)."
9. "You better say your prayers."
10. "You might want to think twice about that."

Some of the most classic Implied threats—those repeated by many spurned spouses—are ones that have originated from great feature films. Here are a few of the most memorable:

1. "You're gonna be sleeping with the fishes."
2. "Go ahead, make my day!"

3. "I'll be back."
4. "I'll make you an offer you can't refuse."
5. "You will never see the light of day."

One last note about Implied threats: They tend to be the most common. Why? Because most people do not like confrontations, but under duress they will face off with their perceived "Tormentor" by saying things that are ominous in concept, but vaguely stated. As I mentioned previously, Real or Implied, these two threat categories are of equal concern.

IMAGINED: These types of threats are usually non-verbal in nature but still leave a person to wonder what terrible fate might befall them. Some of the most popular of this variety include the following:

1. A cold, icy stare accompanied by a sinister smile.
2. A hateful stare with eyes that could burn holes in the intended target.
3. A sly, quick chortle—a stifled, sarcastic laugh.
4. The index finger drawing an imaginary line across his/her throat.
5. The squealing of tires.
6. The pounding of a fist on a tabletop.
7. The slamming of a door.
8. Angry footsteps.
9. A mocking "tsk."
10. The middle finger.

PANORAMIC VIEW

Going back to the scenarios at the opening of this chapter, you may realize now that each illustrated a situation that depicted a particular "threat" in the threat Trilogy: Real, Implied and Imagined.

In Scene One, Dennis was virtually on the edge of losing all control when Courtney refused to pick up the phone and talk to him. His parting words, "okay, that's it," were certainly a perfect example of a garden-variety Implied threat, one that he may or may not have acted out. Was Dennis going to kill Courtney, trash her house, slash her tires or cut off all spousal and child support? Courtney was left to worry about the "what if's" and the "how soon's." Clearly, a hell no one should have to endure.

In Scene Two, we learned that Faith had feared her ex might make good on his threat to take the children to his native country. Ostensibly, Fahid had suggested many times he would abscond with the children, yet Faith felt helpless to do anything about such threats. She lived in a constant state of anxiety over his threats, however, and ultimately realized her greatest fears. He did not bring back the children as scheduled, she couldn't contact him, and she discovered his phone had been disconnected.

In Scene Three, there is no question that Mort was tormented by speculation as to what Laverne had in store for him. When you have had an intense relationship or marriage, you come to know a person's nuances and subtleties well. Although Mort had no idea what Laverne's glare (a look that could kill!) would mean in "payback" terms, he clearly *imagined* some horrific event would eventually befall him. Instincts play an important part in staying on top of this threat category, for what may be imagined one day could well come to fruition.

These three scenes—and others on similar themes—are played out all day, every day. Any of them look familiar to you?

If so, should you worry? Review your answers in Chapter Four where you were asked to identify your ex type. If you identified your former mate as a "Cooperator," no problem. You need not be concerned. Cooperators generally do not make threats, even idle ones. People who make threats are those who become dejected, feel desperate or hopeless. Most Cooperators may experience some disappointment in the demise of the marriage, but they are ready to move on, and that is obvious in their demeanor and attitude. However, the Cooperator does not fall within the majority: The bulk of those who are engaged in dismantling a close, intimate relationship, can and do become desperate at one point or another, and thus fall within one or more of the ex types.

If you count yourself as one of those among the other ex types, or your ex is easily recognizable within the group, then you may have cause for concern, for each of the others I profiled in that section are all potential candidates for making and carrying out threats.

THE EX TYPE AND THREATS

To refresh your memory, the other types I described in Chapter Four (sans the Cooperator, of course) consisted of the following: The "Intimidator," the "Passive Aggressive," the "Terrorist," the "Manipulator" and the "Victim." As I mentioned, some types overlap. For the purpose of clarifying how each of these ex types figures into the threat dynamic, I am taking a moment to address which types are prone to which kinds of threats.

It goes without saying that the Terrorist clearly falls within the grouping that is apt to make Real threats. They are pedigreed Control Freaks! In their frustration and anger they need a target—usually they pick the individual (or individuals) that have caused them emotional, psychological and/or legal distress. Do not ever take a Terrorist's threat lightly. The only positive about this type is that you usually know where he/she is coming from because they are fairly outspoken about their intentions—you are cognizant of what they plan to do. Though it may be painful for you to handle the truth, that you yourself may well be a Terrorist "operative," come to grips with the reality of it now, and vow to make a change. No one likes a bully. No one feels good about keeping company with someone who plays the villain. If instead you choose to own up to being a Terrorist, and decide to remain one, be aware it is an admission that you have zero control!

The Intimidator may or may not pose Real threats, but he/she surely will offer up Implied threats. In fact, the latter is his/her favorite. Do not forget, Intimidators need control, and one way to get it is to make oppressive overtures toward the other party—to make them feel less than and to keep them behaving submissively and operating in a state of fear and anxiety. Nothing evokes obedience better than a good threat! Threats are often what the Intimidator thrives on—they are what he/she uses to feel or stay "on top" in many of the Typical Wars. If you look into your internal mirror and see yourself as a full-fledged Intimidator, get a psychological grip, and while you are at it, a psychological makeover. If you don't, most people will not find you very desirable after a while.

Both the "Manipulator" and the "Passive Aggressive" will rarely, if ever, make open or Real threats. They are masters at Implied threats and can also dish up huge portions of Imagined Threats. The Manipulator can send you running around in mental circles imagining, and trying to determine, if you have been threatened. The Passive Aggressives can do the same, but their tact is even more pervasive. The Passive Aggressives often funnel their threats via the children, friends, business associates and others with whom you may have regular contact. One good example is the children coming home from a weekend visitation to report that Dad was spending most of the weekend cleaning his rifle. He/she could also pull your best friend aside at a party and infer that he/she knows exactly where you kept your nude photos—the ones you took on a lark and have since regretted. Passive Aggressives are quick to say: "Who me...*threaten?* You must be kidding. I have no idea what you're talking about."

Do not be fooled by the "Victim" ex type: They are much the same as the Passive Aggressive. They just seem to whine when making Implied threats. They may say things to your mother offhandedly with a big sigh like, "I have so little to live for anymore." They are easy to spot, these Victim Threateners, for they imply or present imagination-type threats through a "Poor Me" mask. Beware of the Victims, for they can be as threateningly crafty as any one of the other types.

Once again, if you stumble upon a glimpse of yourself while looking closely at any of these descriptions, find appropriate means to reorient your thinking and redirect your actions. Remember, you will have much greater success at control when you discontinue making threats, whether Real, Implied or Imagined. I cannot stress this enough: Those who make any type of threats are only trying to manage their desperation. But also remember this: Desperate people do desperate things.

LISTENING TO YOUR GUT

Whether or not you should take heed as a result of a threat is often a dilemma. I always advise my clients to pay close attention to their instincts. If something just does not feel right, pay attention to that feeling. I know many clients who had a "nagging suspicion" their ex was about to attack—to act out a threat. I never take such information lightly. Together, many clients and I have devised strategy based on a type of "circumstantial" evidence that his or her ex may strike. Even if your ex has never engaged in physical violence in the past, or appears to have always been passive and non-reactionary to situations that might send others into a complete frenzy, do not overlook your gut feelings. We hear of many spurned spouses who kill exes, for instance, whose friends and neighbors describe them as the last person they thought would ever kill someone, burn down the house, or run away with the kids, etc. When you consider that you may know your ex more intimately than anyone else, your instincts can prove invaluable. I had a business associate who told me tearfully about her best friend, a woman who filed for divorce after 13 years of marriage. Her husband, an engineer for a large petroleum company and a quiet sort, seemed nonchalant about her request for a divorce. He agreed to move out of the house and told her he would hire an attorney who would contact hers. This woman told my friend something did not feel right. She said she could not put her finger on the problem, but expressed worry. Two days later, my friend was aghast and devastated when she learned he had returned to the house ostensibly to pick up the rest of his belongings, and instead killed his estranged wife and himself. The couple's two children were at school. To this day, my friend still talks about this horrible event whenever the subject of intuition comes up. My suggestion to anyone going through a breakup is to not be overly paranoid, but do not underestimate the vibes—those feelings that say something is not right.

What about threats that are made when someone is under the influence of drugs or alcohol? Should these threats be taken seriously or dismissed? It depends on the person and the circumstances. My advice is never to take a threat lightly just because someone was drunk when they made it. The threat had to originate from somewhere in that person's mind. It could be they blurted it out (and lucky for you to find out about it so you can take precautions), or it could be someone was just blowing off steam. It is up to you, always, to decide under these circumstances—when your ex was loaded or drunk—whether you need to worry. Go with your gut.

I have come to rely on my intuition and not only out of a personal philosophy, but also due to one particular experience that still haunts me to this day. A female client, mother of three children, who insisted her ex-husband was neglecting the children, retained me. She implied that her children were in danger of her ex-husband hurting them in other physical ways. Something felt uncomfortable to me. After carefully weighing my commitment to representing her interests, I called her and politely explained I did not feel I was the right attorney for her case. I had a feeling—deep inner gnawing—that something was off—but I did not know what. Approximately two years later, long after I ceased representing the woman, I learned she had killed her children and herself. I shudder when I realize how powerful and accurate my intuition was. Do not underestimate that inner voice that often speaks to you, for very often it speaks the truth.

When my clients are dealing with Implied or Imagined threats, I always ask them to take a silent moment and see if their gut reaction is sending out a real or false alarm. I am recommending that you do the same.

HIDE AND SEEK REFUGE

You may be asking: What should I do if I have been threatened? There are many remedies available to you whether the threats you are receiving are Real, Implied or Imagined.

Let me first address Real threats, the ones that are openly expressed, because these tend to go hand-in-hand with physical danger. If your ex is threatening to take your life or the lives of those around you (your children, your parents, your friends and/or your business associates), call the police and your attorney. The police should be able to help you while the incident is happening, the attorney, after the fact. The attorney can assist you in seeking a Restraining Order. While such a drastic measure may shock your ex into backing off of Real threats (because to act on such suggestions or continue to make them usually means arrest and incarceration), still be careful! Restraining Orders are only a piece of paper, and many of those who obtained them have been murdered or beaten or have had their possessions destroyed.

If your ex demonstrates threatening behavior in your presence (like when he returns the children after visitation and thrusts his fist through the door), call the police immediately. They can issue an EPO (an Emergency Protective Order). This document will tide you over until your attorney gets a Temporary Restraining Order followed by a Permanent Restraining Order (usually effective for three years, and can be renewed, as needed, thereafter). If you should get a Permanent Order, you do not need to have your ex inflict injury or damage before calling the authorities. You can call if he/she comes near you (the judge may order he/she stay at least 100 to 200 yards away from you) or makes any additional threats against you.

You can also seek help from your therapist who, together with your attorney, may suggest you reside in a domestic violence shelter for a time, or assist you in moving away, or in with those who are equipped to provide safety. Ever since the famous O.J. Simpson case, more attention than ever before has been paid to physical violence and the threats that precede it. While Simpson may have been acquitted of criminal charges, he was found responsible for the wrongful deaths of Nicole Brown and Ron Goldman in a civil action, and there is also no dispute that he accosted Nicole Brown Simpson and acted out many of his Real threats. As Nicolle Simpson pleaded for help during one 911 call we heard his chilling words in the background:

> *"Could you get somebody over here now, to…Gretna Green. He's back. Please?"*
>
> *"What does he look like?"*
>
> *"He's O.J. Simpson. I think you know his record. Could you just send somebody over here?"*
>
> *"What is he doing there?"*
>
> *"He just drove up again. (She begins to cry). Could you just send somebody over?"*

I have supported many women's shelters and those that assist men who are also victims of domestic violence. Indeed, it was reported by former LA District Attorney, Gil Garcetti, that one third of all domestic violence cases involve men as the victims. I have been a big fan of Break the Cycle, an organization based in Los Angeles, with several other centers around the country, that are in operation to help youth with domestic violence issues. Such organizations warn people who fall victim to threats to ignore apologies, gifts and other tokens that are geared to throw the victim off-guard and make him or her think future threats might be meaningless. I say once a person makes Real threats and acts on them, take them seriously and always opt for safety. I also say pay close attention to Implied threats, for they could portend of danger if they go unheeded.

In terms of Imagined threats: It's time to call your therapist and ask for help in neutralizing such fears. This mental health professional can aid you in reasoning with such threats and also guide you to the proper persons (your attorney and/or the authorities) if they think any Imagined threat might materialize into some type of danger.

What should you do if your ex acts on a threat?

There is little difference between what can result from a Real and an Implied threat. If someone says "I'm going to kill you," or they make a point of letting you know they just got a new gun, the end result can be the same: Disaster. So, again, call the police! Tell your attorney and your therapist; but in an emergency, only the police can help. If the situation warrants, ask that they assist you in securing your safety and that of your children, immediate family and any others you feel may be at risk. Conversely, if you are the person making the threats, know that you have a major lack of personal self-control and you should reach out for help. There are many who will be glad to assist you.

The following list of specific remedies to staving off the consequences of Real or Implied threats may help. To those faced with threats, these tips have proven very useful.

- If you feel comfortable, arm yourself. Though you may need a concealed weapon permit (some states require them) and instruction on how to safely use a gun, this might be a good remedy.
- Take a martial arts class or some other self-protection workshop.
- Carry mace, pepper spray, a big metal spoon and even an ear-piercing whistle.
- Call 911 if you are in danger (calling your attorney for *immediate* help will not result in *immediate* protection).
- Keep important phone numbers with you at all times (police, domestic violence hotlines, family, friends, etc.).
- Tell as many people as you can about any viable threats, and ask them to be vigilant along with you.
- Develop code words to use with friends and family to let them know when you are in immediate danger.
- Make a list of safe havens—and keep the list in an easily accessible place—if you need to get away in a hurry.
- Find a person or place where you can leave emergency money, keys, clothes and important documents.
- Join a support group for victims of domestic violence, or a group of recent divorcees who find they are dealing with similar threat issues.
- Update, review and practice your safety plans regularly.
- Ask your attorney whether or not a restraining order would be appropriate. If so, get one. Make sure (if you have children) that you drop off a copy at school, the local police station, the daycare center and other places where your ex may come in contact with your children. Also, have one in your desk at work, in your car glove compartment, at home and on your "person".
- If you are remaining in the house you both resided in, have the locks changed and install an alarm system, or change the code, and always set it, even when you are in the home. Do not allow the children to take their house keys to your ex's when they go for visitation (your ex may have copies made).
- Try not to be alone in isolated areas.

- Make an escape plan in case you need to leave home or the office immediately.
- Keep a log of all threats—dates, times, places—Real, Implied and Imagined. Share this log with your attorney and your therapist (and police investigators if appropriate).

Realize that if you are the Threatener and you tell your therapist you plan to hurt someone, your therapist is obligated to report it. Be careful how you vent your frustration—choose your words wisely. This information can be used against you, especially in court hearings and proceedings.

It is now time for you to take a short quiz to see how you fare in the Threat Department. The majority of those going through divorce or a relationship breakup make some kind of threat— Real, Implied or Imagined. I am not chastising you if you have been a Threatener or allowed yourself to be a victim (or been both!), I am simply asking that you manage your threat issues, because they are linked closely with your ability to assume, establish and maintain control. The questions are as follows:

1. Describe yourself:
   Threatee _____
   Threatener _____
   Neither _____
   Both _____

2. Describe your ex:
   Intimidator _____
   Passive-Aggressive _____
   Terrorist _____
   Manipulator _____
   Victim _____
   Cooperator _____

3. Describe yourself:
   Intimidator _____
   Passive-Aggressive _____
   Terrorist _____
   Manipulator _____
   Victim _____
   Cooperator _____

4. The following are the types of threats made against me or those I fear:
Real ____
Implied ____
Imagined ____
None of the above ____
A combination of the above ____

5. My ex has acted on threats:
Yes ____
No ____

6. If you answered "yes" to the above, describe those threats in the spaces below (feel free to add more than this section provides for). Threats made against me (or those close to me):

_____
_____
_____
_____

7. Steps I have taken to safeguard myself and others against threats:

_____
_____
_____
_____

8. I have discussed threats against me with:
The Police ____
My attorney ____
My Therapist ____
Others ____

9. The threats I have made or responded to with threats of my own have kicked off the following war:
Emotional ____
Psychological ____
Legal ____
All of the above ____

You will note I did not offer questions for the Threatener. I do not want you to incriminate yourself. Even answering questions 1, 2 and 3 by writing the answers in this book could be a problem, if you are the aggressor. Writing down and recording such information in the workspaces of this book might be considered a journal of sorts, and it could be confiscated and entered into as evidence. If you are a Threatener who has made threats, acted upon some of them, or retaliated with a threat, I am asking that you do some real soul searching. Think about the nature of the threats you have made and resolve to change your behavior, no matter how difficult it may be. Know that leaving menacing messages on someone's voicemail, or writing threatening notes, faxes or emails, are all potential bombshells that can get you into trouble. Trying to explain to the police or the judge or the psych evaluator that you were angry at the time, or just kidding, is not going to work. Verbal or written threats have a damaging and lasting effect.

ADDING UP

If you ranked yourself as a Threatener, you should realize that you have relinquished control in the name of threats. This does you no good. In fact, you may find yourself in some horrible bind because of it. Losing your temper, issuing an abrupt threat, and acting on it could drastically change your life. What might feel satisfying for a quick moment in time could have negative ramifications for a lifetime.

If you checked the box "Threatee," are you returning fire by becoming a Threatener? If so, this also is non-productive and demonstrates a lack of control on your part. It can also get you into real trouble.

If you are a Threatee and doing nothing to safeguard your security, you need to take control and ask your attorney to assist you in intervening by showing some legal muscle. You also need to contact the local police if you feel you are in imminent danger. This is another way of asserting control over the situation.

One other way to take control is to make a safety plan, and at the same time, ignore your ex's threats. This is a passive way of saying, "You do not control me with your threats!"

If your ex is anything but a Cooperator, is he/she making threats? If your answer was "yes," get help. If you are not a Cooperator and rank yourself as a Passive-Aggressive, Manipulator, Victim or Intimidator and you are not making threats, good for you. If you are making them, however, first stop yourself from doing so. Next, handle that frustration more positively by asking your therapist to guide you (be careful how you word this to your therapist, as I warned earlier) towards more positive solutions to managing your hurt and anger. If you are a Terrorist, there is no doubt that part of your *Modus Operandi* is to make threats. Doing something about correcting that behavior sets you on the road to a meaningful way of finally gaining and keeping the right kind of control.

Your next set of answers dealt with the types of threats you have been getting. If you are giving any of the trio of threats, get a grip and give up such self-sabotaging behavior! If your ex is making Real threats against you, do everything I gave you to do on the Break the Cycle checklist. If Implied threats are what you are up against, review that same checklist and take necessary precautions. If the threats you are receiving are Imagined, dismiss thoughts of worry and fretting and take a more active stance (Hallelujah: Control!). Talk them over with your attorney and your therapist. Just because you *think or worry* that your ex means something by that "look" or some other questionable inference, does not mean he/she will do anything to hurt you. In the end, go with your instincts. A reasonable way to measure your concern is to look over your answers to questions 4 and 5—has your ex acted on threats? If the answer is "no," then try to gain a rational picture of what might be or could be. In the end, go with your gut. If the answer is "yes," by all means take appropriate steps immediately.

As you listed mentally (but did not write down) the threats you make, you will find a theme—some underlying issue that is bugging you. Work on that problem with your therapist. If you are the Threatee you will also notice a theme. Let your attorney know what you perceive it to be. If you have kept the log I suggested—when you go back to review it with your lawyer— you too will see a very clear-cut pattern. For example, if your ex is always *threatening* you about different ways to get more money from you, you know the issue is a monetary one. This allows you to circle the wagons around those financial things that may need your attention (i.e., keeping your company's books in good order, regularly logging all your expenses for you and the children). If your ex is displaying tremendous jealousy towards a new beau or how your new boyfriend/girlfriend is gaining the affection of the children, then you know it has to do with more personal issues like the inability to let go (these Threateners are often the ones who inflict physical harm, by the way). By answering question 6, you have started on the road to taking control. Just the simple identification of threats made against you allows you to take steps to mitigate such threats. The ultimate result: Control. If you are the Threatener, the answers to these questions pose an introspective look as to what is holding you back from moving on with your life. This understanding clearly gives you a healthy sense of control, not a demented one.

In regard to questions 7 and 8, if you are getting threats and left these spaces blank, you have work to do! You must protect yourself against harm.

If you made mental notes of threats you have made, you must find suitable ways to correct such ill behavior. Do not ignore taking positive steps to correct this behavior for it is a pivotal milestone to your getting a firm grasp on the control you want and need.

The answer to question 9 is also very revealing. If your threats have started a war, is that war absolutely necessary? The only war I think may have to be fought is a Legal one, and only then, as I have stated throughout different chapters in this book, for very good reasons. If you are engaged in any of the Three Typical Wars, are threats escalating the conflict? If so, what does that get you? Grief? Frustration? Despair? Do not say control, because it is quite the opposite. You do not need to make threats to take appropriate action in marital matters. I stress the word "appropriate," because you should never take action unless a situation warrants it. Threats have no place or real purpose in sorting out your marital conflicts. What I hope motivates you against issuing or responding to them with threats of your own is the realization that it broadcasts, "I am so out of control!"

Now that you have tackled many of the mysteries that have caused you to question your sense of control or examine how to better get and keep control, it is time to take a look at some of the other "lists" of dos and don'ts and even a humorous view at how control impacts your life as you wade through the travails of the breakup process.

*Herb prepares to give his
marriage another shot.*

Chapter Ten

THANK YOU MR. LETTERMAN
Top Ten Lists

"I think that sucks, your honor," blurted a 40ish software company owner, tucking a finger between his Adam's apple and the collar of his overly-starched oxford button-down shirt, in search of more breathing room.

"Excuse me, Mr. Lithrom!" It was not a question, but a statement, by a curt and extremely irate female judge from the bench. Leaning closer she added, "If you so much as open your mouth one more time, I will have you removed by the bailiff and I will find you in contempt." She pounded her gavel to emphasize the point.

"I'm sorry, Your Honor," a well-mannered female attorney offered, in a too-late attempt to save her client from total disaster. "My client is distraught over…"

"I don't care what your client is," the judge said, sitting up even straighter, fiddling superiorly with her pearls. "This is a Court of Law, and Mr. Lithrom will conduct himself accordingly…"

Before she could finish the sentence, Lithrom let out with, "Oh pul--leeeeze…"

"Remove him," the no-nonsense judge ordered, her gavel pointing to the bailiff.

◆   ◆   ◆

"And another thing: Your father is an idiot. A complete and total idiot, and I can't even believe I ever married him. What was wrong with me?" sneered the spurned housewife, letting go of the steering wheel momentarily to gesture to the heavens, arms outstretched above her head. Her seven-year-old daughter in the back seat began to cry. Her nine-year-old son tried to distract her. "Hey, mom, we're gonna win at soccer today, don't you think?"

"Yeah, if we ever get there." She threw the sarcastic remark over her shoulder. "Your father is so stupid. What part of 'return the kids by no later than three so I can get them to soccer on time' do you think he didn't understand?"

Showing zero mercy to her daughter, "What are you crying about?"

"I hate it when you and daddy say bad things about each other," she said, wiping the tears and her nose with her sweater sleeve.

Backing off, "Well if he just wasn't so self-centered and full of himself..."

The poor children, they still had another ten minutes to go before they reached the soccer field.

◆   ◆   ◆

He was so angry he ripped open the desk drawers and dumped them on the floor.

"What are you doing, Jake?" asked a distraught mother, not knowing if or how she could get her 36-year-old son under control.

"I'm getting rid of everything that remotely reminds me of her!" he snapped.

"I understand how angry you are honey, and for good reason," the woman who knew him best tried to talk him down. "But don't you need those records for your attorney? I mean if she emptied out the bank accounts and you think she cashed out some of the stocks and bonds, shouldn't you be saving those things as..."

"As what? As what?" the irate son challenged.

"As backup. You will need to prove..."

"Forget it. I really don't care anymore."

With that, Jake scooped up stock certificates, loan documents, jewelry appraisals, and a stack of what appeared to be other original papers and began to feed them, one by one, to the paper shredder.

His mother looked on, hands pressed against her cheeks, horrified.

You may have found all three of these scenes rather amusing, but they do happen. They go hand-in-hand with any one of the Three Typical Wars and they are anything but funny when you take into account the potential consequences. Many who make their way through the trenches of the Divorce Wars are angry, frustrated or so despondent they say and do such things. And they do so despite the repercussions. Control, of course, is at the heart of the need to spout off or behave in counterproductive ways. Some have told me doing so makes them feel like they are gaining in that department. Not so. In fact, they are unquestionably out of sync with their control mechanism altogether!

To some, the scenes above and others like them may appear hilarious (if you are not involved in them). However, they are anything *but* funny to those who get hit as innocent bystanders or to those who are forced to suffer the consequences of their remarks or acts.

When any one of the Three Typical Wars is raging, and people are being pulled taut emotionally, psychologically and legally, they behave in ways that are less than flattering or favorable to them. Indeed, people say things and do things that either seal their fate on the spot (like Lindstrom, who clearly alienated the judge), or create residual effects, like the soccer mom whose children will quite likely harbor resentment and anger toward her for years to come for bashing their father. Or, of course, there's Jake, who foolishly destroyed crucial documents needed to support his claims in his dissolution case. Certainly, he is the one who will have a heck of a time (think Humpty-Dumpty) when trying to put back together all the paperwork he shoved down the shredder. I shudder to think that in his rampage he may also have trashed the only executed copy of his prenuptial agreement, making his case that much harder to prove.

As you may have guessed, I'm big on "paper trails" and record keeping, because as a divorce attorney I have come to know a few things: He who has the most comprehensive trail of paper wins; he who fights with real ammo emerges from the Legal Divorce Wars victoriously; and most importantly, he who wears the white hat emerges with victory and honor. So I caution you: Always think before you speak.

TAKING A LEAVE

I want you to think seriously about avoiding similar mistakes as those in the trilogy of scenes I have described (and others with like themes), but I also want you to lighten up a bit, to partake in some levity as you step back and assess your situation. Part of the problem with people going off on judges, venting out loud, or destroying things they need (like legal papers), is that they have not balanced all their trauma and stress with some modicum of humor.

I realize the messages in this book have given you a great deal to think about, and the tasks I have asked you to do have taken real work on your part. In that process it is not unusual to get laden down with gravity. With that in mind, I am offering some additional do's and dont's, but I am doing so in a different way: With a dash of humor—with a tongue-in-cheek approach.

I am a firm believer that humor is a positive way to make salient points and an unforgettable way of serving as reminders. I also think humor is a terrific way to gain a better perspective under duress. As a way of making you laugh, yet also helping you take heed of what could be regrettable—saying things you wished you hadn't or doing things you might agonize over—I put together suggestions I thought would be interesting and fun, yet also meaningful.

Inasmuch as I am a huge David Letterman fan and truly enjoy many of his "Top Ten" lists, I thought it would be fitting to offer up what I gathered from my research in a much more entertaining way. With that in mind, I have compiled my own ten Top Ten lists. Review these—some are lighthearted and some are serious. Then try out your own. These rundowns are designed to help you clearly identify what you can and cannot tolerate in a marriage, what you would like to change about yourself, and the qualities that you may be seeking in a new mate.

HELD IN CONTEMPT

A few of the lists in my first round are directly related to the opening scenarios in this chapter. I would like you to use them as a backdrop to assess candidly whether or not you see yourself "pictured" in any of the list's itemizations. I will start with the Top Ten things you should never say to the judge.

10. So she gets the gold and I get the shaft?
9. I don't think you would have ruled that way if I'd been a guy (gal).
8. I'm really not comfortable raising my right hand and repeating after anyone.
7. I'm not hiding my income, so help me God.
6. Why are you picking on *me*?
5. No court's going to tell me what to do!
4. You'll have to wait a minute, my cell phone's ringing.
3. I don't have time for this.
2. You're the one who should have a psych eval.
1. With all due respect, Your Honor, have you ever been through a divorce?

Done laughing yet? The remarks to the judge may sound funny to you, but they are all too true and have been said in court during a real hearing. If you find yourself losing your temper, bite your tongue, or shove your attorney's coat sleeve in your mouth for a timeout, but *never, ever* say any of the above to the judge! In fact, remain silent in court unless you are directed to speak. Let your attorney do your bidding.

PARENTS SAY THE DARNDEST THINGS

Here we go now for a Top Ten list of things you should never say about your ex in front of the children.

10. I wish your mother (father) would drop dead.
9. I never loved your father (mother) anyway.
8. One of these days, so help me, I'm going to kill her (him).
7. I'm sorry I did such a horrible job picking your father (mother).
6. So where'd he (she) get the bimbo (bozo)?
5. Thank God you don't look like her (him).
4. He (she) was really bad in bed.
3. Oh, he (she) never loved you kids anyway.
2. She (he) is fat and ugly and really stupid.
1. He (she) does not pay me nearly enough child support.

Shocking? To some maybe, but I know of situations where parents have actually said these things, and worse yet about their exes to their children. Many have no regrets, which I find tragic. That is such a pity because the truth is that the children from broken marriages often feel responsible not only for the divorce, but the wars their parents engage in as well. That's right, they think all the discord is their fault. Be extremely careful how you coin your phrases and what you say in haste and/or anger about your ex.

Next, I have my Top Ten picks of things you should never do to jeopardize your case.

10. Never refer to your holdings as your hidden assets.
9. Never show up late (or early) for a court appearance with a hangover.
8. Never telephone your ex's attorney and tell him/her off.
7. Never bribe the kids into testifying against your ex.
6. Never throw a fit in court.
5. Never act in a threatening or inappropriate manner in front of your ex's attorney.
4. Never toss out a pickup line to the Judge.
3. Never have a wild party on your custodial weekends.
2. Never lose or destroy your important paperwork.
1. Never say, "I'll *never* get through this."

DUMB AND EVEN DUMBER

"Hey, after this is all over, what do you say…how about you and me have a couple of stiff drinks," sheepishly smiled the dashing 40-year-old record producer. "I know a quiet little place with a…"

His bombshell blonde attorney whose spectacular looks were sometimes more a curse than a boon responded, "That is against my policy and that of the State Bar's."

"Who's gonna know?"

"Mr. Martin, you are completely out of line and…"

"Don't tell me other clients haven't asked you out."

Fed up, and never one to tolerate such behavior, she said, "Mr. Martin I find it necessary to refer your case to another attorney."

"Hey, what's the problem for God's sake? I'm about to be single," he leaned over her desk to whisper, *"I found out you're single too, and…"*

"That's enough. You need to leave. I will send your file to a new attorney. Just let me know who you wish to substitute in." She stood and pointed a finger toward the door.

Taking his cue, and his bruised ego with him, Martin nodded politely as he stood and turned to make his exit.

◆   ◆   ◆

She sat, legs crossed, puffing deeply on her cigarette. Her eyes held a Bette Davis chill. *"I don't even know why I ever married you."*

"I think you once loved me," said a brow-beaten husband trying to salvage some semblance of pride.

"Loved you?" a *"hah!"* followed.

"Yes, you said you loved me, Shannon. For three years, every single day, remember?"

"Oh come on, Steve. Isn't it obvious by now?"

"What?"

"It was your money I married, not you, you fool." She stubbed what remained of her cigarette onto the couple's plush stone covered patio deck and let out a snide laugh.

"I don't believe this, Shannon," he said, rising to follow her into the house.

"Well, you should. It's true. Now would you please take those things," she pointed to a stack of belongings on the sofa in their cathedral ceiling living room, *"and get out of here. We're getting a divorce, remember?"*

Steve's worst fears had been realized. Marrying him for his money was something he could have gone the rest of his life without ever hearing her say. It was painful enough.

Martin certainly made a dumb move by hitting on his attorney. It is not only unprofessional for an attorney to "date" or carry on with a client, it is unethical, and in most states, such behavior can get a lawyer disbarred. I have many colleagues who have had clients who have alienated them by engaging in inappropriate conduct, rudeness, uncooperative attitudes, hiding vital information from them or by trying to boss them around. When you are going through a divorce, your attorney must be your strongest ally. Think twice about saying or doing something that may distance him/her from you. It could prove disastrous!

In Martin's case, he had spent four months getting his attractive attorney up to speed. To find and brief another attorney was both time-consuming and costly. So watch what you say and do. You do not want your attorney to fire you, nor do you want to turn your much-needed legal counsel against you. In your Legal War, that person is leading the "charge" and protecting you from the enemy. Be wise. Do not make dumb mistakes.

Naturally, my next list pokes some fun at my choice of the Top Ten ways you can potentially alienate your attorney. Though some may seem far-fetched, they can and have happened. Do not:

10. Make a pass at your attorney.
9. Show up late for meetings and court appearances.
8. Threaten to sue if your attorney botches your case.
7. Tell your attorney you think opposing counsel is doing a better job.
6. Put your attorney on hold while you take another call.
5. Have your retainer or payment checks bounce.
4. Nitpick your attorney's bill.
3. Make negative comments about your attorney's offices (décor, distance, size…)
2. Order your attorney around.
1. Lie to your attorney

Some of those suggestions might seem completely outlandish, but I promise you they are not. And, these are just a few! There are numerous other ways to alienate your attorney. In order to keep with my format, however, I chose to list only ten of them! Now is a good time to ask yourself: Have you done anything dumb to disaffect your attorney?

MONEY TALKS

In Scene Two, Shannon was certainly unnecessarily hurtful to Steve. He had suspected all along that she had married him for his money, but that reality was excruciating to face. Though some people are angry and thus become spiteful, dumb or insensitive, shocking or hurtful remarks should not be flung freely. Most are uncalled for and gain nothing for the person saying them. Do not become one of those people, since such mean or cruel acts can come back to haunt you. Going out of your way to throw a below-the-belt punch at your ex may feel good at the time, but the residual effects or the consequences are simply not worth it. Besides, you ought not to say anything you would not want someone to say to you!

Though I know there are hundreds of things people should never say to their exes, I have taken some of them—the ones I consider to be the most classic or popular—to comprise my Top Ten list in this category. They are:

10. I was never in love with you.
9. You look like hell.
8. The kids can't stand you.
7. Everyone I know is so glad we're getting a divorce.
6. Good luck finding someone who would want you.
5. I only married you for your _____(money, fame, body, prestige…)
4. I was cheating on you all along.
3. You were never good in bed.
2. I can't believe I ever married you.
1. You're not their father. (Toward women: Their stepmother is their real mom).

Again, I am certain some of these have caused you to grin, laugh out loud, or maybe even cringe. As I admonish you in this category—things never to say to your ex—I must revert to my mother's famous words to my brother and me as we were growing up: "If you don't have anything nice to say, don't say anything at all." She was right. Negative barbs at your ex only chip away at your dignity, and who needs that? So, even if your ex is resorting to negative comments, do not stoop to his/her level. It gains you nothing in the bigger picture, except perhaps an unwanted war.

By the way, Shannon's arrogance and hurtful remarks caused her huge problems when it came time for discussions about the property settlement agreement. It took several months to negotiate a settlement, and Steve had become so furious he made it very tough on Shannon. In any kind of a Legal War you certainly do not want to lose control and shoot yourself in the foot!

MEETING YOUR MATE

"The bride looks beautiful, doesn't she?" asked a very attractive 50ish female CPA of the man seated in the pew next to her, a guest who also looked to be alone.

"She sure does," he whispered as they waited for the minister to begin the ceremony.

Stella put out her hand, "Stella Hanson."

"Matt Sterns."

"Nice to meet you."

"You, too. Say, I hate coming to things like this alone, but the bride's father is my client so I…"

"Mine, too." Stella said in a hushed voice.

"There's no seating arrangement specified at the reception table. I already checked it out," Matt was trying to get up the nerve to ask if she might sit next to him.

At the same time Stella and Matt both asked, "Mind if I join you?"

They laughed.

They were married 13 months later.

◆   ◆   ◆

His hair was tousled, he was twirling his key chain, and he was leaning with his back against the bar at Hedricks, a popular pub that attracted the singles crowd. "You look familiar. Haven't I seen you here before?"

The curly-haired redhead, seated at a table in front of the bar, looked away shyly.

"Hey," he said, plopping himself in the empty seat next to her. "You look like Julia Roberts."

"I do?"

"Yeah," he looked around cautiously. "Where's your date?"

"Oh, I came with my friend Jenna. She's in the restroom. I just got divorced and needed a night out. Well, we were just about to leave."

"Well, so was I! He flashed a Hugh Grant grin, his boyish charm captivating even though he was pushing 50. "Where do ya live?"

"Oh just a few blocks from here."

"Yeah?"

Feeling compelled to say something else, the Julia Roberts look alike finally managed, "On Wellington."

"Hey, so do I. No wonder you look so familiar. Say, why don't we ditch Jenna—send her home—let me buy you a drink and I'll give you a ride," he smiled using one of the all time classic worst pick up lines. "I live just around the corner from Wilming…"

"Wellington," she corrected. "Wait, I thought you said you lived on Wellington?"

"Yeah, oh yeah, Wellington. Well see, I used to live there. I live around the corner now. Moved just a few weeks ago…"

Keeping with the Letterman motif, I am providing you with two more Top Ten lists. These include the Top Ten best places to meet a new mate and the Top Ten worst places to hook up with one. Once again, I present these to you tongue-in-cheek!

I will begin with the Top Ten best places to find a new mate:

10. At your best friend's wedding (it doesn't matter how many he/she has had).

9. At the headquarters of your favorite political candidate.

8. At your local home improvement or hardware store (women can never find what they need so the men cruising the aisles are easy recruits for assistance—men hardly shop anywhere else).

7. At the studio of your personal trainer.

6. At someone else's office, not yours.

5. On a ski lift.
4. Through a reputable dating service that finds you the perfect match.
3. At a self-help seminar for divorcees.
2. At your place of worship.
1. At a Sting concert (people of all ages attend them).

As you tuned-in to the wedding scene with Matt and Stella, you noticed that both were business professionals brought together indirectly by someone they knew and respected. A wedding is not a bad place to meet a potential new mate. Everyone is in a good mood, the atmosphere is romantic, and people seem friendlier than usual. Since people usually invite those who are most important to them, and people they obviously like, it can be fertile ground for singles to connect with quality people.

One the other hand, Hedricks, the singles bar, was certainly not a good choice for the pretty redhead. There are good-looking guys (and gals) who troll such venues on a regular basis in search of innocent, newly-divorced individuals on which to prey for sex, money and other favors. A guy I know, who used to head the homicide department for a Southern California sheriff's office, Lieutenant Sim Middleton, once told me that those who allow themselves to picked get up by strangers in nightclubs are perfect targets for rape, kidnapping and murder. The hardest part of his job, he said, was finding the perpetrators of such crimes, for the predators who linger in bars are hard to catch for they often leave no trail; they are hard to trace. A night out on the town with friends for the heck of it might be an okay idea, but be careful who you talk to, and never leave with someone you do not know. Ask for a business card instead and make sure it belongs to him or her. Check this person out thoroughly before agreeing to a follow-up get-together.

Choose wisely those places to meet a new mate! Now divorced, the last thing you want to do is find yourself getting together with someone who might be another divorce candidate, or worse yet, someone who could physically hurt you.

Here is a rundown of the worst places to meet a mate:

10. A laundromat. (If a person does not have his/her own washer and dryer by now, that could be very telling).
9. A bar for singles. (You get my drift).
8. Your attorney's office lobby. (That other divorcee you are suddenly attracted to needs time to "unpack" his/her baggage).
7. Around the water cooler at work.
6. In a parking garage.
5. An Anger Management class.
4. Alcoholics Anonymous.
3. A fast food restaurant.
2. In the car next to you.
1. Jail.

I genuinely hope some of the above provide a few chuckles, but also instill in you some good common sense. After all, at a time like this, good common sense may be the single most important commodity you can latch on to. I say that because you are no doubt currently embroiled in one or more of the Marital Wars and suffering from some distress that tends to pull you off your center. Do not make foolish or impulsive choices just because you want some companionship or because you are on the hunt for a new partner.

THINKING ABOUT MARRIAGE

"Oh, I know he seems kind of self-centered, Portia, but after we're married things will be different." Starry-eyed and noticeably excited about her wedding two weeks away, Gretchen was sure her fiancé, Nathan, would change.

"I sure hope you're right, Gretch," her best friend said evenly, still eyeing the menu, *"Because I think his 'me-first' attitude will drive you nuts eventually."*

"I'm not worried" Gretchen was debating between the Caesar salad and the club sandwich. *"Everyone knows marriage is a 50/50 proposition."*

◆   ◆   ◆

"That's ridiculous, Sabrina. I should be able to splurge on some things." Sabrina's husband Peter went back to reading the BMW manual, feet comfortably positioned atop the coffee table.

"You can't go out and buy a new Beamer when we can't even afford the kids' tuition."

"Oh stop. Hey look!" Peter exclaimed, "It's got a place to plug in my fax machine."

Sabrina could take no more. Finances were always an issue between them, a big issue that was getting even bigger. Peter spent it before he earned it, while Sabrina tried hard to make every penny count.

"That's it, Peter. I've had it."

Peter was deep into page 63, an explanation of how the DVD movie screen descended from the headliner.

"I need to ask you to leave. I can't be married to you anymore."

It was as though he never heard her. "Sabrina, get me another beer, would ya?"

LEAVING YOUR PRINCE/PRINCESS

I do not know if you have been the subject in either of the above scenes or know people who have been, but these two scenarios are similar to the ones I hear about every day. People always have preconceived ideas of what a marriage should be, especially the first time around. Unfortunately, that may well be the case with Gretchen, the hopeful bride. People rarely change, and to expect marriage to redefine a partner's basic character is ludicrous—it is just plain unrealistic. If anything, people's worst traits become more amplified in a marriage. They do not disappear, nor do they become minimized. One sure way to stay realistic about the person with whom you are considering a long-term relationship is to ask yourself from the get go, if you are comfortable with his/her "ways." Once again, people do not "improve" as time goes by and thus the reason many relationships go downhill.

People also find there are circumstances that break up a marriage. Some may seem silly, while others are not. The woman who can no longer take the toilet seat being left up may be acting out from a series of metaphorical experiences resembling that one, like her husband always arranging his environment for his comfort and his needs, and showing complete disregard for hers. (Control issue!) I knew of a woman who once snatched the remote control out of her husband's hand and threw it at the television screen. She then proceeded to pack her bags. She never returned. Apparently she was never given "equal time" with the device, and that one particular incident symbolized her inability to tolerate any more frustration. Remember the "remote control syndrome" in Chapter One, when discussing the Anatomy of control?

A PENNY EARNED IS OFTEN A PENNY SPLURGED

There are many people like Sabrina who fight with their spouses over money. As you may already know, finances are one of the chief reasons people divorce. (Secondary reasons often include lack of communication, problems with the children, cheating, and in-law problems, of course, run close behind!) However, if people have different points of view on how money should be earned and/or spent, it can be a constant irritant and strain on the relationship, ultimately causing the partnership's undoing.

After as many years as I have been in practice, I have heard every reason in the book for getting a divorce regarding finances, but one takes the cake. A dear friend said she had to leave her second husband because she could not handle the Monday morning bookmaker collection calls any longer. It was not so much that she objected to her husband betting heavily on Sunday afternoon sporting events: It was that they often had no money for groceries for the week because of his gambling addiction. "The kids never know if they're having beans and franks or lobster," she admitted one day. "I find myself bulking up on food and cleaning supplies during the good weeks then rationing them out on bad weeks." It was absurd, since her husband was a well-known sportscaster who made a substantial living. But, like Sabrina, she just could not take any more financial uncertainty or her husband's over-indulgences.

It is now time to provide a few more lists that address some of the issues that typically cause divorce and the myths that surround the idea of what a marriage can or should be. I hope they are both helpful and humorously uplifting.

I will start with my favorite, the Top Ten Myths about marriage:

10. We will live happily ever after.
 9. I can have it all.
 8. He/she will complete me.
 7. He/she is my soul mate.
 6. We don't need money; we can live on love.
 5. Marriage will make our relationship better.
 4. We will grow together.
 3. I will *always* love him/her.
 2. Having children will strengthen our relationship.
 1. His/her family/children will learn to accept me.

I like this list so much I feel compelled to offer another complete Top Ten countdown in the same category:

10. I would never cheat on him/her.
 9. We will always be this romantic.
 8. I'll never get tired of him/her.
 7. Love conquers all.
 6. He/she will change once we're married.
 5. Every marriage should be 50/50.
 4. He'll/she'll always be there for me.
 3. Love is bliss.
 2. Till death do us part.
 1. I will never be lonely again.

Well, I am positive there are hundreds of other myths about marriage. Perhaps you have your own! Those who sit on the other side of marriage (divorce) often recall many traditional myths about marriage—myths they completely bought into, until they realized marriage was undoubtedly lots of give and take and a good deal of work. There are many happily married couples who have managed to stay together for decades, but most people, during the "marriage exit interview," say that what they thought a marriage should be and what it turned out to be were completely antithetical. So, before you jump into a new marital union, examine your misconceptions about marriage and the myths that may have prompted them—and deal with them before tying the new knot. In fact, it might be a very good idea at this juncture to make your own list of myths—those theories about marriage you grew up with or bought into and disappointedly learned were not so. It would be helpful to revisit this list as you seriously consider that next relationship commitment. As a divorce attorney, I have learned that many of my clients had a "Hollywood mentality" about marriage. It could be they had seen so many films with happy endings or written or sung so many love ballads they began to believe them. Real marriage, as you now may very well know, is comprised of many complexities. However, many people think the head-over-heels aspect of their relationship will be the mainstay of their marriage. Tragically though, most people who go through divorce have done just that. They get entangled in romantic myths. They did not bargain for the tough times, nor did they factor in the nonromantic moments when he became ill or she lost her job or when they grew apart or what it did to their relationship when one of the children got arrested. So again, examine your myths and make sound decisions, not ones based on a fairytale mentality.

Now it is time for my list of Top Ten things that can cause divorce. Some may cause you to chuckle, but all are legit.

10. One of you thought it was perfectly okay to have just one extra-marital affair.
9. The children from your spouse's former marriage hate you.
8. He/she thinks money grows on trees.
7. He/she is smothering me.
6. You're tired of picking her/him up from the rehab center.
5. His/her idea of a vacation is going somewhere without you.

4. He/she never remembers your birthday or your anniversary.
3. He/she really let him/herself go.
2. He/she thinks holidays should be spent on the golf course; you think they should be spent with family.
1. He/she is controlling.

LEAVE THEM LAUGHING

Before we move on to your homework tasks in this chapter—that of making your own lists—I would like to take this opportunity to offer a Top Ten list of some of my favorite humorous quotes about divorce. Here goes:

10. "I've never been married, but I tell people I'm divorced so they won't think something's wrong with me." *Elayne Boosler, standup comedienne.*
9. "I don't think I'll get married again; I'll just find a woman I don't like and give her a house." *Lewis Grizzard, humorist.*
8. "Divorce is like a root canal; never wanted, sometimes needed." *Elizabeth Griffith, Webmaster of Divorce.*
7. "Marriage is grand. Divorce is about twenty grand." *Jay Leno, comedian and TV talk show host.*
6. "Divorce is most likely to wreak havoc when spouses declare war on each other and draft their kids." *Constance Ahrons, Emeritus Professor of Sociology, USC.*
5. "I am a marvelous housekeeper. Every time I leave a man I keep his house." *Zsa Zsa Gabor, Hungarian-born American actress.*
4. "Marriage is about love; divorce is about money." *Anonymous.*
3. "Love, the quest; marriage, the conquest; divorce, the inquest." *Helen Rowland, American journalist.*
2. "Divorce is a declaration of independence with only two signers." *Gerald F. Lieberman, American writer.*
1. "I guess the only way to stop divorce is to stop marriage." *Will Rogers, humorist.*

MAKING YOUR LISTS AND CHECKING THEM TWICE

Naturally there are dozens of other reasons people file for divorce, but just like most of those I listed in the previous section, perhaps many of yours had to do with control or big or small irritants as well. In any case, the reasons are often very personal. Some are very serious like adultery; others may seem trivial, but small things can bring down a marriage too!

I have had some fun with my Top Ten lists, so now it is time for you to do the same, if you are up for it. If you are feeling more comfortable making your Top Ten lists in a more serious vein, do so—because I realize you may not be feeling necessarily upbeat or detached enough at this point in the marital breakup process to see the humor in anything. In either case, I am now going to ask you to get busy writing down your Top Ten.

ADIOS, SAYONORA AND AUF WIEDERSEHEN

Your first list "assignment" is to jot down your Top Ten reasons for leaving the marriage (if you were the one who called the relationship off). If, on the other hand, you were the one left hanging, so to speak, you can still take a moment to identify the Top Ten things you think caused the demise of your relationship. To get you started, here are some ideas:

10. He/she was a slob.
9. He/she wouldn't do anything about his/her snoring.
8. I was getting tired of asking him/her to sleep on the couch.
7. He/she gave the term "workaholic" a whole new meaning.
6. His/her idea of a great night out was playing poker with his/her friends.
5. It was either his/her way or no way.
4. He/she always made a beeline for our bedroom to watch TV when my parents came over.
3. Cocktails every single day was not my idea of drinking socially.
2. He/she only wanted fun time with the kids, none of the real responsibility.
1. He/she criticized everything from my cooking to the color of my hair.

Now it is time for you to make your list. You may have more than just your Top Ten, but ten good reasons is enough to break up a marriage.

10. _____

9. _____

8. _____

7. _____

6. _____

5. _____

4. _____

3. _____

2. _____

1. _____

Next on my list of lists, are the Top Ten things you will not put up with again in a future mate. Once again, to get your mental juices flowing, here are some suggestions:

10. Cheating on me, even once.
9. Slacking off on commitments to make the household responsibilities a 50/50 proposition.
8. Refusing to discuss our differences.
7. Putting me down in front of friends and family.
6. Dishonesty about bank accounts, like the ones he/she hid from me.
5. Always counting on me to be the one to initiate sex.
4. Emotional immaturity.
3. Drinking to excess.
2. Abusing the children.
1. Hitting me.

Okay, list your Top Ten:

10. _____

9. _____

8. _____

7. _____

6. _____

5. _____

4. _____

3. _____

2. _____

1. _____

EVERYTHING MUST CHANGE

"I'm going to stop spending on things I can't afford and start sticking up for myself rather than allow someone to make me question my self-worth," said Elizabeth, a 20-something coquettish soon-to-be single mom, *"and listen to my head rather than my heart next time!"*

"You go, girl!" Marnie could hardly contain herself. She had seen her closest friend take emotional abuse continually for six years and was glad to learn Elizabeth had finally gotten up the nerve to leave her husband, *"It's about time."*

"Yup."

◆   ◆   ◆

Unshaven, exhausted, and furious over his ex's claim that he had been neglecting their two children during his visitation weekends, Fred stood close to the mirror over the bathroom sink in his apartment and began to rant, "And another thing, you lying (bleep), you are the one who left them standing outside the movie theater waiting for you to pick them up for over an hour, and you're the one who has no money to buy them birthday presents but can buy yourself a new Chevy Blazer, and you're the one who makes promises to them that you never keep

and thennnnnnn has the nerve to tell them we never loved each other."
He was turning red from running out of air. "And, I might add, you
are fat, lazy, self-centered, shallow, unable to carry on an intelligent
conversation, and you are not the center of the universe!"

As we move on and through difficult relationships, we find
things we want to change and things we know we must change,
just like those Elizabeth confided to her best friend, Marnie. In
our second scenario, Fred let us in on what he would have said
if only it would have been appropriate to go off on his ex (it
never is) expressing his innermost thoughts and feelings. He was
smart not to do so, for it would have probably started a War-of-
No-Return. More grief is not what he needed, but venting his
frustrations was. Staring into the mirror and letting loose can just
be good therapy!

Writing down the Top Ten things you would change before
entering into another relationship is a very good idea, and that
is your next assignment. Also, finding ways to blow off steam
without jeopardizing your dignity or starting a war is another
of your assignments in this section.

As depicted in our first scene in this segment, Elizabeth
resolved to make some meaningful changes. While many aspects
of divorce are negative, what can positively emerge from the
ashes is the wish to make changes or to refuse to tolerate the
things in a marriage that left you so unhappy.

Elizabeth may have had more changes she wished to make,
but for now I am going to share with you a list from another
individual, a male friend of mine who shared with me the Top
Ten things he would like to change. Soon I will ask you to do a
little introspection and make a list of your own. For now here's
his:

10. To be more in touch with my real feelings.
 9. Trade less work at the office for more time on a
    relationship.
 8. Taper off my excessive behavior patterns.
 7. Spend more time listening and less time talking.
 6. Let go of the need to always win.
 5. Take my children's feelings more into account.

4. Take better care of myself (diet, weight, exercise).
3. Quit gambling, once and for all.
2. Make an effort to socialize more.
1. Let go of the need to control other people. (Big hurrah for my clients!)

If you do not have a full ten to make up your list of things you would like to change about yourself, include instead at least the things you would like to improve upon. Take your time with this one:

10. _____

9. _____

8. _____

7. _____

6. _____

5. _____

4. _____

3. _____

2. _____

1. _____

The next list affords you the opportunity to vent. I am now asking you to make your Top Ten list of things you would like to say to your ex if only you could. While this is somewhat similar to those things you ought not to say to your ex, this list of what you would say if only you could, *ala* Fred to the mirror, is what I am asking for. The example list I put together—the one to get you thinking—is actually a compilation of suggestions from both friends and clients. Get ready to organize your thoughts for your Top Ten list in this category will immediately follow:

10. Get a life!
9. I never could stand your taste in music; it's corny.
8. I hope you get what you have coming to you.
7. You're a complete phony.

6. I am so sorry I wasted all those years on you.
5. I can't wait to see the look on your face when I show up with someone else.
4. I sure won't miss anything about you, especially your cooking.
3. You have a big ego, but nothing to back it up with.
2. I wish your new husband lots of luck because he's going to need it.
1. If I never see you again, it will be too soon.

Ready? Though I am suggesting you devise your own Top Ten list, if you have only one particular thing you want to say that "says it all," go ahead and use all ten spaces to write it! That will give your one would-be comment more emphasis. Let's get started:

10. _____

9. _____

8. _____

7. _____

6. _____

5. _____

4. _____

3. _____

2. _____

1. _____

YOUR EXIT INNER VIEW

Before calling it quits, I wanted to suggest you also take some time to consider whether or not you might wish to save your marriage or relationship. Since it would be important to identify "why" it would be beneficial to do so, I am now asking that you make a list of your Top Ten Reasons for staying together. I thought it might be therapeutic to make one list that is serious and the other that reflects your sense of humor. To get you started I have provided two samples, one for each list.

Serious Reasons

10. I couldn't live this lifestyle on my own.
9. We have so much in common.
8. I like and respect him/her.
7. The passion we have for one another has never diminished.
6. We have an incredible chemistry.
5. I love the way he treats the children.
4. We share the very same values.
3. He/she has great integrity.
2. I can always depend on him/her.
1. We have excellent communication.

Humorous Reasons

10. Who else will laugh at my jokes?
9. I don't think anyone else can put up with my early morning crankiness.
8. I can always beat him/her at Trivial Pursuit.
7. He/she understands the word "workaholic."
6. He/she tells me my wrinkles give me "character."
5. He/she is the only person I know who can humor my mother.
4. Who else is not going to chastise me for running out of gas on the freeway?
3. If I leave him/her I will have nothing to complain about!
2. Who else will still look sexy in that goofy hat?
1. Most single people out there may be even more neurotic than my wife/husband.

Now it is time to make your own lists. It is also the perfect time for you to reflect on the pros and cons of your marriage or relationship and decide whether it would be prudent to give it one more chance before walking away. To help make that assessment, go ahead now and fill in the blanks below. You do not need to limit yourself to only ten!

Serious Top Ten Reasons to Give it One More Chance

10. _____
 9. _____
 8. _____
 7. _____
 6. _____
 5. _____
 4. _____
 3. _____
 2. _____
 1. _____

Humorous Top Ten Reasons to Give it One More Chance

10. _____
 9. _____
 8. _____
 7. _____
 6. _____
 5. _____
 4. _____
 3. _____
 2. _____
 1. _____

TEACH YOUR CHILDREN WELL

One of the last lists in this chapter has to do with the qualities you would most like your children to learn from you. I am hopeful you will have more than ten, but to list the Top Ten lessons you wish to pass on to them is more important than you may think. You may want to revisit this list often, for it may keep you grounded on those days when wars are waging with your ex and you are running low on resolve. It is also a list you may wish to revise from time to time. Know this: What each of us teaches our children shapes their lives dramatically and permanently. To provide an example, I took my favorites from several lists submitted by those who wished to volunteer them. These are the qualities they most wanted to pass on:

10. Honesty.
 9. Poise under pressure.
 8. Not giving up what you believe in.
 7. Ability to make lemonade out of lemons.
 6. Dignity at all costs.
 5. Self-respect.
 4. Reaching for the stars.
 3. Consideration of other people's feelings.
 2. A strong work ethic.
 1. To love yourself.

BATTLE CRIES

As a bonus, I wanted to include just one more list. I hope it leaves you thinking about the Three Typical Wars. It is meant to offer some sage advice about engaging, or choosing not to engage, in them. Please feel free to make a similar list. Such items make for good inspiration reminders (put them somewhere handy) as you trudge through the trenches of divorce. Here they are:

10. "Victory belongs to the persevering." *Napoleon Bonaparte.*
 9. "The battle, sir, is not to the strong alone; it is to the vigilant, the active, the brave ..." *Patrick Henry.*
 8. "War is cruelty. There's no use trying to reform it, the crueler it is the sooner it will be over." *General William Tecumseh Sherman.*
 7. "Never in the field of human conflict was so much owed by so many to so few." *Prime Minister Winston Churchill.*
 6. "We make war that we live in peace." *Aristotle.*

5. "In war there is no substitute for victory." *General Douglas MacArthur.*
4. "It's no use saying, 'we are doing our best.' You have got to succeed in doing what is necessary." *Sir Winston Churchill.*
3. "If you don't have enough artillery, quit." *General Richard Cavazos.*
2. "It is the unconquerable nature of man and not the nature of the weapon he uses that ensures victory." *General George S. Patton.*
1. "Once we have a war there is only one thing to do. It must be won. For defeat brings worse things than any that can ever happen in war." *Ernest Hemingway.*

My goal in this chapter has been to provide some wisdom, enlightenment, inspiration and, above all, a reminder to keep your sense of humor intact.

Take the liberty of posting your Top Ten lists where you will view them frequently. Often it is a reminder or two of important messages or a bit of humor that can get any of us through a difficult day. Divorce certainly has its share of them!

My final chapter is an important one because it sums up the overall lessons in this book: How to get, gain, assume and maintain control. Moving forward now, I ask you to pay close attention to the messages in this final chapter—they are some of the most important in the book.

Chapter Eleven

GETTING, GAINING, ASSUMING, AND MAINTAINING CONTROL

Tiffany twisted the Kleenex between her fingers, nervously. She kept her hands in her lap.

The attorneys and the rent-a-judge had left the room for a private discussion.

Alone with David now, she felt extremely uncomfortable.

"You look like hell, Tiffany," David sneered, slithering lower in his chair, and assuming an even more macho posture. He raised his eyebrows slightly, suggestively, "Not sleeping well?"

Tiffany pulled resolve from deep within. Her voice was level and strong. Completely shrugging off his question, she said, "Oh, before I forget, can you give this to Jenna when you pick her up from school today? She wanted it for the weekend." Business-like, Tiffany gently slid the small Barbie-doll makeup case across the large conference table.

David reluctantly reached for it. Then tauntingly, "I asked if you were sleeping well, Tiff."

Looking him squarely in the eye and speaking each word slowly, deliberately, and without malice, she leaned forward bravely, "That... is...none...of...your...business, David. Enough. We're here to settle some practical issues, nothing more."

GETTING TO THE BOTTOM

A disappointed David sat by helplessly, realizing he no longer had power over his former wife—control he had not only enjoyed, but relished.

They had been locked in an Emotional War for two years.

Each time they met, David had managed to unnerve Tiffany with ambiguous sexual innuendos—such innuendos hit her "C" (control) spot. He attacked her with what had been the couple's pet phrases, the ones that Tiffany had gone weak in the knees over, many times, after they fought over his infidelity.

Not sleeping well was one of those phrases.

This query, often whispered in her ear as he closed in from behind to embrace her after she had turned away from him in a fit of rage, was David's "come on." It was what he used to entice Tiffany into bed with him.

Tiffany had always taken the bait.

She had let him know early on that sex between them had always helped her sleep exceptionally well, particularly on those nights when she had been stressed with work, or encountered problems with their hyperactive daughter, or when she was riddled with anger over what she suspected were her husband's transgressions. She also let him know that she found him irresistible, despite those times when she threatened to leave him, once and for all. And she made those threats often during their twelve-year marriage. Yet, when she heard him utter those three little words, she had abruptly changed her mind.

Taking her prisoner of (Emotional) War and using sex to subdue her, or make her surrender, was David's weapon of choice. He had mouthed the words (not sleeping well) to her most recently from across the room at their daughter's dance recital. Though they had been separated and going through the throes of divorce for two years, David still tried to seduce Tiffany at every opportunity. Though she resisted, it was painful. She often found herself lying awake at night in a state of passive longing.

But things had suddenly changed.

During this tenth settlement conference (David was not about to let go) I noticed that the cavalier attitude he had worn like a comfortable overcoat from the first time I met him had mysteriously vanished. He had pulled himself up to the table, was sitting straighter, and was grumpily straightening both his tie and jacket lapels. It was an amusing sight. The guy who, moments earlier, had strode into the room in his best "Russell Crowe," was now reminiscent of *Sesame Street's* "Oscar the Grouch." He was noticeably pouting. His irritation level escalated until it reached an irrepressible high. Then in a sudden fit of anger, David stood and wordlessly charged from the room.

The judge called a recess.

There never was another settlement conference with a judge or another hearing. David's attorney and I settled the case. My client had won, big. Not so much in terms of monetary gain, but in reclaiming herself. She had finally managed to escape the holding-cell of her husband's Emotional torment, his sexuality.

GETTING REAL

It had taken time and work and a relentless determination, but Tiffany finally had control. She admitted it was not easy for her, but once she had done it, she realized she had broken the spell; she was fully in control of her emotions, her moods and her self. It was a momentous victory!

Later I asked her what had been the turning point. She told me she came to understand that her only emotional salvation was to win the Emotional War. She could not move forward with her life without it. But coming to grips with that required that she get control—not of David, as she imagined would be the case if she were to prevail, but of herself. It had been a difficult journey up a long and steep mountainside, but she relentlessly set about to claw her way to the top, and she had. Once there, looking down on the huge canyon filled with emotional debris, Tiffany was able to gain a panoramic perspective of their perverse relationship. Only then could she confront David once and for all. And she had, on that momentous day, without anger and without judgment, calmly, with a direct "your line doesn't work anymore" approach. Tiffany no longer wanted David, in any way. It was over; and for Tiffany, so was the war.

GO GET IT

There would have been no war at all during the divorce if Tiffany had not enlisted in it, she finally said to me.

"Yes," I said sympathetically and sincerely, "it wasn't so much what David was doing to you as it was the tapes playing inside your head. Once you can turn them off, or reprogram them, you're on your way to getting control."

"That's true. I can see that now," she said. "I suppose that's what made it easier for me, an understanding that David had no real power over me." She sat silent for a moment and then said, "Wished I had gotten control sooner, earlier...."

"It doesn't matter," I assured her. "You have it now. That's all that matters."

To underscore that point and as a means of celebration, we opened—not a bottle of champagne—but a dictionary. Together we looked up Webster's definition of "get." It explicitly states: To come into possession of; to obtain; to go for and bring back....

If you recall the types of exes listed in Chapter Three, David fit perfectly into the "Manipulator" slot. He was clever, charming and, oh yes, often seductive. Manipulator that he was, David had also hired away from Tiffany the couple's housekeeper, accountant and gardener. Last time Tiffany had spent a day at her favorite spa (a treat in which she indulged only twice a year), David had mysteriously appeared.

Getting control for Tiffany meant cutting all ties with former service providers and employees, and that included her favorite spa. Little by little, she had made those changes. Her only vulnerability the last time we met was with their daughter, Jenna. Fortunately, Tiffany, with the help of her therapist, continues to skillfully navigate through those rough waters.

GIVE TO GET

Are you like Tiffany? Do you need to get control? Let's find out. Jot down answers to the following questions:

1. Do you still feel an attraction toward your ex?
   Yes ____
   No ____

2. Are you affected negatively by the things he/she says to you?
   Yes ____
   No ____

3. In any way, do you feel your ex has a "hold" on you emotionally? (Sexual attraction, self-esteem issues ...)
   Yes ____
   No ____

4. Do your moods largely depend upon how you are feeling about the way your ex treats you?
   Yes ____
   No ____

5. When you come in contact with your ex how do you feel?
   Unusually uncomfortable ____
   Somewhat uncomfortable ____
   Never uncomfortable ____

6. In any way, do you feel your ex has the ability to "push your buttons"?
   Yes ____
   No ____

If the answer is "yes" to any of these first six questions, you have work to do. Unless you answered "never uncomfortable" in question five, you have to strive to come to terms with why it is you feel unusually or somewhat uncomfortable when you are in the presence of your ex. From there you need to overcome the perception that your ex has any type of hold on you now, nor will he/she have any hold on you in the future. While you are asking yourself the six questions above, also ask whether or not you are currently engaged in any of the wars described in Chapter Five (Emotional), Chapter Six (Psychological), Chapter Seven (Legal), or Chapter Eight (Internal Wars).

If the answer is "yes" to involvement in any of the four major war-types, go back and reread those chapters and do the tasks I suggested, because you must come to grips with the reality that, at the present time, you have no control. So, control is what you need to get. Only then can you move on to a more productive and happy life.

"Let the children live with him. Go ahead, tell the judge he can have the sole legal and physical custody he's been fighting for, and I mean SOLE, legal and physical custody!" Then the very calm mother—a calmness I had never seen—went on to add, "If it's better for Scott and Sierra to cut all ties with me, then, fine, I won't even exercise my visitation rights. I can't put them through this anymore."

"But that's asking a great deal of you, Ramona," I told her, ready to go to battle on her behalf. I was certain I would prevail in court. "You better take more time to think about this."

Calmly and very clearly, Ramona said, "I HAVE thought about this! I cannot do this anymore. Really, I can't. The current arrangement isn't doing anyone any good."

"You're entitled to joint custody, even primary custody," I reminded her.

"Yes, I understand all that," she continued very calmly, "but the court can't make my life peaceful, nor can it protect my children from the horror of the past five years. I've come to the conclusion that only I can help facilitate that. Please, I'm begging you, draw up the appropriate paperwork."

Reluctantly, I did.

NO PAIN, NO GAIN

Ramona was a beautiful, smart 30-something actress, a successful one, whose life had turned into a living hell when driven to divorce her possessively jealous husband. Spencer began to engage in a Psychological War to beat all wars! He not only convinced the children that their mother was a bad person, but he also tried to make them believe she was mentally unstable, out to harm them, and did not love them. As bloody battles go, Spencer had done an admirable job to create tremendous emotional and psychological carnage. Scott was 8 and Sierra, 10. The grave psychological damage was beginning to take its toll on both children.

Ramona and Spencer had been married four years and at war for five years, since their divorce. Ramona wanted desperately to end her marriage in an amicable way, but Spencer was an all-or-nothing guy. So far he had managed to get Ramona to fork over most of the couple's belongings and more than his rightful share of the property. It was not enough. He wanted the children, too, completely to himself; and he was relentless, stopping at nothing to get them away from her.

My client had been to therapists, mediators, and relatives —everyone she could recruit for help. Yet in the end, she felt she had no recourse but to give up in order to gain.

Ramona and I talked a great deal about control. She shared with me that she felt she had been in an exhausting tug 'o war with no end in sight, other than letting go of the metaphorical rope. "If there is no struggle, there is no war, right?" she asked one day, finally breaking down in tears. "I mean … I don't know what I mean anymore."

The torment on her face looked like that of a victim in an Alfred Hitchcock thriller, one where the leading lady is staggering aimlessly down a dark highway in the middle of the night trying desperately to get away from her predator. After five years of agony, I could see Ramona was fast approaching a mental breakdown.

I had enormous respect for Ramona because I knew how much she adored her children. Thoughts of Ramona never seeing them again were difficult to ponder.

However, the only way she believed she could gain in Spencer's sinister game of "I'll destroy you and I don't care if the children go down with you," was to completely let go. Ramona was entitled to live her life, something she had been unable to do since the two had separated. That, too, was a factor in her decision.

GAINING STRENGTH THROUGH WISDOM

In Ramona's case, her control issue was not one of helplessly stagnating in a state of vulnerability like Tiffany. In contrast, she had a great sense of self and Spencer knew that. He was well aware he could not disturb her equilibrium...unless he used the only weapon of mass destruction available to him against her: The children. He knew such a tack was probably the only way he could take her down psychologically.

It has been my experience as a legal bystander that often when spurned lovers are angry, they can do the unthinkable; especially when they come to realize that they cannot penetrate another's feelings. Such was the case with Spencer. He could not jostle her emotionally because she had no feelings whatsoever for him, except disgust. Knowing she was repelled by him, Spencer felt the same helplessness a person experiences when firing a gun at someone who is wearing a bullet-proof vest—the rounds powerlessly bounce off the intended target. As a result, the frustration of the shooter escalates and so does the intensity of the attacks. Ergo, Psychological Warfare. If you took my suggestion early on in the book and watched "War of the Roses," you know exactly what I am talking about!

GAINING ON IT

During my many years of practice, I have taken note that once I see the Emotional War cannot be fought (because it takes two to fight it), one or both of the spouses often up the ante—they opt to launch the harmful psychological attack as a substitute. Surely, Spencer felt angst knowing Ramona had no emotional attachment to him any longer. In order to get some reaction from her—any reaction—he would have to do her one better. That meant using the children against her, which he knew would dismantle her mentally. Yes, Spencer knew that would beat Ramona senseless.

In the end, and in her situation, Ramona believed it was the wiser choice to give up the children—for everyone's benefit—in order to gain control of the situation. For if she walked off the battlefield, it would be impossible for Spencer to do anything more to hurt her—impossible for him to continue messing with Ramona's mind. In a valiant effort to end the chaos, Ramona made the ultimate sacrifice for peace and for her children's peace.

In Ramona's estimation there was no other choice.

As Ramona and I thumbed the pages of Webster's, we found several definitions of the word "gain." The one we both felt most aptly fit her circumstances read: "An improvement or advantage." To gain also meant, according to the dictionary, "to outdo the competition."

That said, please do not misunderstand me: Ramona did not want to win the Psychological War at all costs. She did not want to outdo anyone in a Psychological disaster; she wanted to end it. With nothing left to fight over, she wisely realized, the war was, in effect, over. You cannot attack a target that is no longer within range.

As an interesting footnote, though I will not go into detail, two years after Ramona made her decision, Spencer was arrested during a drug smuggling sting and went to prison. Needless to say, the children came to live with Ramona. Last I had heard, all three were thriving in a loving and healthy relationship.

If you are currently engaged in a Psychological War— whether you are the victim or the perpetrator, find a way to end it as I stated in Chapter Six. As in most divorce situations, the big victory is always peace of mind. With Psychological Warfare there can be no peace. Psychological Warfare is the deadliest and cruelest of all.

GAINING INSIGHT

Are you currently embroiled in a Psychological War and in need of gaining on it? Answer these questions to find out:

1. Do you spend a good deal of time trying to outsmart your ex?
   Yes ____
   No ____

2. Are you constantly trying to "decipher" what your ex spouse meant by that (comment, threat, innuendo)?
   Yes ____
   No ____

3. Have you come to accept that being worried, fearful and overly-concerned when it comes to dealing with your ex is just the way it is going to be?
   Yes ____
   No ____

4. Are you constantly thinking about plans and strategies to avert psychological damage, but feel you can never get a foothold?
   Yes ____
   No ____

5. Do you have moments when you second-guess your sanity?
   Yes ____
   No ____

Even one yes means you need to gain on the control front. Start in small ways. If necessary, revisit Chapter Six and your worksheet. A careful review of the answers will bring clarity in the area you most need to gain control. For example, whether you classified yourself as an Attacker or a Defender, do you find a certain enjoyment in the process of getting even? Do you obsess about the state of the war? Are you planning an attack or concocting ways to stave off an attack? Again, if you are still answering any of the questions affirmatively, the idea is to reverse the process.

GAIN PRAISE

Applaud yourself for every step that moves you forward and points toward your progress. For instance, if you have been mindful of the damage the Psychological War in which you have been engaged has done to others, and had not even considered that until now, that is a big gain. If you are in counseling to get a handle on your penchant for engaging in Psychological Warfare, or going to therapy to find a way to extricate yourself from the war game, that is also a gain. Gain in my estimation means obtaining an advantage in terms of working toward control. In Ramona's case, it meant giving everything up in order to gain her peace of mind and reclaim her life. For others, gaining may be a progressive process. Often you cannot expect to get control until you make incremental gains toward it. Inching your way to control will eventually get you control.

Tad walked into the courtroom, his legs carrying him, but barely. They felt leaden... It was as if, he told me later, he was plodding his way through a swamp.

It was the big day. He and his former wife had gone several rounds in mediation and had made no progress at all during eighteen months of purported negotiations.

She wanted physical custody of their three children and the lion's share of his business, claiming she had put him through college, graduate school, and after that, had helped him run his sports medicine clinic by establishing and building the business' customer base. She had also given up her career as a model to stay home and raise their children, though at that time in their live, Tad continued to enjoy the limelight as a former football star. When they finally opened the clinic, she also served on staff for no pay. It was time for Stella to cash in. Or, at least, that is the way she saw it.

When Tad's ex entered the courtroom, she made a grand entrance. The former NFL cheerleader was attired in an unbeatable UmaThurman-dressed-to-kill-winter-white Anne Klein suit.

She confidently followed her attorney to the plaintiff's table, her head held high, the obvious tilt of her nose leading the way. She looked like she had just stepped off the cover of a fashion magazine. Everyone in the courtroom was struck by her.

Even the judge.

Tad had been easily intimidated by Stella, not only throughout their fifteen year marriage, but also during the entire mediation process.

The couple had been unable to resolve their issues and the case had escalated to a full court battle—a Legal War.

Stella felt she had the upper hand. She was not about to let go of her divorce "objectives," and knowing Tad as she did, she felt she could grind him into submission. If she couldn't, she was counting on the court to do it for her. Up to this point, she refused to accept defeat.

As Stella began to sit, she shot Tad a "catch me if you can" look.

Tad sat straight in his chair. He appeared to be unaffected by her entrance. The look on his face did not, in the least, give him away. Inwardly he was feeling demoralized, hopeless and shaken. Outwardly, he looked as tough as he did as an NFL linebacker. He looked to be a formidable foe.

ASSUMING A POSITION

Tad kept his poise under tremendous pressure during the courtroom hearing, but had also made valiant attempts to do so during the many mediation sessions he attended in his quest to settle the couple's issues. In truth, he did not feel in control of his thoughts and feelings, but he "assumed a position" that projected an image of control. This, he told me, when the case was finally heard and ruled upon, was how he had survived it all.

Perhaps it was his many years on the football field that helped—faking out the other side shortly before the snap of the ball. He knew he would have to come across as solid, stable and unfettered, even though he was gripped by fear. When we first met, however, I think Tad had lost sight of the skill that had kept him psyched during many a football contest.

"To take for granted" and "suppose to be true" were just two of the Webster definitions that I read to Tad one rainy Tuesday afternoon, describing what "assume" meant, as we prepared for our first mediation session. "I don't know if I can get control," he said, his shoulders slumped over, his head shaking slowly from side-to-side. "I feel after all this time—all this arguing and going back and forth and the prospect of one day winding up in court—that the circumstances surrounding me are completely controlling my life. I feel I have no say; actually, I feel I'm completely out of control."

"Control isn't out there," I explained, making an indirect reference to Stella, "It's something you have deep within you."

"I don't feel that..." Tad struggled for the right words "...sense of being together at all."

Wanting to meet him on his turf and talk to him in terms I knew he would understand, I approached him like the gruff football coach would a dejected player during a locker room pep talk. "Well, we're going to court tomorrow so you better talk yourself into it."

"Talk myself into it?"

"Yes, assume that you are in control."

He sat silently for a moment, then shook his head, as if he understood the gravity of my words. He knew he would have to pull himself together and come across as steady and solid.

I shared with Tad what I will share with you: A very interesting "performance" trick. It is a technique a dear friend of mine shared with me. This friend is an improvisational comedy teacher and director (and former performer). Improv comedy, of course, is where a troupe of actors takes to the stage fielding random audience requests. It is the responsibility of the improv comedy player to act on those requests in the moment. She told me that the quick wit of the players she directs does not come easily. In "mental boot camp" they have to learn several rules. One of them is "commitment." The improv comedy players' understanding of commitment is to willingly accept any audience suggestion given to them and act it out with no hesitation. Someone might shout out an impossible suggestion, or one that seems difficult to act on, yet the improv players do their best to execute that request. They do so with confidence and poise even if they are experiencing trepidation with regard to just how they will fulfill the assignment! "The audience only knows you're uncomfortable if you let your discomfort or concern show," she explained to me. "But my players step up to the plate every time, putting forth an attitude of complete commitment and control, even if they feel otherwise at that exact moment."

Tad seemed to grasp the concept.

"Fake it, till you make it," was a cliché I wanted Tad to keep repeating to himself.

You, like Tad, may need to pretend to be in control—to psych yourself—in order to get and gain control.

ASSUMING THE WORST

I tell many of my clients to keep the same thought process as Tad—to tell themselves they are in control. Though some clients, like Tad, are feeling delicate and fragile, they can come across as strong and confident in the presence of others, if they are focused on putting forth a demeanor that demonstrates that front. There is much to be said for the dynamics between people who are going through the divorce process and the impressions they make and leave with others. Very often the one who comes across as relaxed, poised and confident is the party that looks good in the eyes of the judge. I have seen many a soon-to-be-divorcee lose it in the courtroom! There have been those who blurt things out (things better left unsaid), those who cower at the sight of their ex (or the judge), and those who wear their emotions on their sleeve.

I am not suggesting you be someone other than who you really are—I am just pointing out that your fate can be decided by how you come across in the courtroom, during mediation, in four-way conferences, or in the presence of your ex. So if you make the assumption you are in control, you will most likely appear to be in control. Such a supposition can very well grow on you. One of the twentieth century's pop psychologists of the PSI World self-help program, Thomas Willhite, used to say, "To think is to create. What are you thinking now?"

MAKING OTHER ASSUMPTIONS

Assuming control may have different relevance and meaning to you altogether. Sometimes assuming control can mean projecting a demeanor that says I mean business and you can't rattle my cage; but it can also mean taking over when the situation or circumstance around you gets out of control. Such situations can run the gamut from your ex telling you off in front of the children to your friends or in-laws attempting to meddle in the affairs of your messy divorce (as you drop the children for a holiday function).

Webster's second definition of "assume" is "to arrogate (claim) to oneself; to usurp (take over)."

I have had many clients who have had to bear the brunt of taking over when they certainly did not feel like it. Some clients were so wrapped up in the aggravation and trauma of the divorce that all they wanted was to wallow in their misery—have someone take over for them. But many times that is a luxury one does not get! If their significant others are behaving badly, if the children are unruly, if family members are asserting themselves in matters that are none of their business, someone has to step up and take the reins. In my years of practice, I have known many clients who wanted to act out; who wanted to metaphorically jump off an emotional cliff, too, but circumstances dictated that they must keep their cool. I have seen people verbally attack one another in mediation, trade looks that could kill in the courtroom, and behave childishly or foolishly in front of the children. With emotions running high through such an ordeal as divorce, it is easy to go from in control to out of control with the flip of a switch.

PRESUMING TO ASSUME

If you are continually exposed to contentious circumstances as a result of becoming embroiled in an Emotional, Psychological or Legal War, it may be time for you to be the "bigger" and the "stronger" person; it may be time for you to assume control. Try to stay above the fray, though I know it is hard to do when you are so emotionally, psychologically or financially vulnerable. But I assure you that you will look back one day and be proud of the way you dealt with a difficult situation, if you handle it well now.

That day in court with Tad was a prime example. He resolved to keep his composure and to assume control of his emotions and the turmoil that was going on inside him and around him. (Fortunately, he had had lots of practice during football games and countless mediation sessions!) As the courtroom proceedings got underway, when Stella caught wind of how composed Tad appeared, she suddenly burst into a fit of anger. She completely lost control when the court awarded Tad joint custody of the children and half of the business assets. She stormed from the courtroom even though the judge ordered her to be seated.

Whether you are assuming control to convey a confident posture or asserting yourself to bring calm and reason to an otherwise unruly situation, your ability to assume control is one more way to get and gain control.

Here are a few questions to determine if you come across as confident and composed when it comes time to impress others that you are deftly in control:

1. Do you appear submissive, downtrodden, nervous or uncomfortable in mediation sessions, settlement conferences, or before the judge?
   Yes _____
   No _____

2. When you encounter your ex in any of the above settings, do you suddenly lose your composure?
   Yes _____
   No _____

3. In the company of others, when someone brings up something your ex has said or done, do you begin to display body language or attitude changes that make you appear less than collected?
   Yes _____
   No _____

4. If you are feeling ruffled in the presence of your ex, his family, his friends, your children or others, are you still able to display a serene countenance?
   Yes _____
   No _____

If you answered "no" to the first three questions, and "yes" to question four, I will assume that you are coming across as convincing in the assuming control department. "Yes" to any of the first three questions, and "no" to question four, is a dead giveaway that you are in dire need of assuming control. Remember what I told Tad: The impressions you make upon others are very important when engaged in any one of the Three Wars. If your opponent thinks he or she has the upper hand because your demeanor makes you look vulnerable, or the judge perceives you as uncontrollable, and opposing counsel sees you as weak, it may work against you. If you have not assumed control, it is now time to do so.

Here is another set of questions designed to test how confident you are in taking the helm when everyone else and everything around you is losing control:

1. When there is a sudden calamity, e.g., someone loses his/her temper, the children throw a fit, your former mother-in-law threatens you, or you are served with court papers, do you handle the situation calmly and smoothly?
   Yes ____
   No ____

2. When your ex embarrasses you in front of the children, your new significant other or his/her new girlfriend or spouse, do you roll with the punches and keep the peace?
   Yes ____
   No ____

3. Though your ex has attempted to keep the war going (whichever type it is), do you step up and do what needs to be done, sensibly and rationally?
   Yes ____
   No ____

If you answered "yes" to all of the above, it is apparent that you are one who is assuming control despite the temptation to get caught up in the chaos that typically surrounds any one of the events inherent in one of the Three Wars. Taking over and handling a situation appropriately and with calm is critical to assuming control.

"I JUST ASSUMED...."

When it comes to grappling with assuming control, I have one all-encompassing edict I pass on to all of my clients. I tell them to always remember to respond, not react. I got this advice from one of my favorite forensic accountants. I even have a yellow Post-it in the pencil drawer of my desk saying, "Do not react. Respond." It is natural for anyone going through such a highly stressful ordeal, such as a divorce or a custody battle, to react to each and every incident that is negative. In the realm of contentious family law disputes, reactions are understandable. Although sometimes it is nearly impossible not to react, it is imperative that you do not. Respond in an appropriate way. This might mean choosing wisely your reply to your ex, or asking your attorney to respond sensibly on your behalf. Under no circumstances should you ever resort to histrionics as a means of "returning the ball," or play tit-for-tat, because this clearly illustrates that your ex has the upper hand. When you respond rather than react, it is you who is in control of your emotions, moods and well-being, not the other party.

For greater clarity, please keep handy the following Webster definitions. One such meaning for the word "react" is, "to act in a manner contrary to some preceding act." However, on the other hand, an explicit definition of the word "respond" is, "to give an answer; to reply."

WE ASSUME

If you are at all familiar with the parlance used in legal matters, you will know that the word "respond" is used constantly. In the case with Tad, he was the Respondent, while Stella was the Petitioner. You will note he was not referred to as the "Reactor"! It is common in most family law disputes for the word "response" to be bandied about—we are often asked to file a response within a given period of time, for instance, or respond to a letter or request by opposing counsel.

To me it is vitally important that you realize how much control has to do with making the choice between responding to something as opposed to reacting to it.

In order to appear to be in control, you need to assume that you are and assume that you will remain in that state! To assume control can also mean reclaiming or taking charge when the circumstances around you are spinning out of control.

When it comes to the assumption of control you may find the word has dual meaning and double purpose to you. For example, you may on a regular basis find it necessary to put yourself across as cool, calm and collected. Simultaneously, you may also be required to assert yourself at pivotal times to take back a situation that is seemingly out of control.

Do not forget that when it comes to a Legal War, like Tad's, the court can often be the entity assuming control (especially if the case is in the hands of such judges as the "Heard-It-Alls" or the "Hammers"). If need be, revisit the list you made in Chapter Seven, the one that chronicled why it would be best to forego a Legal War (especially if you were the "Attacker"). If you are a "Defender" in a Legal War, glance over the list of suggestions on how to stave off a Legal War—the ones that I provided, as well as the suggestions on how to "take cover." Doing your homework in Chapter Seven is an advantageous way to begin to assume control of your situation.

January 12—Dear Diary: Another major scene today! Larissa tells Remington's teacher I don't help him with his homework. Yeah, right! I swear: Her nose is growing longer by the minute! Going to my Zen place to tune out her craziness. What is her problem?! My rational side saved the day! Quick thinking. Told Mrs. Nelson had to take emergency client call. Will call tomorrow to talk to her about Remington's homework assignments for the weekend. Need 24 hours to calm down.

February 23—Dear Diary: Picked up Remington from Larissa's at 4 p.m. Flaunted her new beau again. Like I care. She's pathetic. Remington wasn't ready...again. Who is she kidding? What a game player. Not fair to Remington. He looked stressed. Will ask Dr. Payton what to say to Remington when he gets like this. Geez, will it ever end? Jacuzzi and meditation at 9 p.m. to sleep better. Proud of me. Exactly six months since last Sharper Image shopping binge. Treat myself to double scoop Rocky Road tomorrow after work. Deserve it.

May 10—Dear Diary: Two more days till divorce is final! Yippee! Dr. Payton tells me today not to expect Larissa's scene-making to disappear. Says it might get worse.

Could it get any worse? Guess so. Rem says her beau dumped her. Probably couldn't take her lies. Rem doing much better. Seems to be accepting the divorce. Says he loves us both. Told him he should and I was glad he did. Can't wait for time to pass. Seven more years until Rem is 18. Counting the days...Lost three more pounds. Only eight more to go!

MAINTENANCE PROGRAM

These diary entries were made by Fenton, a pleasant, good-natured, 40-ish real estate agent who wanted to get on with his life. The couple seemed happy according to Fenton. However, when the bottom fell out of the real estate market so did the foundation of their marriage. Larissa was accustomed to spending lots of money on clothes, art and furnishings. When Fenton told her she would have to cut back on her spending she became defiant and began spending recklessly. Her spending and his excesses in food and drink brought the marriage to a final halt after a decade and one son. At first, Fenton was heartbroken. His manner of coping was to over-do in just about every department. To match Larissa's spending, Fenton began a sudden affair with Sharper Image. He could not stop buying "gadgets and gizmos." He could not stop from downing a case of Chardonnay every week, either. He also gained 35 pounds from too many visits to Godiva Chocolatier.

Fenton was at war with the Enemies Within as he desperately sought to ward off the frustrations Larissa caused him. She used their son as a weapon in her Emotional, Psychological and Legal Wars. But Fenton was fairly level in how he handled each battle. Yet when she pushed Fenton's buttons both emotionally and psychologically, he tended to overdo. All indications were that she planned a protracted Legal War. Fenton needed to find a way to keep his excesses under control.

When I first met him, Fenton was in need of help. He had to assume, get and gain control.

I watched him through the control-quest process. It took considerable time and an iron will to get and gain it, but he had. Intense therapy with Dr. Payton and a genuine wish to get on with his life, coupled with an intense love for his son, got him going down the right road. But Fenton was not out of the woods. He had managed to dispose of his Sharper Image catalogues, replace wine in the fridge with Snapple, and cut back on carbs and fat in order to get his belt buckled in its familiar notch. But staying at an even keel would take more than a temporary fix.

Control was what he had assumed, gotten and gained, yes. Now the challenge was to maintain it: A real and ongoing contest for many who pass through the treacherous portals of the House of Divorce. What I try to impress upon my clients, like Fenton and all the others, is that control will probably always be an issue for them. Whether they are trying to manage their feelings or their psychological well-being, or trying to keep from creating situations where they need to depend on legal counsel or the courts to handle their differences, or battling the Enemies Within, they must find a way to keep the inner status quo long after the dissolution is final.

Why is that so hard if you have already gotten and gained control (like Fenton)? Because chances are there will still be ties between you and your ex. It may be the children, family, friends in common or business associates. As such, there may always be a potential for tension and discord. Where there is tension and discord there will always be strife. Where there is strife there is a probable loss of equilibrium, and with that loss, there goes the control one may have had!

What proved instrumental in helping Fenton get and keep his grip were the things he did to keep his peace of mind intact. He kept a diary. Odd you may think for a middle-aged man. Not really. If writing down thoughts for Fenton was cathartic for him, then hats off to Fenton for finding a productive way to stay in control. What was important for him, and what is important for you, is to find a way to maintain control once you get it. But beware, that diary could be "discovered" in a discovery legal war. If you keep a diary, please discuss the risks and rewards of doing so with your attorney.

Back to Webster's for a moment. Though Webster's offers several definitions since the word "maintain" has different meanings, the following is the one I believe most fits as it relates to the context of divorce and control: "...to keep unimpaired or in proper condition." When I shared this with Fenton he had one of those epiphanies—a real Ah Ha! moment.

"How can I do that?" He asked as we wrapped up the necessary details of his divorce the day we sat at the conference room table and he signed final documents. "How do I manage to maintain control?"

Because I believe that is a very personal issue, I said, "That's entirely up to you. Whatever works for you, Fenton."

I have had clients handle themselves brilliantly through the rough waters of divorce, but keeping their cool in check over a long period of time can try their patience and grind down their nerves.

I will offer you the same advice I offered Fenton and other clients. Start by finding your "Zen" place—a quiet and tranquil spot where you can retreat internally to recapture your center. I have clients who imagine themselves at the beach, others sitting peacefully beside a waterfall, some who close their eyes and picture the gentle rustling of leaves. An interesting Zen place belongs to a friend of mine: She imagines floating effortlessly on a magic carpet high above the turmoil of all the worldly things that tend to bother her. The ride is smooth and swift, she says, never turbulent or bumpy! You do not have to experience a Woo Woo or New Age moment— just use a method to calm yourself down—a method that works for you.

After you establish your mental place to go for rest, relaxation, regrouping, and rejuvenation to reclaim your "center," surround yourself with positive triggers to remind yourself that you are in control at all times. Fenton had a saying stuck on file folder labels affixed to his office telephone, his day planner, the refrigerator and the bathroom mirror. It read: Keep Gaining by Maintaining. The message has permeated his psyche. If you have reminders that signal a positive message—one that encourages you to maintain control, like Fenton, keep them handy and visible. They will provide positive reinforcement on a subconscious level. Over time, these ideas will support you when need to fall back on them.

EXTENDED WARRANTIES

There are many other methods for maintaining control, and like my advice to Fenton, it is your job to find out what they are—what works for you—and put them into play. For Fenton it was therapy for a period of time and keeping a diary of his thoughts and feelings—a place he felt safe to vent. If you do not devise a maintenance program and the wars continue to rage (which is the case for many individuals because they continue to face off with their exes), you will live a life where everything and everyone but you is in control. I know that is not what you want.

Here is one simple question to answer that will tell you whether you are maintaining control over your situation at this very moment:

1. Do you sense that no matter what happens with the chaos around you, relative to your divorce and its aftermath, that you always feel strong, centered and able to calmly handle situations as they come your way?
   Yes _____
   No _____

Obviously if the answer is "no" you have work to do. A "yes" would be a major victory, however. The reality is that for most of the clients I have counseled (especially those with children or other family ties) maintaining control is the hardest discipline to master. It requires diligence, follow through, and patience. I have had some clients answer this same question with a "sometimes." That is always good to hear; but my wish is that you manage to get, gain, assume and maintain control all of the time.

Do not forget the overriding message of this book. When it comes to divorce: It is always about control.

I'm a trophy wife.
I got the boat. I got the Porsche.
I got the house. I got the SUV...

EPILOGUE

I first want to congratulate you for working your way through this book and for finishing every assignment along the way. I realize that having done so, took time, patience, introspection, and most of all, a great deal of honesty on your part. Some questions may have been more difficult to answer than others; some assignments may have illuminated truths that were hard for you to face. But most answers to the questions, I hope, provided encouragement and inspiration.

Whatever it is the answers revealed, it is important you realize that coming to grips with where you are in relation to any one of the "Divorce Wars" is critical. Such answers pave the way for you to get, gain, assume and maintain control. The answers to the questions posed also serve to guide you with regard to knowing what appropriate strategies to employ in order to hang on to control, and also how these strategies play out in coming to *resolutions* that prevent, win or end the Divorce Wars.

Therein lies a major purpose of this book: Finding resolutions. For without them you will be stuck in the mire of divorce forever. It is resolution that ensures control.

In addition to congratulating you, I also want to acknowledge you for what it is you are currently going through. Because I deal all day with people who are faced with divorce issues, I know how much courage and resolve it actually takes to handle all the difficulties associated with the divorce process. In fact, I have come to believe that there are few things in life more all-consuming, challenging and devastating than working through a divorce. The mere journey of plodding (or for some, plotting) through the day-to-day practical and emotional issues associated with divorce is no easy feat. Committing yourself to handling these issues productively and wisely deserves respect and recognition. So if you are not already doing so, give yourself credit. I certainly am. You deserve it!

From this point forward, I want you to promise yourself you will stay in control in the positive sense of the word, no matter how tempting or easy it may be to relinquish control at the wrong times, or the wrong places, with the wrong people.

Remember how control factors in, in terms of either kicking off a "Divorce War," or keeping one going. Use control wisely. Find productive and constructive ways to handle your "Divorce Wars," if you happen to be in the midst of any one or all of them, and think about the benefits of avoiding wars altogether.

Though as a divorce attorney I am more interested in resolving issues than fighting over them, many times I do believe there are wars worth fighting. (And fight I will in a bona fide war, fiercely, for those rights or property to which my client is entitled.) But, I also believe there are wars that are absolutely futile. In those instances, fighting a no-win war compounds one's divorce woes and leaves the door wide open for a loss of control. The last thing you want is more grief and frustration! Do not forget that wars can be expensive: emotionally, psychologically, and, of course, financially; especially if they are legal ones. They can also go on for years. So make sure the war in which you enlist, is a viable and sensible one, because once in it, I want you to win.

Always remember you cannot win a war without control.

Before you step onto that battlefield though, here are a few more questions I would like you to ask yourself: Will a war get me what I want? Is a war worth fighting? Is the war in which I am currently fighting, or about to engage in, one I can afford? Will it resolve my issues? If the answer is "yes," by all means proceed full steam ahead. Get yourself a staunch and capable advocate (top-notch divorce attorney) to do battle for you. If the answer is "no," then find alternate ways to seek resolution. A good attorney can help you with that, too.

One more question—the most important question to ask yourself: Who is currently in control? If the answer is "not me," then you have work to do! Go back to the chapters in the book that struck a chord in you. Perhaps you identified with many of the characters in some of the scenarios; maybe some scenes hit home. If so, those are the chapters to revisit (as many times as necessary), to get and *keep* you on a productive path.

Perhaps you are one of the readers who will get through the divorce and find that one day soon, the divorce and the discord associated with it will be safely behind you. Then again, you may also be one of the readers who will be forced to continue communication with your ex. This is usually the case if you have had children with your ex. If you fall into this category, do not pull out your calendar and mark off the days until the children are grown and gone, thinking then the wars will finally end. For even after the children are well on their way to adulthood there will still be major events such as weddings, christenings, holidays, and medical emergencies, where you may be forced to be in touch with your ex. Thus, it is even more important for you to establish control *now* because by doing so you will always keep the discord at bay. You must come to terms with the reality that if you do share parenthood, you cannot completely distance yourself from your ex. That will be impossible. Therefore, if your relationship remains contentious, your "Divorce Wars" may go on forever. They do not have to. You just have to outfox the "enemy." And that doesn't mean continually fighting a war. It just means finding *resolutions* that will guarantee you having the control you need to live your life harmoniously.

And speaking of harmony, I also want you to consider the old adage, "What goes around, comes around." Unfortunately, I have witnessed many individuals who, for spite, continued to inflict emotional and psychological distress on those they perceived to be their enemy or to settle some score. In the end, however, their injustices came back to haunt them. I do not want you living with such regret. I also do not want you stuck in a perpetual struggle for another reason: Very often those that stay mired in the wars take that negative energy into the next relationship.

In Thomas Cleary's translation of Sun Tzu's 2000-year-old literary work, *The Art of War,* there is one chapter (on emptiness and fullness) in which he interprets a particular passage that I like very much. I think it speaks to the issue of remaining in control in the continuous face of the enemy. Tzu says, "Victory in war is not repetitious, but adapts its form endlessly." Cleary explains, "Determining changes as appropriate, do not repeat former strategies to gain victory. Whatever formations opponents may adopt, from the beginning adapt to them to attain victory." Tzu also says, "… the ability to gain victory by changing and adapting according to the enemy is called genius." Remember those words, for adapting may be the key to your ability to maintain control despite the propensity for chaos with your ex over the long haul.

Cleary also writes that the essence of that premier literary classic work (and war manual), used for centuries now, was intended to address the science of conflict. I believe he is clearly talking about control when he translates Tzu's philosophy, like this: "The peak efficiency of knowledge and strategy is to make conflict altogether unnecessary." In his translation of Tzu's Introduction, Cleary also comments on Tzu's comparison of the healing arts and the martial arts. Cleary says, "They may be a world apart in ordinary usage, but they are parallel in several senses: In recognizing that the less needed the better; in the sense that both involve strategy in dealing with disharmony; and in the sense that in both, knowledge of the problem is key to the solution."

My mission with my book has been to help you identify and understand the control issues—where they are creating conflict for you (for every divorce has them)—and to put into play some "arts" (and "sciences" too) that will keep you out of the wars and in control. Only then can you get to resolution.

Once you get to resolution, you can get on with your life. That is what you want, ultimately, is it not?

If I've said it once, I've said it eight times already.
Divorce is all about control!

About the Author

Stacy D. Phillips is a Certified Family Law Specialist licensed by the State Bar of California's Board of Specialization. As an "AV" rated attorney by the *Martindale Hubbell Registry*, she has been listed in *The Best Lawyers in America®* and has been designated as one of the "500 Leading Lawyers in America" by *Lawdragon*. She has received other distinguished honors and accolades over the years, including being named to the *Super Lawyers®* Advisory Board and "Family Law Attorney of the Year" by the Century City Chamber of Commerce. She is named as one of the *Daily Journal's* "Top Female Litigators in California," recognized as one of the "50 Most Powerful Women in Los Angeles Law" by the *Los Angeles Business Journal,* and is considered as one of the "Top 10 Southern California Super Lawyers®" and "Top 50 Female Super Lawyers® in Southern California" by *Los Angeles Magazine* and *Super Lawyers Magazine.*

Phillips, who founded Phillips, Lerner & Lauzon, a full-service family law firm in Los Angeles, represents business executives, entrepreneurs, homemakers, and high-net worth individuals, as well as celebrities and noted personalities in music, film, television, sports and politics in various family matters.

A graduate of Dartmouth College, cum laude with high distinction in a double major, Phillips earned her juris doctorate at Columbia University School of Law. A staunch supporter of victims' rights, in 1994, Ms. Phillips co-authored Senate Bill 924 which extended the statute of limitations period for victims of domestic violence to sue their abusers in civil court. She currently sits on many philanthropic boards concerned with women's and children's rights.

In addition to her work as an author, Phillips has written for dozens of publications such as the *Los Angeles Daily Journal, California Family Law Monthly, Lawdragon, Divorce Magazine, In Touch, Women on Top,* and *Female Entrepreneur.* A regular contributor to the *Huffington Post,* Phillips is frequently quoted in other periodicals and magazines such as *The Wall Street Journal,* the *Los Angeles Times,* the *Chicago Tribune,* the *Los Angeles Daily Journal, Business Week, People Magazine, Us Magazine, Cosmopolitan, Redbook,* and *Town & Country.* In addition, she has appeared on a number of television programs including *Good Morning America, BBC News, E! Entertainment, Entertainment Tonight, Access Hollywood, VH1, Celebrity Justice, Court TV* and *Star TV,* as well as television programs in Japan, France and Hungary to name a few.

Her clients have included Dean Sheremet (former husband of LeAnn Rimes), Bobby Brown (former husband of Whitney Houston), Charlie Shanian (former husband of Tori Spelling), Corina Villaraigosa (former wife of Los Angeles Mayor Antonio Villaraigosa), Kelly Rutherford, Toni Taupin (former wife of lyricist Bernie Taupin), Darryl Strawberry, Darcy LaPier (former wife of Jean-Claude Van Damme and widow of Mark Hughes), Erin Everly (former wife of Guns 'n Roses' Axl Rose), and Jonathan Kaufer (former husband of Pia Zadora) to name but a few. In 2008, she also represented the conservators with regard to Britney Spears' family law matters.

A frequent lecturer, Phillips has spoken to numerous professional groups, bar associations, law firms, legal forums, and women's groups. She has lectured at UCLA, Loyola Law School, Southwestern Law School, Pepperdine University, Western State University College of Law, and Dartmouth College.

The daughter and granddaughter of attorneys (her grandfather and father were partners in the New York law firm, Phillips Nizer LLP, founded by Ms. Phillips' grandfather in 1926), Stacy Phillips resides in Los Angeles with her husband and children.

Stacy can be contacted for keynote speeches and other appearances. To learn more about her, visit her website: www.controlyourdivorce.com.

ACKNOWLEDGMENTS

When my book first came out in 2005, my acknowledgments highlighted those people who encouraged, supported and helped me bring the book to print. I thank all those wonderful folks all over again. For this sixth edition, I am also deeply indebted to so many people. Some of you have been with me since the beginning of this journey and others of you joined me at various points along the way. Whenever and wherever you joined, I thank you. Without your support and encouragement, I never would have completed the task at hand.

At the risk of forgetting to mention someone, I need to give special recognition to a few people.

To my children - Andrew and Ali - one now grown and the other close behind, you remain and always will be the center of my universe. With the benefit of hindsight, I have an even greater appreciation of the role Babs Bloomgarden played in raising Andrew and Ali and for that I am eternally grateful - you did a great job!

To my entire extended family and especially to my father and mother, you continue to be my pillars of support and wonderful role models on this journey we call life.

To my brother Lou and my sister-in-law Jackie, who have certainly taught me that love, hard work, making the extra effort, along with a willingness to share control, are all the things that make any meaningful relationship work.

Devon and Trey you turned out so wonderfully. Your parents did it right.

Much love to my angels, Deb, Linda, Cathy, Lynn and Mary Ann - always there - rain or shine. And to Leah, you were the first to recognize the application of my book to other areas of the law.

To my cousin, Lynn Goddess, who continues to inspire me, and to Lu Katzman-Staenberg who reminds me constantly of the importance of humanity, care, love and dignity in a world that sometimes seems lacking in each.

A special note of thanks to my partners, colleagues and staff at Phillips, Lerner & Lauzon who always remind me to stop and smell the flowers - even if I do not always listen. And a special note of thanks to Tess Gee and Michael Morales who edited this edition. As always, thank you to Jim Doody whose illustrations are an everlasting part of this book.

To all of the judges and their courtroom staff, a personal note of recognition and appreciation for everything you do to ensure that the judicial system works. You experience each day the reality of the events, people and circumstances described in this book. Without each and every one of you, there would be no hope or resolution for those caught in the vortex of preceedings and euphemistically known as family law.

And finally, my T-Bear, my husband and soul mate. You continually urge me to go after my dreams and you are there with me, helping me to make them a reality.